USING AND ANALYSING DATA IN AUSTRALIAN SCHOOLS

SECOND EDITION

DR SELENA FISK

amba press

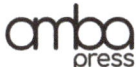

© 2023 Selena Fisk

All rights reserved. No part of this book may be reproduced or transmitted in any form or by any means, electronic or mechanical, including photocopying, recording or by any information storage and retrieval system, without prior permission in writing from the publisher.

Published in 2023 by Amba Press, Melbourne, Australia.
www.ambapress.com.au

Previously published in 2022 by Hawker Brownlow Education.
This edition replaces all previous editions.

ISBN: 9781923116023 (pbk)
ISBN: 9781923116030 (ebk)

A catalogue record for this book is available from the National Library of Australia.

ACKNOWLEDGEMENTS

I think it takes a village to raise a book. I am so grateful for the legends in my village: Tim, Tash, Jhye, Darcy, Carly, Catherine, Anna, Mel, Daniel, Al, Nicola, Liane, Vic, Stacey, Suzanne, Helen, Sarah, Bec and Katie. You are the best humans. Thanks also to Beverly Dann for her ongoing support and encouragement, and for her contribution to this edition.

TABLE OF CONTENTS

Acknowledgements iii

List of examples and templates. vii

About the author xi

Introduction. 1

Chapter 1: Why data? 3

Chapter 2: The power of feedback 25

Chapter 3: Embracing a data-informed culture 37

Chapter 4: How to collect and interpret the data 47

Chapter 5: Using data in your classroom. 67

Chapter 6: Using data in your school 127

Chapter 7: Ensuring that the data has an impact 185

Conclusion 215

References 217

Index 223

LIST OF EXAMPLES AND TEMPLATES

Example 1:	Setting up a spreadsheet at the start of the academic year to establish the ability and potential of a class	69
Example 2:	Using data to identify individual intervention strategies	72
Example 3:	Creating a differentiation placemat to identify differentiation strategies for small groups within a class	74
Example 4:	Tracking class performance throughout a semester or year	76
Example 5:	Investigating strengths and gaps in assessment tasks	81
Example 6:	Calculating the value added for students based on previous achievement	84
Example 7:	Tracking homework	87
Example 8:	Tracking competencies and module completion	89
Example 9:	Tracking progress of students in assessment using the GPA system	91
Example 10a:	Developing a rank order of student achievement using grades	94
Example 10b:	Developing a rank order of student achievement using marks	99
Example 11a:	Developing a rank order of student progress using grades	103
Example 11b:	Developing a rank order of student progress using marks	106
Example 12:	Developing a table of values to show the number of As, Bs, Cs and so on	108
Example 13:	Displaying the spread of student achievement in a box and whisker plot	111

Example 14a:	Graphing progress of individual students over time using line graphs 115
Example 14b:	Graphing progress of individual students over time using colour-coded spreadsheets 121
Example 15:	Using cohort data to identify top performers 129
Example 16:	Using cohort data to identify at-risk students 131
Example 17:	Using data to assist with streaming classes and timetabling 133
Example 18:	Comparing the performance of different classes 138
Example 19:	Calculating individual student grade point averages across learning areas 140
Example 20:	Comparing growth across classes – value added 142
Example 21a:	Considering NAPLAN scale scores over time – tracking a cohort 145
Example 21b:	Considering NAPLAN scale scores over time – tracking a program 149
Example 22a:	My School NAPLAN achievement compared to national averages 153
Example 22b:	My School NAPLAN growth compared to national averages 154
Example 22c:	My School NAPLAN growth compared to schools with similar students 155
Example 22d:	My School NAPLAN growth compared to students with the same starting score 157
Example 23:	Using ACER scale scores to measure progress 158
Example 24:	Creating an ACER difficulty versus percentage correct scatterplot 161
Example 25:	Graphing numerical data 163
Example 26a:	Data wall showing PAT achievement data 164
Example 26b:	Data wall showing PAT progress data 165
Example 27a:	Data wall showing NAPLAN achievement data 167
Example 27b:	Data wall showing NAPLAN progress data 168

Example 28a:	Data wall showing all attendance data	169
Example 28b:	Data wall showing top attendance data	170
Example 29a:	Data wall showing all behaviour reports	171
Example 29b:	Data wall showing best behaviour reports	172
Example 30:	Data wall for literacy or numeracy	173
Example 31:	Thematic analysis of classroom walk-through data	177
Example 32a:	Tracking student wellbeing using a purchased product	180
Example 32b:	Tracking student wellbeing with a home-grown survey	181
Template 1:	Exploring and analysing different types of data	194
Template 2:	Exploratory analysis	200
Template 3:	Bright spots	204
Template 4:	Intervention and areas of concern	206
Template 5:	Data plan	209

ABOUT THE AUTHOR

Dr Selena Fisk has sixteen years' teaching experience in state and private schools in Queensland, Australia, and in comprehensive schools in South London, England. Following three years in the role of Head of Physical Education in South London, where she learned about the power of feedback and transparency of data with students, Selena began a Doctor of Education degree at the Queensland University of Technology on her return to Australia.

Selena has held a range of leadership roles in London and in Queensland, including learning area-specific leadership (physical education, mathematics and science) and whole-school curriculum and pedagogy (in Catholic identity, student data and performance, and leading learning, data and curriculum change). The diversity of leadership roles that Selena has held throughout her career as a teacher has strengthened her passion for seeing students as individuals who fiercely need adults advocating for them and seeing what they are capable of.

In 2017, Selena started her data consultancy practice, Aasha for Schools. In this capacity, she works with teachers, middle and senior leaders, schools and systems to help teachers and school leaders see the inherent good that data can bring, as well as the benefits of using data to develop thriving learning communities through data storytelling. In 2019 she published the first edition of *Using and analysing data in Australian schools* and was named one of ACEL's New Voice in Educational Research scholars. In the same year, Aasha for Schools was recognised as one of the Top 50 Organisations in Education at the GFEL awards in Dubai. In 2020, Selena published her second book, *Leading data-informed change in schools*.

INTRODUCTION

The ultimate purpose of taking data is to provide a basis for action or a recommendation for action.

(Deming, 1942, p. 173)

Teachers in Australia are increasingly told that student data is important. The Alice Springs (Mparntwe) Education Declaration, the Australian Curriculum and the Australian Professional Standards for Teachers all direct teachers to use student data in their teaching, planning and feedback (see Education Services Australia, 2019; ACARA, 2014; AITSL, 2011). Australian media perpetuates the notion that student data is one of the most important measures of school and teacher success, and recent research discusses the importance of data literacy and analysis for educators. In many cases, however, teachers are unsure about which data to collect, how to analyse it and how to translate the data into storytelling and action so that its use benefits the young people that they aim to serve.

I have worked in a number of roles that have allowed me to engage in conversations with senior and middle leaders, teachers, students and parents about student and school data. The recurring theme that I hear from colleagues at all levels is a desire to learn more and do more, tempered with uncertainty about where to start. The use of data in schools has evolved throughout many teachers' careers, and most did not undergo formal training in how to use data at university or college. Understandably, many find it challenging. University degrees are slowly catching up, but the subjects and training in data use and analysis, at this stage, are only reaching our youngest teachers. To make matters worse, the Australian media regularly reaffirm the importance of student data and external testing by comparing states and individual schools with achievement or outcome measures, and reporting on NAPLAN testing results and tertiary entrance ranks without any real understanding of the growth that has occurred or the context of the school.

Prior to becoming a full-time school data coach and consultant in 2020, I taught in schools in Brisbane, Australia, and in London, England, for sixteen years. In that time, I developed my understanding of how data can be used, trialled different approaches with teachers and students, and implemented whole-school tracking and monitoring processes. From 2011 to 2017 I also completed a doctoral thesis that focused on students' perceptions of feedback. The process taught me a lot about the power of feedback and the impact that data and feedback can have on learners. I know that teachers want to do the best for their students, and students want to know their data, but there are gaps between the expectations we have for teachers and their skill sets, and the reality is that developing new skills takes time. Teachers' workloads are increasing, and they are being asked to do more and more planning, data collection, analysis and differentiation than ever before. In my experience, teachers also judge the effectiveness of professional learning sessions on whether they learned any new skills that they can put into practice. Taking all of this into account, the second edition of *Using and analysing data in Australian schools* dives even deeper into the 'why' and 'how' of data and provides additional specific examples of approaches to using data in the classroom or at a group or cohort level.

Chapter 1 explores the 'why' of data and discusses some key research and contextual factors impacting the use of data in Australian schools. Chapter 2 investigates the impact of feedback in schools and particularly focuses on the use of sharing information and data with students to improve outcomes. Chapter 3 covers three elements that are key to embracing a data-informed culture: growth mindset, positive psychology and grit. Chapter 4 discusses the types of data that are available and most commonly used in our schools, such as NAPLAN bands, stanines, GPAs and Z-scores. This chapter also discusses the importance of triangulation and colour-coding in assisting with data use and analysis.

Chapters 5 and 6 explore the ways data can be used in classrooms and schools respectively and provide a series of examples with step-by-step guidance for using different data strategies. Each example also contains tips for implementation, suggestions for using the data with students and the ways the specific type of data can be used. The examples offered in Chapters 5 and 6 are strategies that have worked for me at different times and in different contexts. The list is certainly not exhaustive and not all the examples will be relevant at all times, but the data strategies I detail are sure to be helpful if you look for opportunities to use them.

Building on the focus on mindset and feedback of earlier chapters, Chapter 7 centres on ensuring data achieves its desired impact. Exploring ways that data can be used in feedback to students and to celebrate success, it also discusses developing data protocols and holding data-informed conversations in teams. Chapter 7 also includes templates for data reviews that can be used by classroom teachers and middle or senior leaders.

I hope that you find this book useful and engaging, and that it encourages you to develop your own ideas and adapt the examples provided where possible. These are not the be-all and end-all of data strategies for schools and classrooms, but they do offer a range of ideas for teachers and school leaders looking to develop their skills in using data. I am excited to share these ideas with you, and hope you enjoy the data as much as I do. Have fun with it!

CHAPTER 1
WHY DATA?

Used intelligently, evidence is the teacher's friend.

Sir Kevan Collins, *Education Endowment Foundation guide to becoming an evidence-informed school governor and trustee*

In the movie *Good Will Hunting* (Van Sant, 1997), the main character Will, a cleaner at the Massachusetts Institute of Technology (MIT), is an undiscovered genius. After Professor Gerald Lambeau puts a challenging maths problem on a blackboard in the corridor, Will completes the puzzle and his genius is identified. Professor Lambeau tries to find work for Will, but Will is not sure which career path to take. When Will is in the discernment phase, another MIT professor says to him, 'Most people never get to see how brilliant they can be. They don't find teachers that believe in them. They get convinced they're stupid' (Van Sant, 1997). I believe that school data, when used well, gives teachers an opportunity to see how brilliant their students can be. When teachers see and celebrate the strengths of their students, students feel that their teachers believe in them and see their inherent worth. This can have a significant impact on their well-being and self-identity.

Data is increasingly being used to orient school improvement efforts in Australia and around the world, and data is now seen to be driving educational change (Bishop & Bishop, 2017). There are a number of reasons why this is the case, including international comparisons such as the Programme for International Student Assessment (PISA); internal influences such as the Australian Institute for Teaching and School Leadership (AITSL) teacher standards, the Australian Curriculum, the National School

Improvement Tool (NSIT), the National Assessment Program – Literacy and Numeracy (NAPLAN), the Alice Springs (Mparntwe) Education Declaration and the My School website; as well as the broader effects of living in an age of technology, accountability, globalisation and international mobility. Australian teachers are expected to use data to inform programs, differentiate instruction and modify practice. No matter what the reasoning, the reality is that data use and analysis are here, our schools are measured by it and our students are compared using it. There is no escaping the data.

Unfortunately, however, many educators have developed a negative perception of school data, and this is largely due to the media and some of the existing literature. We regularly hear that data should not drive what we do, that data is impersonal and that students are much more than numbers. But then quotes such as 'You can't manage what you can't measure', often attributed to the physicist William Thomson, the first Baron Kelvin, are used in the context of schools. Some authors compare schools to systems with inputs and outputs that we can discuss, measure and modify (see Desautels & McKnight, 2016). But my view is that data use in schools should always be about more than the numbers. We cannot reduce our students solely to numbers, to their statistics or to their positions in data visualisations. I believe that data has incredible potential in our schools and that using data can actually help us to know and cater for our students better. Much like in *Good Will Hunting*, data can show us how brilliant our students can be. Sometimes what the data tells us might even differ from a student's perception of themself – or from our perception of them. Using data to learn about our students and help them succeed is the number-one priority. Any improvement in NAPLAN or other standardised test scores as a result is a bonus.

In her book *Grit: The power of passion and perseverance,* Angela Duckworth (2016) talks about developing a theory. She states,

> A theory is an explanation. A theory takes a blizzard of facts and observations and explains, in the most basic terms, what the heck is going on. By necessity, a theory is incomplete. It oversimplifies. But in doing so, it helps us understand. (p. 41)

This book is exactly that. I have taken a blizzard of facts and observations about data in Australian schools, and I intend to explain what the heck is going on. I acknowledge that I simplify the data story in a way that is incomplete, but I do so to demonstrate the power of data in education and support you to implement exciting new approaches to using data in your own school. It is incomplete because data does not always tell us everything about a student or a class. Every educator knows that it is teachers' knowledge of students and families, when combined with data, that provides the fullest picture.

I use data, but I believe in people. Those two things are not mutually exclusive. This book is about that overlap.

The international context
Dr Beverly Dann
University of the Sunshine Coast

As experienced educators, we understand the need to use data to inform each developmental step along a student's learning journey. The same could be said about data use by the Australian Government that leads to changes in our education system and influences the advancement of teaching and learning. Various government entities collect data from a range of international sources such as the Organisation for Economic Co-operation and Development (OECD), who believe in the development of better policies for better lives. Our own Alice Springs (Mparntwe) Education Declaration aligns with the OECD vision to develop an education system that promotes excellence, equity, wellbeing and a socially cohesive society.

The OECD created the Programme for International Student Assessment (PISA) to determine the capacity of fifteen-year-olds around the world to problem-solve and contribute successfully to society. This age was chosen because most countries allow students to drop out of high school and go to work at fifteen. Australia has participated in PISA since 2000. Over this time Australia's results have been gradually trending downward with mathematics as our lowest scoring subject, with a drop equivalent to approximately one school year of learning (ACER, 2019).

Other standardised tests in which Australia participates include Trends in International Mathematics and Science Study (TIMSS) and Progress in International Reading Literacy Study (PIRLS). Australia's results indicate that, since 2007, we are mostly maintaining with slight improvement in reading and Year 8 mathematics and science; however, a decline is shown for Year 4 students in mathematics (Thomson et al., 2017; Thomson et al., 2020). The low student scores demonstrated across these three international tests as well as our own NAPLAN test confirm that the results demonstrating little to no change since 2008 are accurate and that the areas of underachievement need to be addressed (ACARA, 2019).

To take a closer look at what is happening in classrooms and school communities, the administrators of these tests survey principals, teachers, parents and students to gain information about teaching qualifications and experience, home-life conditions, and teaching conditions and programs in schools. This information gives us the opportunity to learn from the successes and difficulties of other countries, allowing governments and school leaders alike to consider new ideas that may suit their contexts and goals.

In addition to the subject and survey data, these tests also provide data on demographics such as gender, cultural background, languages used at home, successful teaching strategies and more. This information helps us to see if we are making improvements in specific areas over time. For example, knowing from the data that Aboriginal and Torres Strait Islander students are not progressing at the same rate as non-Indigenous students, we can explore how other countries have handled similar disparity in achievement, potentially resulting in new ideas to consider for the Australian context (Thomson et al., 2020).

> Other influential resources are the reports written by experienced researchers tasked with investigating Australia's standing regarding school processes, teaching practices, learning environments, community involvement and more. These investigations occur with the purpose of improving education outcomes because this has a direct impact on future economic and social opportunities. Some reports such as Action now: Classroom ready teachers (Teacher Education Ministerial Advisory Group, 2014) suggest changes in initial teacher education programs and the creation of school mentoring programs. Another report, entitled How the world's best-performing school systems come out on top (Barber & Mourshed, 2007), identifies the main driver of variation in student learning in schools to be the quality of teachers. Building on these reports, the 2018 report Through growth to achievement from the Australian Government's Department of Education and Training recommended a number of further changes to improve teaching and learning in our schools.
>
> Together, these reports identify strengths and weaknesses in our education system. They provide a range of recommendations to be considered at the federal level. For example, the recommendations to improve teacher preparation programs by requiring teachers to pass a literacy and numeracy test as part of their initial teacher education programs at university became a reality for pre-service teachers in Queensland in 2017. Other examples include recommendations to establish practices, such as creating conditions for teachers and schools to collaborate, that enable students to reach their full potential, as well as recommendations requiring a focus on maximising learning and achievement while supporting teachers to cater for diverse learners in their classrooms (Department of Education and Training, 2018). All of these recommendations include learning how to use data and feedback to improve student engagement and learning in schools.
>
> Australia's teachers participate in professional learning and collaboration with their colleagues to improve teaching and learning, but they have indicated a need for more support and training in teaching students with diverse needs (OECD, 2019). Research clearly shows that teachers are central to improvement and excellence in education; we know that an excellent teacher can account for up to 30 per cent difference in student achievement (Department of Education and Training, 2018). Reaching excellence means providing opportunity for teachers to have professional collaboration, to develop effective formative assessment and feedback skills, and to monitor progress and maximise learning in the classroom.

THE POWER OF 'WHY'

Thought leader Simon Sinek (2009, 2017) proposes in his Golden Circle model that effective leaders and organisations need to harness the power of 'why' when leading change, rather than relying on the 'what' or the 'how' only. Sinek states that while every organisation knows what they do, only some can articulate how they do it and very few can articulate why. The 'why' sits in the centre of the Golden Circle deliberately, as it is the core purpose or reason that an organisation exists – and it is what makes the change in question important. Sinek also postulates that if you do not start with the 'why', leaders and organisations are less likely to get on board with the change agenda and, understandably, less likely to succeed.

So, what is my reason, or 'why', for using data in schools? My 'why' is the young people that are positively impacted by our understanding and use of their data. I am motivated and driven by the learnings that I can find in data about students, classes, cohorts and schools because I have experienced the positive impact that data can have hundreds of times in my career. I have seen data improve individual student performance in classrooms and standardised tests, cohort achievement in school learning areas and standardised tests, and overall school achievement. I love catching out students who have unidentified potential. I love the data-informed conversations I have with students and parents about what I have found. I love proving that students are better than they say and believe they are.

It is important to point out at this stage that I advocate for being *data informed*, not *data driven* – even though the latter term is used occasionally by key organisations in Australia (see ACER, 2017). The term *data driven* has the potential to instil fear of stifling micromanagement, intrusive checking and inflated accountability for the people involved. But that is *not* how data should be used. On the other hand, the term *data informed* is based on an 'understanding that data will inform rather than drive decision making because there are rational, political, and moral elements in decision making and data is only one important element in the process' (Shen et al., 2012, p. 3). Being data informed provides us with new possibilities 'to attain a deeper level of understanding about the complexities of teaching and learning, and to learn how to maximize educators' efforts to meet students' needs' (Knapp et al., 2006, p. 2). It means that data informs what we do – along with our own personal ethics, the understanding and knowledge of teachers and students, and individual contexts. We are not driven by numbers or blinkered into being unable to see anything else.

CRITICISM OF DATA USE IN SCHOOLS

Despite my own personal position on using data, I am aware that there is criticism around the world about the use of data and statistics in schools, and I do not want to shy away from it here. In *Who's afraid of the big bad dragon?*, Yong Zhao (2014) discusses the Chinese education system and warns the United States and other Western countries against following the Chinese lead too closely in their efforts to achieve higher educational outcomes. Early in the book, Zhao discusses the introduction of the *'No Child Left Behind'* policy in the United States, which was instigated by President George W Bush in 2001. A part of this new policy was the use of standardised testing, which Zhao likened to a Trojan horse: full of authoritarianism, similar expectations and a 'sameness' for all students. His perception is that the standardised testing currently in place in China limits creativity and innovation, and forces students to make being test-savvy their number-one priority. Zhao reports that students and parents are driven only by a desire to succeed in these tests and argues that this is not something Western nations should aspire to, warning that other countries will fall into the same trap if they try to replicate China's processes. In saying this, Zhao's interpretation of the Chinese system appears very different to the way I see standardised testing functioning in Australia.

Further, when providing a historical context for the current testing regime and excellent PISA scores in China, Zhao discusses the success of leader Deng Xiaoping who came to power in 1978. Zhao reports that under Deng's leadership, the Chinese were granted new economic freedom and opportunity. When discussing the achievement of people in rural areas over the three decades of Deng's leadership, Zhao states,

> It was not foresight or wise planning by the central government that led to China's global rise. On the contrary, it was gradual withdrawal of government planning and regulation to create an environment that allowed people to exercise their autonomy. As Deng said, if the government deserved any credit, it was for leaving people alone and letting them be – which had been the fundamental principle of good governance in ancient times. (2014, p. 60)

Although he was discussing economic freedom, Zhao uses this story to argue his point about data and standardised testing: that government control limits freedom, creativity and innovation. He applies this perspective to the education system in China, wildly criticising the government and culture for having unfair expectations on students around academic performance and upward social mobility, and a system and culture that limits students' freedom, creativity and innovation. His key message for Western countries is to not aspire to be China, because theirs is a broken system, driven by test scores, that prioritises test success over anything else.

In 2017, a thought leader I have a lot of respect for, John Kotter, wrote an article titled 'The problem with data'. Although talking more broadly about organisations, rather than educational institutions specifically, Kotter states,

> data is essential to running organizations: putting together any rational plan; knowing whether you are operating on-plan or off; keeping things under control; finding and responding to immediate problems . . . Data has also emerged as a great potential asset in inventing the future – especially going beyond traditional numeric strategy exercises. We are told it can help us speculate intelligently about customer needs in new ways, even inventing entirely new ways of serving those needs. Then it might guide the allocation of resources to create a prospering future. (2017, pp. 4–5)

When applied to the context of education, I believe the points that Kotter makes in this article are relevant. He talks about data helping us speculate about customer (student) needs in new ways and identifying new ways of serving those needs. This is true – data can tell us more about what our students need, and we can adjust our strategies for individual students accordingly.

In the second half of the article, Kotter talks extensively about two neurological responses – survive and thrive – and discusses these elements in terms of using data in organisations. *Survive*, he reports, is fear driven, focused on accountability and does not promote a positive working culture. *Thrive*, on the other hand, is freedom to do and be, with confidence in one's ability and path, and no fear. The problem with data, Kotter suggests, is that its use too often overstimulates the survive neurological response and often crushes the thrive response, even when that is not the intention.

There is no doubt that data can be scary and have the capacity to indicate trends that may not sit well with us. Nobody likes knowing that despite their best efforts a particular student did not pass a learning area or a class did not perform to their potential in a standardised test. I certainly don't encourage school leaders to use data to check on staff or to set unrealistic targets that place excessive pressure on teachers. Kotter is right: organisations should use data in a way that helps employees to thrive and flourish, rather than activating the survive response – and that extends to the way that data is used in schools.

However, if a student is below the national minimum standard in their NAPLAN writing result and in the lowest stanine in a standardised reading comprehension test, that student is potentially going to struggle to be a literate and engaged member of society in the future. Although we do not want to activate a survive neurological response in teachers, do we not have a responsibility to learn from the data and help this student? Do we not *want* to help this student improve? Wouldn't you, as an educator, rather acknowledge the potential you have to positively affect a young person's life by focusing on developing their literacy skills than take the data personally or ignore it altogether? I know I would.

Despite his sentiments about data, Kotter believes that it is possible that data can be used to activate the thrive neurological response. But he acknowledges that this is not done regularly enough. Kotter states that activating the thrive response can be done by being aware and mindful of the survive response, and then asking rational and logical questions about the data to understand more about what the data is saying. Kotter advocates for asking 'Do I really need this data?' and 'Why do I need it?' to prevent the over-activation of the survive response. Further, given the significant amounts of data available nowadays, Kotter suggests throwing away one old report each time a new data report is generated!

Sharratt and Fullan – who are well known for the phrase *putting faces on the data* and their 2012 book of the same name – do not necessarily introduce and frame data positively. Even though they recognise data's inherent value and impact on educational outcomes the authors state, 'education is overloaded with programs and data', and 'technology accelerates the onslaught of data' (Sharratt & Fullan, 2013, p. 45). This makes the data seem a bit scary – no doubt particularly scary to those who are not sure how to use it in the first place! But as advocates for using data in a humanistic manner, Sharratt and Fullan go on to say that 'all this information goes for naught unless educators can put faces on the data at all points on the learning continuum and know what to do to help the children behind the statistics' (2013, p. 45).

Interestingly, Sharratt and Fullan surveyed 507 teachers about why putting faces on the data is important. The survey respondents stated that putting faces on the data helps them to know students, plan for students, ensure responsibility for students and assess progress. Consequently, they explain that 'educators need to know that every child is learning by making ongoing assessments and incorporating that information about each child's learning into daily instruction – a non-negotiable practice' (2013, p. 46). Understanding the individuals behind the numbers is vital to helping achieve this goal, and by putting faces on the data, educators are encouraged to remember the young people they are analysing the data for.

The final criticism, for lack of a better word, of data use is that data never considers every possible angle of a problem, nor does it have the answers or solutions. Data generates its meaning and impact when we associate the statistics or numbers with our own experience, understanding and interpretation. The numbers by themselves mean very little. For example, Knapp et al. (2006) specify 'data by themselves are not evidence of anything, until users of the data bring concepts, criteria, theories of action, and interpretive frames of reference to the task of making sense of the data' (p. 10). Similarly, Charles Seife (2010), in his book *Proofiness: How you're being fooled by the numbers*, states:

> *For a non-mathematician, numbers are interesting only when they give us information about the world. A number only takes on any significance in everyday life when it tells us how many pounds we've gained since last month or how many dollars it will cost to buy a sandwich or how many weeks are left before our taxes are due . . . We don't care about the properties of the number five. Only when that number becomes attached to a unit – the 'pounds' or 'dollars' or 'weeks' that signify what real-world property the number represents – does it become interesting to a non-mathematician. (p. 9)*

Seife is absolutely correct. In schools, a NAPLAN scale score, a stanine, a grade point average (GPA), a rate of value added or a stand-alone learning area result all mean nothing unless we understand benchmarks, learning areas and students. We need to be able to understand the context of the numbers so that we can work out what each student's achievement means and what they need. We also need this context to be able to use data to compare students with their peers, compare them with the nation, compare within groups, change programs and modify instruction for students who need it.

DATA LITERACY, DATA VISUALISATION AND DATA STORYTELLING

Unfortunately, this interpretation of the data (and the context) is not often done for us in schools. Data collection is one step, but it is the least important. Having spreadsheets and data stored on computers and data walls has no impact on student outcomes unless we truly understand what the numbers mean and learn to interpret the results in a manner that helps students in the future. In 2017, the Australian Council for Educational Research (ACER) published an article titled 'Data-driven improvement in schools'. The article talks about the need for teachers to be using and analysing data to differentiate instruction, to cater for individual needs and to improve educational outcomes. The contributors to the article state that the key part of using data comes after the collection phase – it is what is done with the data that is most important.

Using data effectively in schools involves three key elements: data literacy, data visualisation and data storytelling. All three of these are essential for data to be translated into actionable and tangible change.

Data literacy

The first element is data literacy, which entails understanding the data itself. Numbers don't mean anything to us unless we understand the context around them, such as what is low, average or high, what is assessed (and not assessed) with each task, and what individual criteria results mean. When we have good data literacy skills, we understand the data quickly and learning about the metrics doesn't delay the next steps.

Data visualisation

Next is data visualisation. This is where the data is made beautiful, where it is converted into graphs, tables or other visual renderings to make trends more easily identifiable. In schools, data visualisations are sometimes done for us in pre-packaged learning management systems, data dashboards or visualisation platforms. These visualisations are often big picture and can be super helpful. They are often also 'unbreakable', in that we can use them and not alter or edit them. On the other hand, some schools develop their own data visualisations to support bespoke tracking, reporting and feedback. This is done with spreadsheets and programs such as Power BI and Tableau. Extensive training and time are necessary for educators to build the skills to develop beautiful dashboards in Power BI and Tableau, but for some schools and educators the outcomes are absolutely worth the investment. Regardless of the technology, spreadsheets can be generated by almost anyone who wants to do further analysis of the data, or to view it in a slightly different way. Spreadsheets are highly customisable and are far easier and quicker to master than Power BI or Tableau. Having good data visualisation skills means you can generate the visualisations that you need, and you are able to read and interpret the visualisations that are provided to you.

Data storytelling

The third important part of using data effectively is data storytelling. This is where data literacy and visualisation combine with a deep understanding of the trends and the students represented as educators look for actionable stories. Data storytelling humanises the numbers and returns our thinking to our students and what they need from us.

It ensures that students are at the centre of our use of data, allows us to see what our students need next and prompts us to think about the ways that we could support them.

Despite the fact that storytelling is the most important of the three elements discussed here, the time dedicated to this practice is often insufficient. In fact, organising and presenting data can take up to 80% of an analyst's time (Jones & Pickett, 2019). Time is in short supply in schools, and so much of it is taken up displaying the data we collect that storytelling is left to do later or in teachers' own time – or forgotten entirely. Sure, visualisation platforms can help us with this (if they generate the dashboards we need), and when we have good data literacy we can use the numbers more quickly, but time still needs to be spent organising what information is needed when and by whom. The other challenge is that, even if time is allocated in department or full staff meetings, many staff don't know how to tell stories with their data. They're not always sure what questions to ask, how to ask them, or how to explore options for change with others. This is particularly challenging for teachers who haven't shared their data before; it can be pretty scary to open up results and begin talking their students' achievements, because what will people think if we don't have the answers? But we need to start having these data-informed conversations and looking for the stories in the data if we want to make a real difference and meet the unique learning needs of every student.

DATA DEMOCRATISATION

The normalisation of sharing of data with colleagues, in planning meetings and in conversation with leaders, parents and students represents a shift that is occurring in a range of industries: the move towards the third generation of business intelligence and data democratisation (see Marr, 2017; Qlik, 2019).

In the past, in what was called the first generation of business intelligence, only key senior figures had access to business analytics. The data was often held by the leader or tech team and were often viewed and discussed by only a handful of key staff. In schools, this was often the principal and deputy principal. The second generation of business intelligence saw the broadening of this access to a larger group, but the analysis, discussion and narrative were still controlled by the few. In schools, this began with the principal and deputy sharing data and summaries with the wider leadership team and even middle leaders. However, when this happened, educators were often under strict instructions to not share the data or insights with others. We are now moving into the third generation of business intelligence, in which organisations are building a data democracy that allows staff access to data that they need, when they need it (Marr, 2017).

In schools, that means open access to standardised testing results and increased transparency between teachers, parents and students. Some systems even provide organisation-wide access to all student and class data. These shifts have been supported by investments in technology, the introduction of middle leadership roles to build the capacity of staff, and more open classrooms than ever before. This approach doesn't extend to highly sensitive or confidential information, but relates to summative, formative and standardised assessment results.

The shift from first-, through second-, to third-generation business intelligence has taken years in some cases and has happened more rapidly in others. Every organisation is somewhere along the journey. This, like all change, is affected by leadership priorities, staff capacity and resource investment. It is a shift that takes some thinking and can be a bit daunting for people who have never had access to data before, but it is key to opening up and normalising data-informed conversations.

Throughout my career, I have seen many teachers collect data and – unintentionally – do nothing with it. I have spotted data walls sitting behind teachers with little understanding of the information they held, meaning 'the faces on the data' had no impact on actual programs and strategies. I have witnessed school leaders identify an area of weakness to be addressed in a particular cohort, only for the data and insight to not lead to any changes to programs, to approaches or for students.

The reality is that we are all at different stages with our knowledge of collecting, understanding, using and analysing data – and that is absolutely okay. At this point, I would like you to think about where you sit with using and analysing data in your classroom or school. In Robert J Marzano's *The New Art and Science of Teaching* (2017), he outlines forty-three elements that constitute good teaching. When discussing these elements, Marzano advocates for monitoring teachers' progress toward the goal of embedding these elements in their classrooms. Data use and analysis are not specifically identified in *The New Art and Science of Teaching* (other than broadly in 'Element 2: Tracking student progress'), but Marzano does suggest a developmental scale for classifying teachers' skills in each teaching element at one of five stages: 'not using', 'beginning', 'developing', 'applying' and 'innovating' (pp. 103–104).

Although these five skill levels were not articulated with school data and learning analytics in mind specifically, they provide a sound structure that we can adapt (as I have in table 1.1) to evaluate how we use data in the classroom.

Table 1.1. Developmental scale for using data in the classroom

Not using	I am unaware of the existence of data, do not understand it or do not engage with it.
Beginning	I attempt to use data in my work, but there are flaws in the way I use it or my methods are incomplete.
Developing	I use data in my role, but I do not monitor the effect that it has on students.
Applying	I use data in my practice and I monitor the extent to which this impacts my students and their learning.
Innovating	I have a high level of expertise in using data and I modify my practice for individual students in my class.

SOURCE: Adapted from 'Developmental scale for elements', *The New Art and Science of Teaching*, Marzano, 2017.

Take a look back at this progression and think about where you would be positioned. Have you progressed recently? Have you moved along the continuum during your career? Or are you at the very first stage, where you have been for most of your career? It really does not matter where you are – it is more important that you can recognise your starting position and set goals to move along the continuum. When I started my teaching career in Australia I was in the 'not using' category, but during my time in the United Kingdom, with the help of highly skilled leaders and fellow middle leaders, I moved into 'beginning', through 'developing' and then into the 'applying' stage for using and analysing data. It was not until I returned to Australia and worked specifically in a role in which I was focused on student data and performance that I moved to the 'innovating' stage. This progression – for me – took about fifteen years! But it doesn't need to take you as long.

In *The New Art and Science of Teaching*, Marzano (2017) also talks about deliberate practice: the idea that expertise takes time and requires deliberate practice for skills and effort to come to fruition. This applies to all of our skills as educators, not just Marzano's forty-three design elements – and learning to use and analyse data is no different. The reality is, like any skill, it takes time. Through using data, you will continue to improve your computer skills, continue to learn new ideas and ways of using and analysing data, and you will possibly spend time making a spreadsheet that you don't end up using. Know that this is all part of the process, and that you will become quicker, more efficient and more discerning in how and when you use data as you go on. It will get better!

ASSUMPTIONS ABOUT DATA

Before discussing the contextual expectations that are affecting Australian teachers' use and analysis of data, it is important that I share my personal beliefs and assumptions about data.

We all come to the data conversation with different experiences, backgrounds and beliefs. Wherever you are on your data journey, pause and think about your fundamental beliefs about data. Are they inherently positive? Are your perceptions motivated by a survive or thrive neurological response? Do you believe that data has a place in our schools? Why or why not?

Once you have done this, read over my beliefs about data. I come to this conversation with the following beliefs and presuppositions:

1. Data provides us with useful information about student potential, which can sometimes be different to what we think.
2. Everyone can learn and improve with effort and application.
3. Using data can motivate and engage students.
4. Data can be inaccurate or may not truly reflect a student's ability.

5. Data should be used to inform planning, programs and differentiation.

6. Data can surprise us – and for the right reasons.

7. Data should be used to catch out students (not teachers), whether they are underperforming, flying under the radar or achieving great results.

There are so many reasons I have developed these beliefs, but it is largely because of what the teachers and students I have worked with, learned about and supported have taught me. My Year 11 General Certificate of Secondary Education (GCSE) physical education students in the United Kingdom taught me about the power of data and feedback to motivate and engage students because they used formative assessment results to direct revision and set goals. My all-boys mathematics A class – in which nine students had failed Year 10 mathematics, but only one went on to fail Semester 1 in Year 11 – taught me the power of tracking homework, having clear and transparent data systems, and involving students in the process. Ava, who for years had worked at a C in mathematics and then achieved an A+ on an algebra test in Year 8, reminded me that students are not limited by their previous results. Harry surprised me for the right reasons and was identified as a twice-exceptional student (meaning he had a verified disability as well as an exceptional IQ) when, despite his disability and disengagement in school, we realised he was in the ninety-ninth percentile in a national norm-referenced test.

While I have lost count of the number individual students, class groups and cohorts I have seen rise to a challenge, achieve their goals or exceed their own – and others' – expectations, some stories stick out more than others. In my most recent teaching role I met a student called David in a supervision lesson. I had heard about David and the time-out cards that he used during the day, which excused him from part of a lesson whenever he needed it. David was frequently suspended and engaged in re-entry meetings, and was regularly the topic of discussion in the staffroom for his disruptive and disengaged behaviour. In this supervision lesson, I logged onto the ACER online platform to check the results of the Progressive Achievement Test (PAT) that we had recently undertaken for reading and mathematics. I noticed that David was in the top five students in his year group.

I started up a conversation with David and showed him where he was positioned. He did not believe me at first, but when he realised that I was indeed telling the truth, he was really proud and surprised, and tried to hide his smile from me. I love feedback and good news stories, so I emailed all staff to tell them that David was in the top five students in his year group for this test and asked them to give him a pat on the back when they saw him next.

In the coming days, so many teachers thanked me for letting them know – it was the first positive academic feedback they had received about David in months. A couple of weeks later, we recognised our top five achievers and improvers for each PAT test in an assembly. I told David on the Tuesday – literally as he was being suspended – that he was getting an award on the Friday. He responded, 'I don't even know if I'll be allowed back by Friday.' Thankfully, when Friday came, David was at school. He got up, received the award and sat back down, choosing not to line up with the other recipients at the front of the assembly. I was confused as to why he did not line up with the others, so I asked around. It turned out that for the three days prior to the assembly, a middle leader and David's mother worked with David to encourage him to get up and receive the award. He was embarrassed and shy, because he had never stood up in an assembly to receive an award before and he did not want to. Thankfully, through their encouragement and negotiating that he could receive the award and sit straight back down, David agreed. I am still so glad that he did.

Students like David are the reason that I am so passionate about using data. I subscribe to the belief that our number-one priority as teachers is providing the best education for the young people that we teach. Our kids should be front and centre. Ultimately, using data should be about looking for the positives – the 'bright spots' – and for what students *can* do, rather than viewing data from a deficit model and only looking for things they *cannot* do. It is about using data to help individuals and cohorts flourish, and activating the thrive neurological response for both students and teachers. Data should always be used to identify areas of strength and to develop understanding of the areas requiring attention. The fact that using data is a contextual expectation of Australian teachers is just one aspect of the data story – stories like David's are the real reason I do what I do.

USING DATA IS AS MUCH PASTORAL CARE AS IT IS CURRICULUM

I hope it is clear at this point that although there are policy and framing documents in place that explicitly outline the expectation that Australian educators use data, it's not just a question of compliance. I believe that data can be used well and that it can truly benefit our teaching, our programs and, ultimately, our students. In fact, I believe that using data effectively is as much pastoral care as a curriculum responsibility. In the schools that I have worked in as a teacher, pastoral care and curriculum leadership roles have been separated. In fact, a friend and colleague recently asked whether a new incoming teacher was more 'curriculum' or 'pastoral', because if they were the former, they would find it tricky to succeed in that particular (sometimes quite difficult) context!

However, I strongly believe that these are actually intertwined, because data doesn't have to be limited to just learning analytics information, and, regardless of what we collect and measure, the outcome should be helping us know more and do more for our students. Yes, department heads might track the number of As or Ds in a cohort, look at problem-solving results in Year 8 mathematics classes, or investigate Year 10 music responding criteria results from a curriculum perspective. But when teachers and school leaders use data to confirm what they think about a student, recognise a student's ability in a particular area or identify a need for teaching to be differentiated for particular students, they are demonstrating a greater understanding of the abilities of their students and using the data to raise their own expectations and encourage students to do and be better. When we use data to help students flourish, to build their self-confidence and to reward their hard work, we are looking after and celebrating the humans in front of us. Having high expectations of students means we are more likely to have students who reach their potential, and consequently have more options available to them post-schooling. Furthermore, when a teacher uses data to modify a teaching program, differentiate instruction, celebrate success or raise expectations, this is catering for the needs of more students. How is this *not* pastoral care? As Desautels and McKnight (2016) state, 'Schools are not machines. Schools are a network of human beings who feel, think, behave, and function within a human system that is alive and never static. Schools are living systems!' (p. 3). When we view the education system as dynamic and students as individuals with different needs, we re-shape our approach to education and begin to treat students as the individuals that they are.

We have all heard and experienced the notion that students do not learn content; they learn teachers. We also know that developing relationships with students is key to success – now more than ever. Desautels and McKnight (2016), in their book *Unwritten: The story of a living system*, discuss the need for students to have teachers in their lives who see them as thriving young people with potential, who treat them with compassion and who they work with to achieve success. The authors argue that students deserve teachers who see their potential and help them to harness their strengths. In fact, they state 'programs do not change people. People change people' (Desautels & McKnight, 2016, p. xi). Desautels and McKnight (2016) talk about 'turnaround teachers' – that is, teachers that positively affect, motivate and inspire individual students to do more and be more. A key characteristic of turnaround teachers has to do with being able to see the potential and the strengths of their students, rather than focusing on their students' weaknesses.

The point – echoed in the saying 'if you judge a fish by its ability to climb a tree, it will live its whole life believing that it is stupid' – is that every student has potential and every student can succeed. It is our role as teachers to nurture students' abilities, build their self-worth and show them how they can be active, engaged and good global citizens. If we don't, who will? We don't want kids growing up thinking they're stupid. In gathering information from all types of sources, we can support students to flourish and find their 'thing'.

Perhaps I have a biased perspective, but I believe that more of the extant literature about data promotes knowing the potential of our students and tracking their progress than the opposite. An example of this is in the work of Lyn Sharratt and Michael Fullan (2013), who promote the human aspect behind the data and report that teachers have a responsibility to help students get better at the one thing that will stand them in good stead for the rest of their lives – their education. Their focus is on the individuals and the impact that effective teaching has on them, and they propose fourteen parameters for improving student achievement (Sharratt & Fullan, 2013). Relevant to using data in schools is the shared beliefs and understandings that every student 'can achieve high standards given the right time and the right support', and that having high expectations for students in addition to early and ongoing intervention is essential (Sharratt & Fullan, 2013, p. 45). In fact, Sharratt and Fullan mention early and ongoing intervention twice in their list of fourteen parameters, which is telling – we need to constantly adapt to our students' strengths and modify programs where needed. This is truly catering for their needs and doing whatever we can to help them succeed. We can – and need – to use data to achieve this.

A benefit of Sharratt and Fullan's work is that it is full to the brim with examples of system-wide improvement. Specific school examples are less common, but that does not mean that the improvement Sharratt and Fullan discuss cannot be replicated in individual schools and classrooms. After discussing improvements in the district of Sanger, California, Sharratt and Fullan (2013) state,

> This process can be replicated anywhere. However, this will require shifting the role of data from an anaemic list of statistics and punitive accountability to the daily learning that comes from informed and committed groups of leaders and learners understanding the students behind the statistics. (p. 48)

Sharratt and Fullan call on teachers, leaders and learners to engage in the data and to understand the individual lives that are represented by the numbers.

In Australia, recent framing documents such as AITSL's teacher standards and NSIT are changing the expectations for Australian teachers to use data, feedback and assessment regularly in their practice. Where using data was never previously explicitly outlined, the 2008 Melbourne Declaration on Educational Goals for Young Australians shaped this significant change in Australian education. The subsequent Alice Springs (Mparntwe) Education Declaration of 2019 has increased these expectations even further. The following sections discuss the expectations of the AITSL standards and the NSIT for Australian educators with respect to the use of data.

AITSL STANDARDS

The AITSL (2011) standards outline seven standards for teacher professional practice under three domains: professional knowledge, professional practice and professional engagement. Under the domain of professional knowledge sit Standard 1, 'Know students and how they learn', and Standard 2, 'Know the content and how to teach it'; under professional practice sit Standard 3, 'Plan for and implement effective teaching and learning', Standard 4, 'Create and maintain supportive and safe learning environments', and Standard 5, 'Assess, provide feedback and report on student learning'; and under the domain of professional engagement sit Standard 6, 'Engage in professional learning', and Standard 7, 'Engage professionally with colleagues, parents/carers and the community' (AITSL, 2011, p. 4). Teachers operate at one of four levels of proficiency in each focus area within each standard: 'graduate', 'proficient', 'highly accomplished' or 'lead teacher'.

Using data to differentiate, modify programs, cater for student difference and celebrate success addresses elements of Standards 1, 2, 3 and 5 from the AITSL teacher standards. Across six focus areas, Standard 1 outlines the expectation that teachers will understand the characteristics of their learners and cater for the needs of the students in front of them. Using data is explicitly outlined in the descriptor for a lead teacher in Focus area 1.5, 'Differentiate teaching to meet the specific learning needs of students across the full range of abilities' (AITSL, 2011, p. 11). But becoming a lead teacher in almost all of these focus areas requires the use of data in some way, though it is not explicitly referenced. Evaluating, modifying and ensuring programs cater for the needs of all students, including Aboriginal and Torres Strait Islander students, students with diverse backgrounds and students with a disability, relies on the collection of both qualitative and quantitative data to measure the impact of programs and evaluate teacher effectiveness.

Standard 2 contains a focus area that refers to data specifically; Focus area 2.5, 'Literacy and numeracy strategies', refers to a lead teacher being able to use student data and research-based knowledge to monitor and evaluate the impact of teaching strategies in their school (AITSL, 2011, p. 13). Like in Focus area 1.5, lead teachers are required to use student assessment data because literacy and numeracy strategies should be informed and motivated by an understanding of student performance and research-based knowledge.

Much like Standard 1, many aspects of Standard 3 require the use of data even though it is not stated explicitly. Engaging parents in the learning process, reviewing teaching and learning programs, reviewing pedagogy and strategies, and having high expectations are all required of teachers if they are to become lead teachers in Standard 3. Using student assessment data is mentioned directly in the descriptors for Focus area 3.6, 'Evaluate and improve teaching programs', because there is an expectation that teachers use student assessment data to evaluate and improve teaching programs beyond graduate level (AITSL, 2011, p. 15).

Finally, Standard 5 outlines the expectation that teachers will collect, analyse and report on data for their classes and in their schools. This is the standard in which the expectations around data, feedback and assessment are most clearly articulated. All five focus areas within Standard 5 relate to collecting, analysing and using data. Most specifically, Focus areas 5.1, 'Assess student learning', and 5.4, 'Interpret student data', refer explicitly to using student data (AITSL, 2011, pp. 18, 19). In particular, as a starting point, a graduate teacher in Focus area 5.4 must 'Demonstrate the capacity to interpret student assessment data to evaluate student learning and modify teaching practice' (AITSL, 2011, p. 19). While this might seem like a relatively low benchmark, it is expected that skills in interpreting student data increase beyond a 'capacity to interpret' as teachers progress through proficient, highly accomplished and lead teacher levels.

NATIONAL SCHOOL IMPROVEMENT TOOL (NSIT)

Since 2013, the NSIT has shaped reform and improvement agendas in schools in Australia (Bishop & Bishop, 2017). The NSIT is an evidence-based framework that was developed by ACER as a means by which to monitor school progress and improvement. The NSIT tool evaluates schools across nine domains:

1. An explicit improvement agenda
2. Analysis and discussion of data
3. A culture that promotes learning
4. Targeted use of school resources
5. An expert teaching team
6. Systematic curriculum delivery
7. Differentiated teaching and learning
8. Effective pedagogical practices
9. School–community partnerships (ACER, 2016, p.iii)

Of most relevance to this discussion on data is Domain 2, 'Analysis and discussion of data'. When detailing the aims of Domain 2, the NSIT states,

> *A high priority is given to the school-wide analysis and discussion of systematically collected data on student outcomes, including academic, attendance and behavioural outcomes, and student wellbeing. Data analyses consider overall school performance as well as the performances of students from identified priority groups; evidence of improvement/ regression over time; performances in comparison with similar schools; and, in the case of data from standardised tests, measures of growth across the years of school. (ACER, 2016, p. 4)*

Schools are rated 'outstanding', 'high', 'medium' or 'low' in each of the nine domains. Consequently, schools receive nine overall scores for the domains, meaning that they might achieve better in some areas than others. A school that is rated outstanding in Domain 2 is described in the following way:

> *The principal and other school leaders clearly articulate their belief that reliable data on student outcomes are crucial to the school's improvement agenda. The school has established and is implementing a systematic plan for the collection, analysis and use of a range of student achievement and wellbeing data. Test data in areas such as literacy, numeracy and science are key elements of this plan.*
>
> *Data are used throughout the school to identify gaps in student learning, to monitor improvement over time and to monitor growth across the years*

> of school. A high priority has been given to professional development aimed at building teachers' and leaders' data literacy skills. Staff conversations and language reflect a sophisticated understanding of student assessment and data concepts (e.g. value added; growth; improvement; statistical significance).
>
> Teachers are given test data for their classes electronically and are provided with, and use, software to analyse, display and communicate data on individual and class performances and progress, including comparisons of pre- and post-test results. Teachers routinely use objective data on student achievement as evidence of successful teaching. (ACER, 2016, p. 5)

I think it is fair to say that achieving the outstanding rating for Domain 2 is a pretty tough ask! Systematic plans, identifying gaps in student learning, monitoring growth and progress, prioritising data literacy professional development . . . The task is huge! All with very little training provided to schools as to how to use the data, graduates officially needing to demonstrate only a 'capacity to interpret' data, and some schools and systems only just starting to employ people with added responsibility for learning analytics and student data.

Although the NSIT provides feedback on how schools can move up the continuum, I wonder how many schools in Australia are capable of achieving this in Domain 2 during a review cycle. I know there are plenty of teachers and school leaders in Australia that have the desire to use data at this level, and indeed many of these individuals have the skills. But I wonder how many entire schools are in this position. When discussing the NSIT, ACER's Robert Marshall reported that the biggest challenge with using data is the development of school systems and processes by which they can be used (ACER, 2017). Further, Professor Amanda Datnow stated that educators must have a clear plan when collecting data: knowing what they are collecting, why they are collecting it and what they intend to do with it (ACER, 2017). But how do schools create these plans, systems and processes if they're not sure where to start in the first place?

Even though it is clear that the AITSL teacher standards and NSIT direct our attention to using and analysing data, there is little specific guidance about what this actually looks like. The expectations are clear. Teachers just now need to know *how* to go about using data in a way that is effective and efficient – and has an impact.

MEASURING PROGRESS AS WELL AS ACHIEVEMENT

> I'm a very serious 'possibilist'. That's something I made up. It means someone who neither hopes without reason, nor fears without reason, someone who constantly resists the overdramatic worldview. As a possibilist, I see all this progress, and it fills me with conviction and hope that further progress is possible. This is not optimistic. It is having a clear and reasonable idea about how things are. It is having a worldview that is constructive and useful. (Rosling, 2018, p. 69)

When discussing the use of student data, we usually hear about achievement. When states are compared in NAPLAN results, the media talk about achievement. When we award students learning-area prizes in schools, we celebrate achievement. When students are accepted into universities with a 'top-down' entrance system, where the highest achieving student applicants are offered a place, this is based on achievement. Of course, recognising achievement has a purpose – we should always reward and recognise students who work hard and achieve great results. However, this isn't the only type of data that we should be collecting, analysing, using and celebrating in schools.

There are many students in our schools who, despite their best efforts, will not dux a learning area, achieve all As on their report, or perform at three or four bands above the national minimum standard in NAPLAN tests. When we only recognise achievement, this significant number of students is not seen or celebrated. The reality is that there are many students who persevere and persist to make gains in a particular criterion or writing genre, or to finally move from a C grade to a B grade in a learning area. For these changes to occur, a student might have significantly changed their approach, sought and acted on feedback in different ways to how they had previously, or changed their home or school routine to improve. The students who make these changes and who make progress, should be recognised and celebrated in the same way that our highest achievers are. And teachers should have access to information that shows the progress that each student is making.

Australian teachers are increasingly expected to measure growth rather than achievement alone, but guidance about what this looks like is quite limited. Progress measures are referred to in the NSIT's descriptions of Domain 2 and schools rated Outstanding, with both referring to the use of data to measure growth and improvement, not just achievement (ACER, 2016). Similarly, a 2017 publication from ACER stated that evaluation of student data should be used to inform teaching so that students progress with their learning. In this article, the contributor Robert Marshall stated that Australian schools often have access to grades from summative assessments, but do not typically collect data on student progress. More recently, the Alice Springs (Mparntwe) Education Declaration has further raised the expectations on teachers to assess, collect, monitor, adapt to and feedback information about progress and achievement. In fact, in this document, progress is mentioned twice as often as achievement!

Australian policy and framing documents are not the only resources that draw our attention to the notion of progress measures. In Carol Dweck's (2010) work on mindset, she identifies the need for teachers to recognise effort and progress as a method by which to create a growth mindset in the classroom. She states that teachers might do this implicitly through increasing the difficulty of tasks so that students see themselves achieving and completing tasks that they may not have been able to before. But Dweck also states that teachers can demonstrate progress explicitly: by providing a pre-test and then testing after the unit. This process shows students – because they achieve higher results in the post-test and have made clear progress – that their intelligence is not fixed and that they can make progress and increase their achievement with effort. In her subsequent work, Dweck (2015) has found that focusing on developing a culture of growth mindset raises student motivation and achievement. If we consider these findings in the context of learning area results, NAPLAN data and ACER percentiles, we can potentially increase student motivation and achievement by focusing on their progress.

John Hattie (2017) expresses similar sentiments about measuring growth in the context of NAPLAN results, arguing we should focus more on measuring progress than on comparing achievement against averages. After all, 'we do not send our students to schools to maintain the average; we do not ask teachers to teach to the average' (para. 4). Rather, Hattie continues, we seek to 'add value' to students' capabilities. He frames the problem – and the solution – like this:

> . . . teachers have few, if any, assessments that can measure an individual student's growth over time. We need to make it easier for teachers to do this. We need to back our teachers to win. We need to help them collect, interpret, use and share meaningful progress data. We need to empower teachers to immediately take action where it's needed. When teachers have access to information about individual students' progress they can be more targeted in what and how they teach. They can identify gaps early, including areas where a student may have missed core concepts in learning. (para. 28–31)

Hattie argues that by focusing on progress rather than solely achievement, teachers can be more strategic in their pedagogical choices and targeted in their differentiation. This knowledge of student progress can be tied to resourcing, supporting teachers where necessary and catering for the needs of all students. This, Hattie states, leads to empowerment of teachers, students and parents, which will lead to improved outcomes.

Like the challenges that Hattie mentions, in my experience, there is limited authentic progress tracking in Australian schools. Sure, there are annual reports and newspaper articles that demonstrate the movement of a school from year to year, or that detail the progress being made by a whole system. There are a handful of schools I have worked with that show authentic progress on semester reports. But progress – which has the potential to motivate and empower – is not being truly harnessed in Australian schools for individual students. So what does it look like in real schools with real students?

To me, progress is about those incremental steps forward students make. As a noun, *progress* is defined as 'a proceeding to a further or higher stage, or through such stages successively'; 'advancement in general' and, most relevant to our purposes, 'growth or development; continuous improvement' (Macquarie Dictionary Publishers, 2021). As a verb, its meanings are 'to advance' and 'to go forwards or onwards' (Macquarie Dictionary Publishers, 2021).

Given these definitions, I believe that true progress tracking shows student growth and development over time – from the starting point, through the incremental steps, on to their achievement of a goal. Some students will make these incremental steps quicker than others and their end products or goals might differ, but if we are truly and authentically tracking progress, we are keeping track of how students are building their skills at points along the way, and we are looking back at how these compare with previous outcomes. Tracking progress is not only about assessing summatively at the end of a six-month period and making a comparison back to the previous reporting period; we need systems and strategies to help us track the steps forward that happen along the journey. While summative assessment can contribute to tracking and the discussion of progress, it must be viewed and visualised longitudinally and alongside formative tasks to form a picture of the progress a student is making.

In Chapter 5 there are some examples of the ways in which progress can be tracked by a teacher in their classes. Looking forward, the National Learning Progressions and Online Formative Assessment Initiative will, in the not-too-distant future, hopefully provide a mechanism with which this can be done centrally (Education Services Australia, n.d.).

This chapter has covered a number of uses for data and the ways data can lead to action. Data should be used and analysed by teachers to change programs, develop strategies and differentiate for students' individual needs, helping them reach their potential. Students should be front and centre when we talk about using and analysing data, because ultimately they are the ones who are affected by the way we use it – or don't use it! Teachers having both access to and an understanding of student data is the first part of the puzzle. We have a long way to go before all Australian teachers are comfortable with this and using truly evidence-informed approaches that harness the power of data storytelling.

Taking a different perspective, many students rarely know their data. This is because teachers often do not often share it with them in a way that is formative and leads to future growth and improvement. Too often, it sits on data walls in offices, on computer programs or laptops, and never makes it to the key recipients: that is, the individuals who have the most control over their progress and achievement, the students. This contradicts the extensive amounts of literature that tell us that feedback is one of the key influences on student achievement. Therefore, the following chapter considers the impact of feedback, and discusses how and why data should be used in feedback to and with students.

CHAPTER 2

THE POWER OF FEEDBACK

... teachers seldom provide the types of feedback interventions identified as effective to improve learning and development.

(Gamlem, 2015, p. 462)

Using data to plan units, differentiate lessons and celebrate success are just a few of the uses for data in our schools. At the same time, we also know that feedback to students is an important factor in improving academic achievement (Black & Wiliam, 1998). Effective feedback improves the quality of a student's work and builds the motivation and confidence of the learner (Brookhart, 2011). Therefore, providing feedback about student data can have an impact on performance. But much of the existing literature in the field of feedback discusses feedback on class formative or summative tasks and does not critically consider the role of sharing data with students.

Seeing as the power of feedback is so clearly documented in the literature, it is possible that teachers could also use standardised-testing data in feedback to improve outcomes and results. For example, NAPLAN and ACER's PAT may not currently be used in feedback to students, but why aren't they? If research tells us that feedback has a significant impact, and we want students to improve in literacy and numeracy, why would we not share that information in feedback to students?

DEFINITIONS OF FEEDBACK

The term *feedback* was originally used to describe the gap between an output signal and a pre-determined reference level in electronic and electrical circuits. Feedback would provide information to the circuit on its output, to adjust the gap between the expected outcome and the actual outcome of production. The concept of feedback appeared in education literature in the second half of the twentieth century, when Kulhavy (1977), an educational psychologist, stated that feedback was more complex than the traditional systems approach. He stated that although educational feedback could be a simple yes–no response, it could also appear anywhere on a continuum, all the way through to significant corrective feedback to modify and improve the task. Kulhavy identified that educational feedback has two functions: it provides information to a learner about their progress towards the task goals and leads to the learner making adjustments to their work.

Six years after Kulhavy's work, Arkalgud Ramaprasad (1983) identified that feedback did not have a commonly agreed upon definition in management theory. Ramaprasad defined *feedback* as 'information about the gap between the actual level and the reference level of a system parameter which is used to alter the gap in some way' (p. 4). Even though Ramaprasad's definition includes the action of the recipient after they have received feedback, his definition – like Kulhavy's – relies on the receptive-transmission view of learning. In this type of learning, feedback is seen to be a 'gift' from an 'expert' to a recipient, the aim of which is to close the gap in some way (Askew & Lodge, 2000). In their publication on three views of feedback and learning, Askew and Lodge postulate that feedback in this manner is less effective than the other two types of feedback – constructivist and co-constructivist – where students are involved in the process.

In the field of psychology, Kluger and DeNisi (1996) reviewed quantitative feedback literature and conducted a meta-analysis that considered over three thousand articles relating to the impact of feedback. Prior to their work, there had been significant differences in the literature regarding the effect size of feedback. For the purpose of their study, Kluger and DeNisi defined feedback as 'actions taken by an external agent to provide information regarding some aspects of one's task performance' (1996, p. 255). Unsurprisingly, through their meta-analysis they also found that feedback is effective.

Possibly the most influential review of feedback literature to date has been that of Black and Wiliam (1998). Even though their findings are now over twenty years old, their work is still consistently used and referenced today. Black and Wiliam state that a feedback system provides:

- *data on the actual level of some measurable attribute*
- *data on the reference level of that attribute*
- *a mechanism for comparing the two levels and generating information about the gap between the two levels*

- *a mechanism by which the information can be used to alter the gap. (1998, p. 48)*

Black and Wiliam's definition extends previous work by providing more guidance about identifying and comparing two sets of data, leading to an adjustment of practice, knowledge or skill to bridge the gap between the desired and actual levels.

Around ten years after Black and Wiliam's work, Hattie and Timperley (2007) published their findings on feedback in the classroom context, where they recognised that few studies had previously investigated classroom feedback, even though *feedback* was a term that was regularly used by educators and in the literature. Just as Black and Wiliam's work was seminal in the broader field of feedback, Hattie and Timperley's (2007) has been key in education and is regularly referred to in educational feedback literature. Hattie and Timperley defined educational feedback as:

information provided by an agent (e.g., teacher, peer, book, parent, self, experience) regarding aspects of one's performance or understanding. A teacher or parent can provide corrective information, a peer can provide an alternative strategy, a book can provide information to clarify ideas, a parent can provide encouragement, and a learner can look up the answer to evaluate the correctness of a response. Feedback thus is a 'consequence of performance'. (2007, p. 81)

Although Hattie and Timperley's definition is specific to education and identifies the importance of the role of teachers, parents, peers, learners and resources, it still has room for growth. What it offers in the context of the literature is that there is no mention of a 'gap', moving our understanding of educational feedback from receptive-transmission into the realm of the constructivist (Askew & Lodge, 2000). As outlined, this type of feedback is more effective than the receptive-transmission view of learning belonging to previous feedback definitions because it means that students and teachers construct their understanding together rather than teachers being the 'experts' that 'gift' students feedback in a one-way interaction.

CHARACTERISTICS OF EFFECTIVE FEEDBACK

Needless to say, defining feedback in an educational context has not been straightforward. But even more complex is finding a definition for effective feedback. The literature has proven that feedback is effective, but that not all feedback types have the same impact. Yet the extant literature again lacks a common definition of effective feedback, relying on lists of characteristics of what effective feedback looks like, rather than clearly defining the term.

A key contribution in the area of effective feedback was that of Kathleen Brinko (1993), who developed an understanding of effective feedback in the context of university lecturers by considering W questions for both the person giving the feedback and the person receiving the feedback. The six W questions are who, what, when, where, why and how, denoting the following avenues of inquiry:

- 'who' – the people involved in the feedback process
- 'what' – the content or information conveyed to the recipient
- 'when' – relating to timing
- 'where' – the location in which the feedback is delivered
- 'why' – the purpose of the feedback
- 'how' – the mode in which the feedback is delivered.

The 'where' and 'why' of effective feedback are excluded from Brinko's investigation, because it is assumed that feedback is generally delivered in the classroom or on classwork, and the 'why' is explained in other research about the power of feedback. Brinko also notes that the 'what' of feedback is the most complex of the W questions, and details lists of factors that contribute to the effectiveness of feedback.

Nearly twenty years after, Bain and Swan (2011) brought together Brinko's work with that of Scheeler et al. (2004). Scheeler et al. also sought to identify the characteristics of effective feedback, but in the field of providing teachers with feedback on their teaching practice. Though its original context is slightly different, this list of six ideal characteristics and conditions of effective feedback compiled by Bain and Swan (2011) has been used extensively in the context of effective feedback for school students:

1. *Feedback is most effective when it comes from multiple sources including the recipient and is shared in a variety of modes (Brinko, 1993).*
2. *Feedback is most effective when the standing or status of the source is lower or equivalent to the recipient (Brinko, 1993).*
3. *Feedback is most effective when it is immediate (Brinko, 1993; Scheeler et al., 2004).*
4. *Feedback is most effective when it contains accurate irrefutable evidence (Brinko, 1993).*
5. *Feedback is most effective when it is positive, specific and corrective (Brinko, 1993).*
6. *Feedback is most effective when the information shared is focused and concrete (Brinko, 1993).*

(Bain and Swan, 2011, p. 675)

Despite creating yet another list of the characteristics of effective feedback, Bain and Swan did not define effective feedback itself. Similarly, Wylie and Lyon (2015) did not define effective feedback but stated that it 'must identify gaps between the desired learning goal and the student's present status, provide actionable suggestions for how to close the gap and students must then act upon the provided suggestions' (p. 142).

It is difficult to know why these key authors in the field did not define effective feedback. Is it because a definition would be useless? Would a definition for effective feedback just say, '*Effective feedback* is feedback that achieves all of the aforementioned characteristics'? Why can't effective feedback be defined as 'feedback that achieves its purpose – it provides information on performance, compares the work to a set measure and provides information on ways the student could improve'? The literature tells us that feedback is differentially effective – some feedback is a complete waste of time and effort, and misses the point. Given the impact that we know it can have, I struggle to understand why effective feedback has not yet been clearly defined in the literature.

It could be possible that a definition for effective feedback has not been generated because it is, in fact, difficult to define and measure. How does one exactly measure the impact of feedback if the feedback was corrections on an essay draft, or guiding verbal feedback during an assessment lesson? Much of the feedback that teachers issue in class is qualitative, and so it is difficult to ascertain its impact. Students might report that watching a video performance of their volleyball spike and talking through their technique with the teacher improved their skill. A teacher talking through a series of steps to complete a mathematics problem might help a student identify their error and improve their work in the future. But unless a grade was assigned to the specific skill or level of understanding beforehand (which in itself is difficult) and then compared with a grade afterwards, it is quite difficult to measure the impact of qualitative feedback – and, consequently, progress.

THE IMPACT OF FEEDBACK

Despite the lack of a commonly accepted definition for effective feedback and the most useful definition of feedback being over ten years old, there is no doubt about the impact that feedback has on a learner. There is no shortage of literature in this area, with Bangert-Drowns et al. (1991), Jackson (2018), Kluger & DeNisi (1996), Kulhavy & Stock (1989), Sadler (1989) and Zacharias (2007) all demonstrating a range of different effect sizes for feedback. The literature makes it clear that the impact of feedback is differentially effective depending on the type of feedback offered. Therefore, even though teachers can give students significant amounts of feedback, it does not always translate into improvements in academic performance (Hattie, 2009).

As I've already noted, one of the largest studies on the effectiveness of feedback was that of Kluger and DeNisi in 1996. Their meta-analysis of over 3000 studies found that feedback positively affected performance, on average, 0.41 of a standard deviation than for people who did not receive feedback. An easy equivalent that they use to illustrate this finding is that of a student moving from the fiftieth to the sixty-sixth percentile on a standardised test (for example, the ACER PAT). Other authors had previously attempted to measure the impact of feedback but had achieved quite mixed results (see Bangert-Drowns et al., 1991; Crooks, 1988; Natriello, 1987). Consequently, Kluger and DeNisi's work, although over two decades old, is regularly referred to and seen to be the key initial publication that acknowledges the significant impact that feedback can have on a learner.

Two years after Kluger and DeNisi's meta-analysis was published, Black and Wiliam (1998) performed their review of the impact of formative feedback. Using previous work by Crooks (1988) and Natriello (1987), and comparing eight major studies of formative assessment, they found that the effect size of formative assessment and feedback can be as high as 0.7. Given that Hattie (2012) talks about an effect size of 0.4 being the 'hinge point' – the point at which an educational intervention becomes worthwhile – these results suggest formative assessment is a worthwhile strategy. Black and Wiliam (1998) state:

> *formative assessment does improve learning. The gains in achievement appear to be quite considerable, and as noted earlier, among the largest ever reported for educational interventions. As an illustration of just how big these gains are, an effect size of 0.7, if it could be achieved on a nationwide scale, would be equivalent to raising the mathematics attainment score of an 'average' country like England, New Zealand or the United States into the 'top five' after the Pacific Rim countries of Singapore, Korea, Japan and Hong Kong. (p. 61)*

But a key finding from all of the literature on the impact of feedback is that the effect size varies considerably, and it is largely dependent on the type of feedback issued (see Hattie, 2009; Hattie & Timperley, 2007; Kluger & DeNisi, 1996). For example, Hattie and Timperley (2007) found considerable differences in effect size, depending on whether feedback contained cues (effect size 1.1), reinforcement (effect size 0.94), praise (effect size 0.14), rewards (effect size 0.31) or punishment (effect size 0.2). Hattie and Timperley also found that to be effective, feedback must answer three questions: 'Where am I going? (What are the goals?), How am I going? (What progress is being made towards the goal?), and Where to next? (What activities need to be undertaken to make better progress?)' (2007, p. 86).

Not only does feedback relay information about student goals, progress and strategies for the future, Susan Brookhart (2011) states that it is also an opportunity for students to be shown something about their work that they had not previously identified themselves. Feedback allows students to reflect and make modifications and helps them to be successful and achieve their goals.

FORMATIVE AND SUMMATIVE ASSESSMENT

Classroom data and feedback are usually generated by student performance in class tasks and assessment. Depending on the purpose of the assessment and the way the feedback is provided, it is described as being either formative or summative. But the ideas of formative and summative assessment, and the formative and summative ways in which this data is shared and used with students, is still evolving. Bloom et al. (1971), writing in the *Handbook on formative and summative evaluation of student learning*, discuss and compare formative and summative assessment. In this discussion, Bloom et al. recognise Scriven's (1967) explanation of the terms, and describe the differences between formative and summative approaches as follows:

> *the main purpose of formative observations . . . is to determine the degree of mastery of a given learning task and to pinpoint the part of the task not mastered . . . The purpose is not to grade or certify the learner; it is to help both the learner and the teacher focus upon the particular learning necessary for movement towards mastery. On the other hand, summative evaluation is directed toward a much more general assessment of the degree to which the larger outcomes have been attained over the entire course or some substantial part of it. (Bloom et al., 1971, p. 81)*

In addition, Bloom et al. (1971) identify three defining characteristics of formative and summative assessment:

1. Purpose (for helping the student learn, or for grading).
2. Timing (frequent or at the end of course).
3. Level of generalization (narrow, small tasks, compared with broad assessment). (p. 81)

The most important factor of these three is the timing in which the formative or summative assessment is performed (Newton, 2007). Identifying a task as formative or summative depends on whether it is performed at the end of the unit to summarise learning, or throughout the unit in smaller and more regular tasks. However, Black and Wiliam's (2003) explanation differs to that of Bloom et al.'s, reporting the 'use of the terms "formative" and "summative" applied not to the assessments themselves, but to the functions they served' (p. 623).

Ultimately, whether something is formative or summative depends on not only the nature of the task, but also the way the data and feedback are used. Summative assessment data can be used formatively, and something that was planned as a formative task may not actually be used effectively in formative feedback. Similarly, I believe that standardised testing data can, although it is technically a summary of skill and understanding, be used formatively and beneficially in our schools.

While these types of testing don't tell us everything we can know about a student, they can provide an accurate representation of their potential or ability in a particular area. More often than not, the data is a good reflection of student ability, so why would we not capitalise on this accuracy? Take for example a group of students who achieved good results in their Year 7 NAPLAN assessment and are now getting ready to sit their Year 9 tests. It might be useful and beneficial to talk with students about the things they did well in the previous test as a way to boost their confidence and self-belief. Further, a student who is underperforming in mathematics while also placing in the upper two bands in the NAPLAN numeracy test might benefit from having a conversation with their mathematics teacher about their potential in that particular learning area. Having the standardised testing data to prove a student's ability provides solid evidence for a conversation on their potential, rather than vague or nonspecific information that the student may disregard. Finally, a cohort of students might benefit from a conversation about their potential regarding NAPLAN performance, previous school-leaver data and their Year 12 outcomes. This conversation and insight into their potential could lead to improved educational outcomes.

Though standardised testing has its limits, why would we not want to share successes and challenges with our students? I do not believe that teachers should disregard all of this data because a small number of students might underperform on the day of the testing or because they may fundamentally disagree with the testing in the first place.

CONCEPTIONS OF ASSESSMENT

In addition to understanding formative and summative assessment, and holding different beliefs about learning, teachers also have different conceptions of the purpose of assessment. This in turn impacts the way in which they use and view assessment and student data. The three key conceptions of assessment, as identified by Brown et al. (2011), are:

1. assessment as improvement of teaching and learning (improvement)

2. assessment as making schools and teachers accountable for their effectiveness (school accountability)

3. assessment as making students accountable for their learning (student accountability). (p. 211)

Using these three conceptions of assessment in their research in Queensland schools, Brown et al. found that primary school teachers perceive that assessment improves teaching and learning; however, secondary school teachers believe assessment holds students accountable for their learning.

In a different way of looking at assessment, Newton (2007) argues that the purpose of assessments should be classified as either judgement level, decision level or impact level. *Judgement-level assessment* is defined as 'the technical aim of an assessment event (e.g. the purpose is to derive a standards-referenced judgement, expressed as a grade on a range from A to E)', while *decision-level assessment* relates to 'the use of an assessment judgement, the decision, action or process which it enables (e.g. the purpose is to support a selection decision for entry to higher education)' (Newton, 2007, p. 150). Finally, *impact level assessment* concerns 'the intended impacts of running an assessment system (e.g. the purposes are to ensure that students remain motivated, and that all students learn a common core for each subject)' (Newton, 2007, p. 150). In the way that it is usually used in Australia, summative assessment has a judgement-level purpose. On the other hand, formative tasks inform the decision level.

Another factor worth considering when thinking about conceptions and the purpose of assessment in Australia is the way that assessment is changing in an increasingly technologically mediated learning environment. Cope and Kalantzis (2015) suggest the emerging assessment model, which is being seen more and more in our schools, differs quite significantly from the more traditional assessment model. Some of the characteristics of these models are compared in table 2.1.

Table 2.1. Characteristics of traditional models of assessment compared with emerging models of assessment

Traditional assessment model	Emerging assessment model
Assessment is external to learning processes; 'validity' or alignment of the test with what that been taught is a challenge.	Assessment is authentically embedded in learning; 'validity' is less of a challenge.
Limited opportunities for assessment result in restricted datasets.	There can be many small data points during the learning process. These include diagnostic and formative data.
There is a conventional focus on summative assessment.	There is renewed focus on formative assessment.
Summative assessment is an outcome- or end-view of learning.	Summative assessment is a progress view, using data that was at first formative to trace learning progressions; feedback is recursive.
Assessors are experts or teachers.	Assessments are crowdsourced and moderated from multiple perspectives, including from learners themselves and their peers.
There is a focus on individual memory and deductions leading to correct or incorrect answers.	There is a focus on knowledge representations and artifacts that acknowledge textual provenance and trace peer collaborations.
Assessments are of fact and correct application.	Assessments are of complex epistemic performance and disciplinary practice.
Assessment experts as report grades.	Learners and teachers are data analysts with the support of analytics dashboards and visualisations.

SOURCE: Adapted from Cope & Kalantzis, 2015

Cope and Kalantzis (2015) report that assessment is moving from being external to the learning process to a point in which it is embedded in learning. The notion of data is changing as there are more opportunities for small data collection and assessment points throughout the learning process. Consequently, the focus shifts from large summative assessments that generate infrequent data to formative assessments that generate more frequent data. Most relevant to this discussion on the use of data and feedback, Cope and Kalantzis refer to a shift from the teacher's responsibility being just reporting grades to becoming data analysts who use analytics dashboards and visualisations to represent student performance with and for students.

This final point of Cope and Kalantzis's emerging assessment model is increasingly prevalent in some teachers' and leaders' practice in Australia. For some, there has been a shift from traditional to emerging models of assessment, where there has been a complete reframing of the role and purpose of assessment in classrooms and schools. Some teachers and leaders are data analysts, who use visualisations and dashboards of student data in their work. However, the shift into this space is a slow one and the outcomes of this practice have major implications for pedagogy and skill development.

Another interesting notion in the emerging model of assessment is the reference to students being data analysts, as this is a significantly different conception of assessment compared to the traditional model. For students to become data analysts, they need teachers who are analysts themselves. In my doctoral research, many students expressed a desire to know about their data and performance, reporting that they wanted to learn more about how they were progressing (Fisk, 2017). As much as this is great for students, and potentially represents a massive shift in pedagogical practice, it requires upskilling of students by teachers who may not have had adequate training themselves.

ASSESSMENT *FOR* LEARNING, ASSESSMENT *AS* LEARNING AND ASSESSMENT *OF* LEARNING

Assessment for learning is 'the process of seeking and interpreting evidence for use by learners and their teachers to decide where the learners are in their learning, where they need to go and how best to get there' (Assessment Reform Group, 2002, p. 2). More specific to the Australian context, Val Klenowski (2009) defines assessment for learning as 'part of everyday practice by students, teachers and peers that seeks, reflects upon and responds to information from dialogue, demonstration and observation in ways that enhance ongoing learning' (p. 264).

The term *assessment for learning* was originally made popular by Black and Wiliam (1998) and became increasingly accepted following Wiliam's (2011) review of the practice. The Assessment Reform Group, which was formed in 1998 and included both Black and Wiliam, has become well-known for its list of assessment for learning principles. Expanding on its definition, the Assessment Reform Group (2002) states that assessment for learning:

- *. . . is part of effective planning*
- *focuses on how pupils learn*
- *is central to classroom practice*
- *is a key professional skill*
- *is sensitive and constructive*
- *fosters motivation*
- *promotes understanding of goals and criteria*
- *helps learners know how to improve*

- *develops the capacity for self and peer assessment*
- *recognises all educational achievement . . . (p. 2)*

In a perfect world, assessment for learning brings students to the fore, where they become 'self-monitoring, modifying and improving aspects of a performance that have yet to reach the desired standard' (Dixon et al., 2011, p. 366). Although most of the definitions of feedback offered earlier in the chapter have been criticised for aligning with the receptive-transmission model of learning, assessment for learning fits in the co-constructivist model of learning as students and teachers collaborate and feedback occurs in a loop between both parties.

The reality is that assessment for learning is different to assessment *of* learning and assessment *as* learning. Assessment of learning is a summary: it provides an overall picture of how a student has performed at the end of an assessment period. But assessment for learning is embedded in the learning process and helps the learner develop their own understanding of their performance, which ideally leads to improvement in the future. Meanwhile, assessment as learning is when learning occurs through the assessment task itself.

There is some confusion about the different terminology of assessment for learning and assessment of learning, and formative and summative assessment. Some literature states that assessment for learning is not synonymous with formative assessment, neither is assessment of learning and summative assessment. Rather, the terms *formative* and *summative* directly relate assessment to the 'function it actually serves' (Wiliam, 2011, p. 16), while categorising assessment as *of* and *for* learning refers to the 'purpose for which the assessment is carried out' (p. 16). Further, it is possible that a summative task may provide feedback that is used in a formative manner to improve practice in the future. It is also possible that a formative task might be undertaken without the resulting feedback and data being used in a way that assists the student to improve. Therefore, formative and summative use of data and feedback may not always directly align with formative and summative assessment.

Assessment of, for and as learning are key concepts that are important for educators in Australia. The shift towards assessment for and as learning, and away from solely assessment of learning, is largely a result of the Melbourne Declaration on Educational Goals for Young Australians, which for the first time referred to different types of assessment at a national policy level (MCEETYA, 2008). The Melbourne Declaration introduces the concepts of assessment of, for and as learning by explicitly discussing their use in this key document.

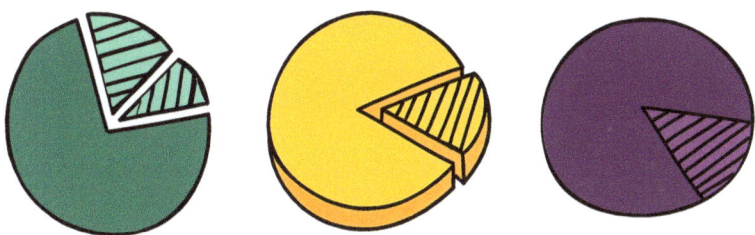

CHAPTER 3

EMBRACING A DATA-INFORMED CULTURE

You never know who will go on to do good or even great things or become the next great influencer in the world – so treat everyone like they are that person.

Kat Cole, 'See what's possible, and help others do the same'

In the different roles in which I have worked with data, I have witnessed a myriad of teacher, parent and student perceptions about its use. I have heard members of all three groups speak negatively about NAPLAN testing, I have heard questions about the validity and relevance of the ACER PAT program, and I have heard all sorts of qualitative and anecdotal justifications for high and low marks. I have had people say to me, 'Oh I get it, but I'm not a numbers person,' or my favourite, 'Oh yeah, but Selena, I'm a humanist.'

On the other hand, I have worked with people that are better mathematicians than I, who have their own brilliant spreadsheet strategies, visualisation platforms and tracking mechanisms. I have worked with a lot of people who are enthusiastic about using data and are willing to learn. Irrespective of how you have come to read this book, you obviously have an interest in student data and in using it further. To do that, you are already recognising the value that it brings and embracing the idea of a data-informed culture in your classroom and school.

Our willingness to embrace and use data is influenced by a range of factors: our colleagues, our experience with data, our existing beliefs, our information technology skills, the school climate, our previous training (or lack thereof), the views and skills of our leadership team, and our willingness and ability to learn and adapt to new priorities in education. In this chapter, I will address three key factors and their impact on the use of data in your classroom and school: mindset, positive psychology and grit. Each of these three factors has received extensive coverage in educational literature of late.

In our context, *mindset* refers to the way in which a person views their intelligence and abilities – and whether they have a fixed mindset or a growth mindset makes a difference. Your mindset – and those of your leadership team, colleagues and students – about data, will significantly affect (and indeed determine) the data-informed culture in your school. *Positive psychology* is 'the study of the conditions and processes that contribute to the flourishing or optimal functioning of people, groups, and institutions' (Gable & Haidt, 2005, p. 103). When discussing data use and data cultures, positive psychology reminds us to use data for the right reasons: to contribute to the flourishing and optimal functioning of our colleagues, teams and students. *Grit* – as popularised by Angela Duckworth's 2016 book of the same name – refers to the amount of effort a person puts into a task and how persistent they are, which Duckworth found counts twice when translating talent into achievement. Grit relates to the way in which we use data and feedback with students to develop their 'grittiness', as well as our own persistence when it comes to sticking with developing data skills. I know you will be able to identify examples of times when a well-calibrated mindset, positive framing or persisting with a task led to improved achievement for a student, you or a colleague. This chapter will consider these three factors and discuss the impact and relevance of these factors on using data and embracing a data-informed culture within your school.

MINDSET

Much literature discusses the importance of mindset. A 2017 McKinsey and Company report (Mourshed et al., 2017) investigated the factors that influenced student achievement in the 2015 PISA testing in over seventy countries. The authors found that there were two major impacts on student performance: providing opportunities for direct teaching and inquiry-based learning, and the mindset of the learner. The report found that in almost all regions in the world, mindset (both general mindset and mindset toward the learning area) was one of the most important, if not the most significant, impacts on achievement. In fact, as shown in figure 3.1, students in North America who were from the bottom socio-economic quartile, but who had a well-calibrated mindset, outperformed students in the top socio-economic quartile with poorly calibrated mindsets.

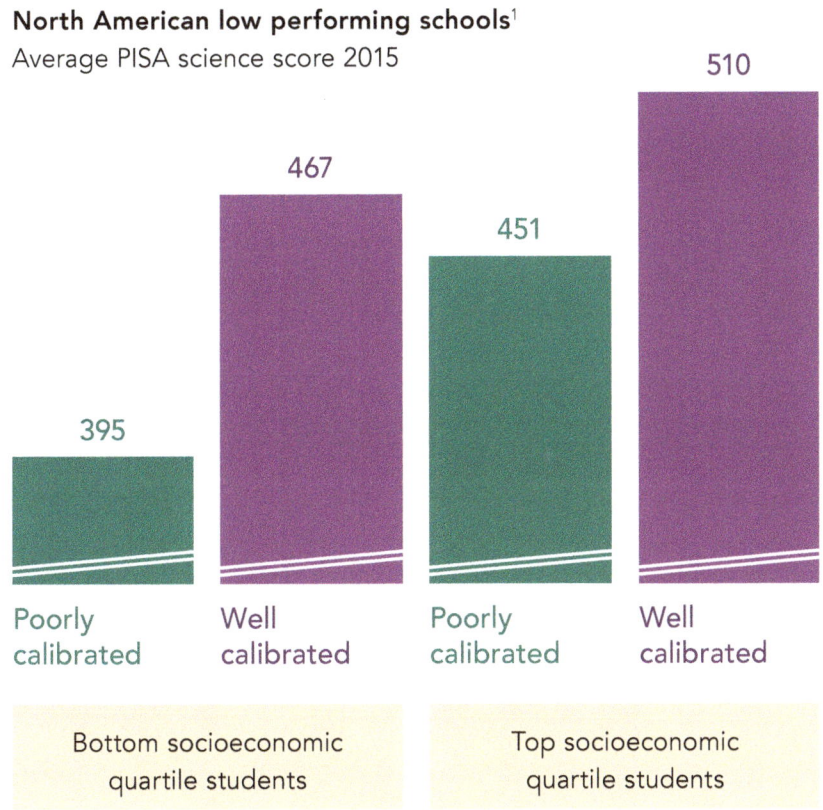

Figure 3.1. The effect of mindset on the results of bottom and top socio-economic quartile students' results in 2015 PISA testing

SOURCE: Mourshed et al., 2017, p. 5

What does this mean? Mindset matters. Having the right mindset means that our students are more likely to outperform those from higher socio-economic groups and achieve above and beyond what they would have with a poorly calibrated mindset.

Growth mindset has received a lot of attention of late, thanks largely to the work of Carol Dweck (2006). Dweck categorises two types of mindset: fixed and growth. Someone with a fixed mindset believes that intelligence is set; they have what they are born with and, therefore, do not believe in the power of improvement through effort. Someone with a fixed mindset believes that their intelligence cannot improve or change no matter what they do, whereas someone with a growth mindset believes that intelligence is constantly evolving and that with work and effort it can be improved. A person with a growth mindset believes that, over time, intelligence increases (Dweck, 2006, 2010). Carol Dweck talks about the power of 'yet': a person with a growth mindset, when faced with a challenge, perceives that they cannot do it 'yet'. This statement is telling. A person with a growth mindset inherently believes that even when they face challenges, they will inevitably be able to master the skill or knowledge required to overcome them with practice. But a person with a fixed mindset sees a challenge as something that might catch them out and show that they are not as capable as people perceive (Dweck, 2006, 2010).

Dweck talks about the importance of school culture in building a growth mindset in students. One of the key contributors to student mindset is providing feedback on the effort, process and persistence that they have demonstrated (Dweck, 2010). Dweck states that emphasising for students that learning takes time, and that it cannot be rushed, is key to developing this school culture of a growth mindset. The key messages that teachers should be relaying to students to build a growth mindset culture are that students can be as smart as they would like to be and that their intelligence can change over time.

For our students, this means that we have a responsibility to develop their growth mindsets by discussing effort, talking through process and encouraging them to persist through challenging tasks, rather than giving up easily. One of the ways that we can do this, Dweck (2010) states, is by providing feedback to students on their effort. This might be done qualitatively by engaging in a conversation about the things they tried, how they reframed the problem and tried again, and the sorts of things that students thought during the process. But we can also provide data for our students that reports on their effort. We can show students – through progress marks, judgements and formative assessments – that they can get better, that they are getting better and that their intelligence is not fixed.

Although Dweck's work and the McKinsey and Company publication focus on student mindset and achievement, the mindset of teachers and school leaders is also incredibly important. Growth mindset applies in the workplace too – we and our colleagues have assumptions about whether or not others can change (Dweck, 2007). We know that one of the major influences on student achievement is the teacher, and we know about the impact of growth mindsets. Therefore, teacher mindset counts. I am sure we can all recount our favourite teacher, and I am sure some of the consistent characteristics attributed to them would be that they smiled, cared and had high expectations. I think it would be highly unlikely to hear of a favourite teacher who had low expectations, or who believed that their students were destined for failure. Our favourite teachers were filled with hope. They could see our potential – perhaps even when we could not – and believed that we had something to offer the world.

You may have heard the saying often attributed to Henry Ford, 'Whether you think you can or you can't, you're right.' When discussing teacher mindsets, I would also say it is true that whether teachers think their students can or they can't, they're right. The mindset of teachers affects the mindset and achievement of students, and the mindset of school leaders affects the mindset and achievement of teachers. A teacher's belief in a student's potential will have a great impact on that student's self-belief. A teacher's mindset toward using and analysing data will affect the people around them and influence the level of engagement students have with the data.

This is a significant shift for teachers. But as Tracey Ezard states in her 2015 book, *The buzz*, education is changing and it is no longer possible to remain indefinitely comfortable. This is certainly true across all aspects of education – including the use of data. Change happens, change is necessary and change brings better outcomes for our students. Teachers model learning by being learners themselves through constantly seeking feedback and by adapting and modifying their approaches. Using data is no different. It can be scary, it can be daunting, and it can, unfortunately, trigger fear. But as Tracey Ezard points out, we need to be comfortable giving it a go without necessarily knowing what it will look like in the future. Curiosity and growth mindset are key elements of learning intelligence, as people with a strong sense of learning intelligence often reflect, 'I wonder . . .?' and question, 'What if . . .?' If we, as educators, can move beyond our fear of failing and past our deeply embedded beliefs and assumptions about our skills and intelligence, it can be deeply transformative and satisfying. As long as our approach is guided by our own principles and ethics, and we care for the humans in front of us in our classrooms, our growth mindset will help us to learn new skills and enable us to see that data has great potential.

John Hattie (2012) refers to the teacher also being a learner in his work on visible learning. He talks about the importance of making teaching clear and visible to students; however, in turn, the teacher learns from students about their needs and so also becomes a learner. Hattie also states that teachers who learn from their students have more success as they become deliberate change agents. Using data fits into Hattie's views on the teacher learning about and for the student, because data helps us see learning from the student's perspective. Data shows us students' strengths and weaknesses, some of which may have been less obvious in other assessments. As Tracey Ezard (2015) states,

> *teaching is no longer a one-way street of information, facts and authoritarian insights. Effective teaching relies on continuous feedback loops, reflection and shifts in approach. If we don't see the process of teaching as a robust two-way learning process we are doomed to forever 'do what we have always done' and not respond to the changing needs of our students. (p. 11)*

Your mindset is a key factor in determining whether the way you use data in your classroom and school will be successful. Know that the process will take time, that you can and will get better at it, and that by using data well with students you are also developing understanding of their capacity to grow and improve.

POSITIVE PSYCHOLOGY

Positive psychology is a relatively new field of psychology and gained momentum following Martin E P Seligman's Presidential Address to the American Psychological

Association in 1998 (Linley et al., 2006). Over the years, *positive psychology* has been defined in a number of ways. For example:

> Positive psychology 'is nothing more than the scientific study of ordinary human strengths and virtues. Positive psychology re-visits 'the average person,' with an interest in finding out what works, what is right, and what is improving. It asks, 'What is the nature of the effectively functioning human being, who successfully applies evolved adaptations and learned skills?' (Sheldon & King, 2001, p. 216)
>
> Positive psychology is the scientific study of optimal human functioning. At the meta-psychological level, it aims to redress the imbalance in psychological research and practice by calling attention to the positive aspects of human functioning and experience, and integrating them with our understanding of the negative aspects of human functioning and experience. At the pragmatic level, it is about understanding the wellsprings, processes and mechanisms that lead to desirable outcomes. (Linley et al., 2006, p. 8, emphasis in original)
>
> Positive psychology is the study of the conditions and processes that contribute to the flourishing or optimal functioning of people, groups, and institutions. (Gable & Haidt, 2005, p. 103)

Positive psychology is quite different to the traditional, broader field of psychology, as it is hope-filled. Positive psychology was established out of an identified need to focus on what leads to human flourishing, engagement and happiness, and so focuses on maximising strengths in order to overcome adversity. This is seen to be the opposite of traditional psychology, which focused on solving problems, mental illness, diagnosis and repairing things that have gone wrong – a deficit model. Psychological inquiry had traditionally asked, 'What is broken?', 'What doesn't work?', 'What needs to be fixed?' and 'How can we fix it?' In contrast, positive psychology asks, 'What works?', 'What is right?' and 'What is improving?' (Sheldon & King, 2001). But positive psychology does not only consider human flourishing and the positives; it focuses on the entire person – the good and the bad. It does not ignore the negatives but investigates human flourishing through focusing on our strengths, virtues and the positives.

Positive psychology relates to us as individuals and to the organisations in which we work. According to Seligman & Csikszentmihalyi (2000), positive psychology is about three key areas: 'well-being, contentment, and satisfaction (in the past); hope and optimism (for the future); and flow and happiness (in the present)' (p. 5). They continue, 'At the group level, it is about the civic virtues and the institutions that move individuals toward better citizenship: responsibility, nurturance, altruism, civility, moderation, tolerance, and work ethic' (Seligman & Csikszentmihalyi, 2000, p. 5). Organisations that are grounded in positive psychology uphold processes and structures that promote flourishing, and have philosophies and approaches that guide and motivate the people within that organisation. Although discussing positive psychology in the context of psychologists and their work, Seligman and Csikszentmihalyi (2000) state that psychologists' best work is not in repairing the weaknesses of their patients, but in amplifying and focusing on their inherent strengths. Indeed, when listing the contexts that should develop cultures that focus on strengths, the authors mention schools.

In a school context, employing positive psychology means that teachers focus on students' strengths rather than weaknesses. As educators, this means that we inherently focus on what our students can do and celebrate achievement with them when they succeed, rather than believing students are not capable or not talented. When using data, that means that we are looking for good news stories to share with students, their parents and our colleagues. We enjoy looking for data that proves potential, rather than dwelling on low results. In the case of a student achieving below the national averages or below most other students, positive psychology means that we inherently believe that the student has potential and we look for ways to assist, rather than thinking that they have a fixed mindset and intelligence and are destined to always achieve the same results. In the context of teachers working with data, positive psychology means that we believe in the strength and benefit of collecting data and that we do not view it as a negative. We view and use the data as a way of identifying strengths and celebrating achievement, and we see the potential in the data.

In a way, two of the shared beliefs and understandings identified by Sharratt and Fullan (2012) in their fourteen parameters for increasing student achievement – which I introduced in Chapter 1 – are particularly relevant here:

> *1a) Each student can achieve high standards given the right time and the right support.*
>
> *. . .*
>
> *1c) High expectations and early and ongoing intervention are essential.*
> (Sharratt & Fullan, 2012, p. 11)

These two factors reflect the notion of positive psychology in that student achievement and teacher intervention are viewed positively from a strength-based perspective and with a growth mindset. The perception here is that all students can and will achieve with the right support in place. Although Sharratt and Fullan do not refer to positive psychology explicitly in their work, the concepts of looking for the positives and being hope-filled certainly permeate the fourteen parameters.

GRIT

If you have not yet read Angela Duckworth's 2016 book *Grit: Why passion and resilience are the secrets to success*, add it to your wish list. While mindset and positive psychology are important, they fall short without *grit*: the persistence and tenacity to keep trying when things get difficult. Duckworth ties a range of psychological factors together eloquently and beautifully in her book, in a way that will have you thinking 'Yes!' while you are reading.

Duckworth (2016) states that grit is a key factor in achievement, and that it trumps previous academic results, teachers and home contexts. People who defy the odds and achieve above and beyond are, as Duckworth puts it, 'especially gritty'. Throughout the book, Duckworth recalls a host of examples about times that grit has beaten talent – in the military, spelling bees, Olympic swimming and academic pursuits, just to name a few. Duckworth developed the 'grit scale', devoting this period of her life to learning more about grit, effort and achievement. One of the stories she shares is about her using the grit scale with Scripps National Spelling Bee contestants in the United States, where she found that grit could be used to predict how far students would progress in the competition. The students who achieved highest on the grit scale progressed further through the competition than students with a lower score on the scale.

Another story that Duckworth shares is the story of Scott Kaufman, a psychologist with degrees from Carnegie Mellon, Cambridge University and Yale. As a child, Scott was put into a class for students who found learning difficult, in a school for students with learning disabilities. Thankfully, a special education teacher recognised Scott's potential, in what would turn out to be a critical turning point for him. As a result of the teacher showing Scott that they believed in him, he worked hard, improved his results and increased his engagement in school. He said, 'I was just so driven to show someone, anyone, that I was intellectually capable of anything' (quoted in Duckworth, 2016, p. 32). Like Scott Kaufman, we probably all know examples of successful people who had teachers that did not think they would amount to much. You might be thinking of a student you taught or a celebrity's success story – or it may have even happened to you. The story of Scott Kaufman is a great example of grit; he worked his way out of having difficulties with learning, eventually graduating from the some of the most highly regarded universities in the world. In addition, it is an example of a single teacher seeing the inherent possibilities for a young person, showing them that they believed in them and supporting them to improve. It truly shows the impact that knowing and believing in our students can have on their lives.

At this point, you might be wondering what a discussion on grit has to do with being data informed. On one level, your success as a teacher with using data in your classroom and school will be dependent on how gritty you are. You might be talented, you might have skills in this area, but effort and persistence will ultimately determine whether or not you succeed. Using data well is not just something you can either do or not do; it's a skill that you can and will get better at with time and effort.

Grit is also important for our students in their academic pursuits. But what data does is provide feedback on how students are moving from talent to achievement. Take for example Duckworth's (2016) equations on how to move from talent to achievement:

talent × effort = *skill*

skill × effort = *achievement* (emphasis in original, p. 42)

According to Duckworth (2016), talent must be multiplied by effort to develop skill. Once skill has been developed, further effort is required to experience achievement. Interestingly, effort features in both equations, meaning, as Duckworth states, that effort counts twice. Skill does not develop without effort, no matter how talented one is, and achievement does not develop without further effort.

So, what does this have to do with using data? In Chapter 2 we explored the importance of feedback and discussed the impact that feedback can have on student achievement. Assuming that Duckworth's theory of talent, effort, skill and achievement is correct and relevant to the Australian school context, data and feedback allow us to provide information back to students about how they are progressing through these talent-to-achievement equations. Take, for example, formative feedback and feedback from assessment for learning, which provide information about how a student might improve their work without being final. This feedback provides information on the student's approach, effort, strategy and understanding, and if the student acts on that feedback they can improve their work. As shown in figure 3.2, using Duckworth's equations, formative feedback or assessment for learning can provide additional feedback on a student's effort. It can also provide information to the student about their mindset and approach to the task.

On the other hand, summative feedback is final and sums up student achievement or skill. This information does not necessarily feed into information about the student's effort, but it does provide fixed feedback about skill or achievement. For that reason, I have modified Duckworth's equations to include the role of feedback in moving from talent to achievement.

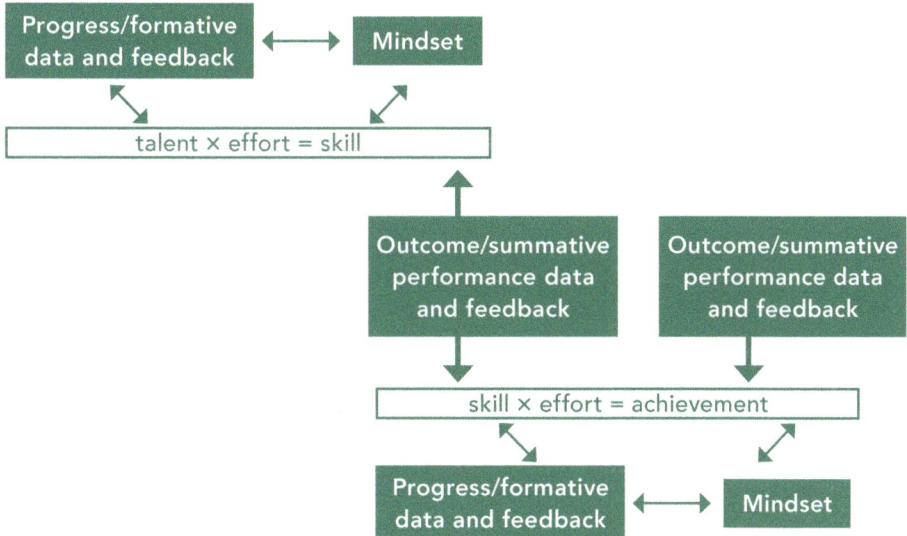

Figure 3.2. The way formative and summative feedback provide data on effort, skill and achievement in Duckworth's (2016) equations

SOURCE: Adapted from Duckworth, 2016

In her book, Duckworth talks about Jim Flynn, the New Zealand social scientist who discovered that significant improvements have been made over the last century in intelligence quotient (IQ) scores – termed the Flynn effect. To explain the improvements in IQ over the last century, Flynn discusses the improvement in basketball over the same time period. He states that the improvements are due to television and what he calls the 'social multiplier' effect. Flynn argues that basketball is an exciting game to watch on television, so once more people had televisions in their homes, basketball's popularity increased. Because people could see professionals sinking reverse lay-ups and three pointers, kids began practising these skills. Eventually they got better at them and enriched the learning environment for all the other kids that they played near and with.

I cannot think of a better way to describe the use of data to improve student achievement than Flynn's description of basketball improvements, and the term *social multiplier*. We can use data to show students that they are more capable than they think, to compare students to where they are in relation to their goals, and to celebrate with them when they achieve their goals. With success, students will start to aim higher and perform at a higher level, and when one student starts to do this, other students see it and start to improve with them. It is like being in a sports team: the most growth happens when you see and play with players that are a higher level than you, you learn and improve because of them.

This chapter has considered the role of mindset, positive psychology and grit in using data in schools. No matter whether you see your role as a teacher as a job, a career or a calling, your willingness, mindset, grittiness and the way in which you frame the data will determine how successful you are at using it. Likewise, the way in which you frame data use to students and colleagues will affect the mindsets of others. Using data can be hard, and there are some teachers who find using spreadsheet software and visualisation platforms difficult at the best of times. But persistence and effort will develop your skills and lead to achievement.

CHAPTER 4

HOW TO COLLECT AND INTERPRET THE DATA

Sometimes, like geological upheavals in a landscape, data surprise us and mark our current views as falsely secure and prone to reversal.

(emphasis in original, Matters, 2006, p. 7)

Now that we have discussed the 'why' of data, the power of feedback and the importance of a growth mindset, positive psychology and grit, let us now consider the data we can collect and use in Australian schools. Although different contexts have different data available, some examples of data that you may have access to are:

- National Assessment Program – Literacy and Numeracy (NAPLAN)
- Australian Council for Educational Research (ACER) Progressive Achievement Testing (PAT)
- ACER Middle Years Ability Test (MYAT)
- Diagnostic Reading Assessment (DRA)
- Allwell testing
- formative assessment results

- summative assessment results
- previous learning area results
- sight words testing
- grade point average (GPA)
- Year 12 exit results
- attendance.

Much of this data will already exist in your school in some form or another. You might already be generating the data, but you may not be storing it in a way that supports its use and analysis. It might be on profile sheets, in spreadsheets or on assessment cover sheets. You also may have it in visualisations on your school dashboard, but you may not be putting the necessary context or interpretation around the data to build an understanding of what it all means. The reality is that all these different data sources require different contexts for them to make sense – for example, NAPLAN bands are not the same as PAT stanines. For this reason, this chapter discusses the most common data in our schools – NAPLAN data, ACER results, GPA and Z-scores – along with colour-coding and triangulation to provide a context around the data.

UNDERSTANDING NAPLAN DATA

NAPLAN data is reported to schools as individual question responses, in overall scale scores and in bands. Depending on the way in which your school or system publishes this data, they may be recorded in any of these formats. Bands are potentially the easiest way to store the information because they position students in one of six categories in relation to the national minimum standard (NMS). Using bands tends to be easier than analysing significant quantities of scale scores, which requires teachers to learn cut-offs for each band to identify quickly what is 'below average', 'average' and 'above average'. Although the scale scores offer more granular detail about the performance of each student, they are compounded by the fact that NAPLAN national average scale scores change yearly and are different for each year group. You can build your knowledge of scale scores and start to use them to dig deeper after you have mastered the bands (if you really want to!).

The changing NMS and different use of bands for different year levels can be particularly confusing for teachers who teach across a number of year levels. For example, the NMS moves from band 2 in Year 3, to band 4 in Year 5, to band 5 in Year 7 and to band 6 in Year 9. Therefore, if you teach Years 7 and 9, you must remember that 'band 5' at each of those stages means something quite different (that is, *at* the NMS versus *below* the NMS). It is also important to remember that student results are not reported above or below the bands shown in figure 4.1. For example, a Year 3 student's lowest possible band is a band 1 and the highest is a band 6 – no matter how high their achievement. Whereas a Year 9 student's lowest reported band is band 5 and the highest is band 10.

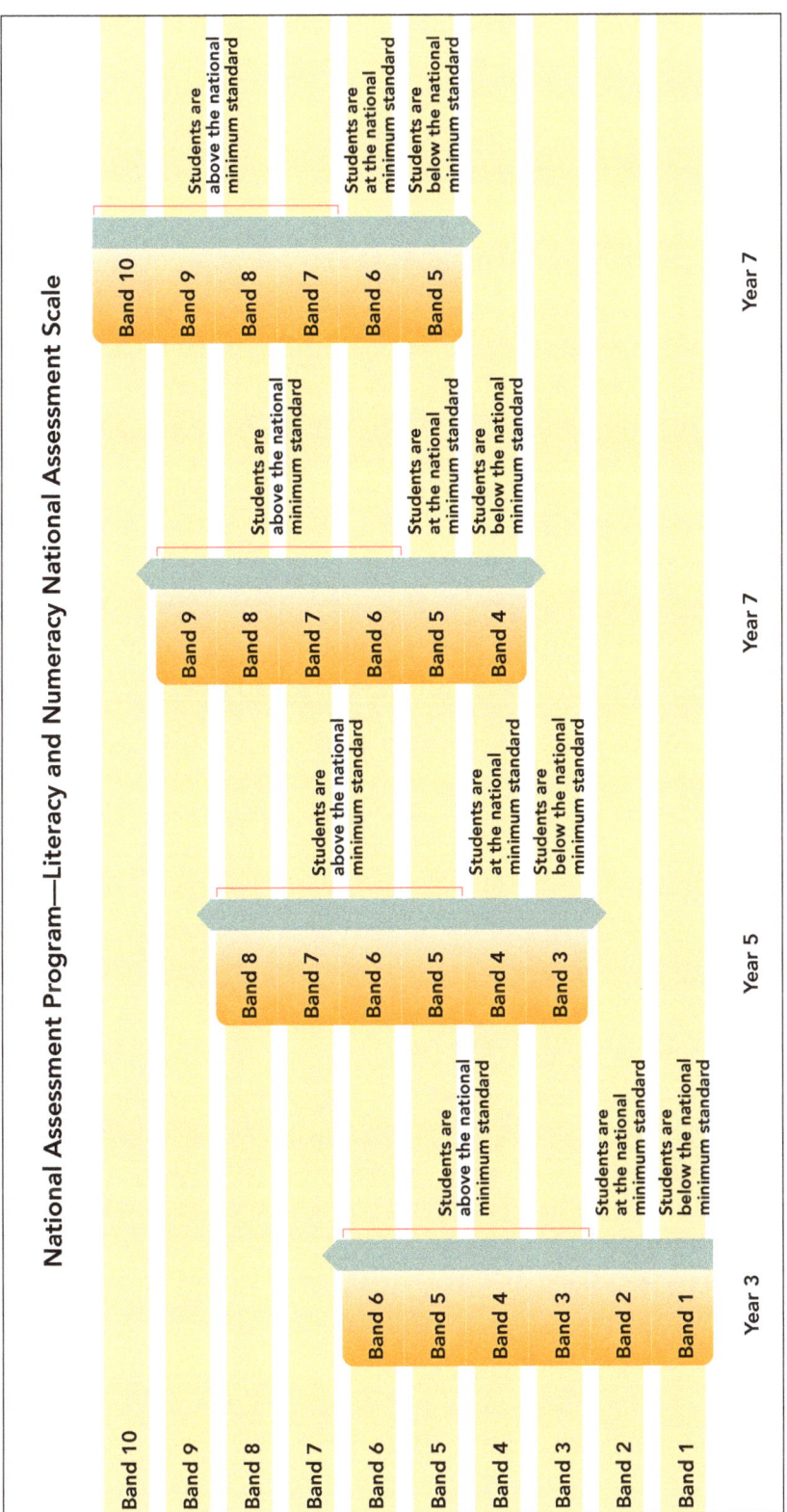

Figure 4.1. NAPLAN assessment scale

SOURCE: National Assessment Program, n.d.

© Australian Curriculum, Assessment and Reporting Authority (ACARA) 2011 to present, unless otherwise indicated. This material was downloaded from the National Assessment Program website (https://www.nap.edu.au/results-and-reports/how-to-interpret) (accessed 24 August 2021) and was not modified. The material is licensed under Creative Commons Attribution 4.0 International (CC BY) licence. ACARA does not endorse any product that uses ACARA material or make any representations as to the quality of such products. Any product that uses ACARA's material should not be taken to be affiliated with ACARA or have the sponsorship or approval of ACARA. It is up to each person to make their own assessment of the product.

Another way of understanding the bands, rather than using the different band numbers for different year levels, is to consider the student's band position relative to the NMS. This can be seen in some of the labels in figure 4.1. The lowest band in all year levels is called 'below NMS', the second lowest is 'at NMS' and then no matter what the band number, the first one above the NMS is 'NMS plus 1' (NMS+1), then 'NMS plus 2' (NMS+2), then 'NMS plus 3' (NMS+3) and 'NMS plus 4' (NMS+4). The benefit of using this terminology is that it can be used regardless of the year level that the data aligns with.

Irrespective of the year level, the bottom two bands (below NMS and at NMS) are often referred to as the 'lower two bands'. Those in the middle (NMS+1 and NMS+2) are called the 'middle two bands' and the top two bands (NMS+3 and NMS+4) are called the 'upper two bands' (sometimes shortened to U2B). Grouping students as being in the lower two bands, middle two bands or upper two bands can be used with cohorts to identify required extension or intervention programs, just as the advent of a significant number of students in the top or bottom bands can be used to inform programs and strategies.

When interpreting NAPLAN longitudinally, it is important to understand that if a student stays at the same level (for example, NMS) across year groups, they will still progress through the band numbers, from Year 3 to Year 5, to Year 7, to Year 9. This is because to progress from NMS in Year 3 (band 2) to NMS in Year 5 (band 4), to NMS in Year 7 (band 5) and NMS in Year 9 (band 6) requires a higher level of knowledge and skill. This applies to every level relative to the NMS. Thus, if a student is at NMS+4 in Year 3, and stays in NMS+4 until Year 9, they would have moved from band 6 to band 8, to band 9, to band 10.

Understanding NAPLAN bands can be difficult enough, but it is further complicated by the fact that it differs from ACER PAT, where students can make progress but stay in the same stanine.

UNDERSTANDING ACER DATA

ACER hosts a range of testing, including PAT in reading, PAT in written spelling and grammar, PAT in mathematics, PAT in science and the MYAT. These tests usually report student achievement in scale scores, percentiles and 'stanines', which is a norm-referenced comparison against all students nationwide who have previously competed the tests. Compared with NAPLAN bands, some educators may perceive that ACER results are easier to interpret, because the stanine and percentile system might be more familiar or because they remain consistent across year levels. Like NAPLAN, the ease of interpreting the data will depend how your school records it, but if you are new to using data, you might find ACER stanines and percentiles easier than learning the cut-offs for the scale scores.

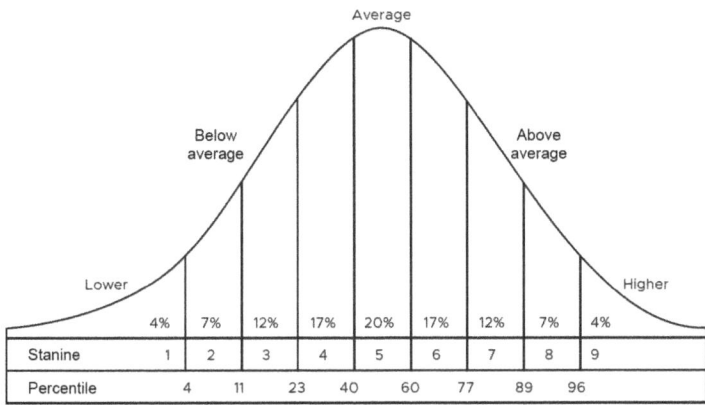

Figure 4.2. Stanine scores

As shown in figure 4.2, each stanine contains a percentage of the results of the overall student population. Stanines 1 and 9 are the top and bottom 4 per cent compared with all students who have completed the assessment previously, stanines 2 and 8 each represent 7 per cent, and stanines 3 and 7 represent 12 per cent of participants. It can be seen that the percentages function as a bell curve, with the middle 54 per cent of student results in stanines 4–6. Generally, students in stanines 7–9 are considered to be above average, stanines 4–6 are considered average and stanines 1–3 are below average.

Unlike NAPLAN bands, consistent performance and growth in assessments mean that stanines often do not change from year to year. Therefore, if a student performs around the fiftieth percentile in Years 5, 6, 7 and 8, the student would be in stanine 5 each year that they take the test. This differs to NAPLAN bands where students are expected to progress up the band numbers as they age.

Table 4.1. Example results for an average student making progress from Year 5 to Year 9

Test	Year 5	Year 6	Year 7	Year 8	Year 9
PAT in reading comprehension	Stanine 5 (50th percentile)	Stanine 5 (50th percentile)	Stanine 5 (50th percentile)	Stanine 5 (50th percentile)	Stanine 5 (50th percentile)
NAPLAN reading	NMS+1 Band 5		NMS+1 Band 6		NMS+1 Band 7

As illustrated in table 4.1, a student who performs in the fiftieth percentile/stanine 5 of PAT in Reading and makes expected progress from Year 5 to Year 9, would continue to achieve in the same stanine each year that they take the test. This is expected progress, as the student's scale score would increase each year to stay in the fiftieth percentile. But if the student consistently performed at NMS+1 on NAPLAN tests from Years 5 to 9, the band numbers would increase from band 5 in Year 5 to band 6 in Year 7 and band 7 in Year 9. This is why there is sometimes some confusion among teachers, because there are different measurements and progress expectations in the different tests. Further, because this information is not often compared in this manner, teachers often have to work this out for themselves. Numbers mean one thing – it is the understanding and context we put around the numbers that helps us put them to use in our schools.

While this example and discussion has been about ACER PAT (as it is commonly used in Australian schools), the explanation of stanines and percentiles applies for any other school assessment that uses this terminology.

UNDERSTANDING GPA

Other than NAPLAN and ACER data, another data source that might be available in your school is a grade point average (GPA). A GPA can be used to measure student progress and achievement across learning areas. Usually, the fifteen-point scale is allocated according to the A+ to E– scale and a score is allocated for each of the student's learning areas. This fifteen-point scale is shown in table 4.2.

Table 4.2. GPA fifteen-point scale allocation

Grade	Score
A+	15
A	14
A–	13
B+	12
B	11
B–	10
C+	9
C	8
C–	7
D+	6
D	5
D–	4
E+	3
E	2
E–	1

A GPA can be used to average the performance on an individual assessment when multiple grades are given for different criteria. For example, if a student achieves a B– for the 'acquire' criterion in health and physical education, a B– for the 'apply' criterion and a C– for the 'evaluate' criterion, we would add the numerical value for each grade together (10, 10 and 7) and divide by how many numbers there are (3):

$$\frac{10 + 10 + 7}{3} = \frac{27}{3} = 9$$

$$9 = C+$$

Note: this calculation will often result in a decimal. In most cases you should not round the decimal up to the next number – instead use the whole number to discern the overall grade.

More commonly, GPAs are used at a school level to generate a picture of how a student has performed across all of their learning areas. Using the same process, the score for each learning area result is added together and divided by how many learning areas were studied. Once a GPA is generated for each student, they can be used to measure and compare students in cohorts and compare progress across semesters. Some schools award students with the highest GPAs and students who make most progress on their GPA at the end of the academic year.

UNDERSTANDING Z-SCORES

A statistical measure that I often see used in schools is the Z-score, which is a measure of the distance of an individual student's result from the class or cohort average. A Z-score is positive or negative, and the number represents standard deviations from the mean the result. A result above the class average would be a positive Z-score, and a result lower than the class average would be a negative. The higher the Z-score, the higher the result (and the further above the average), and the lower the Z-score, the lower the result (and the further below the mean). A Z-score that is equal to zero means that the student's result is the same as the class or cohort average.

As shown in figure 4.3, a result that is between −1 and +1 standard deviations – that is, within one standard deviation of the average – means that it sits within 68.2 per cent of the results for the class or cohort. A score within two standard deviations accounts for 95.4 per cent of all the data, and within three standard deviations is 99.7 per cent of the data.

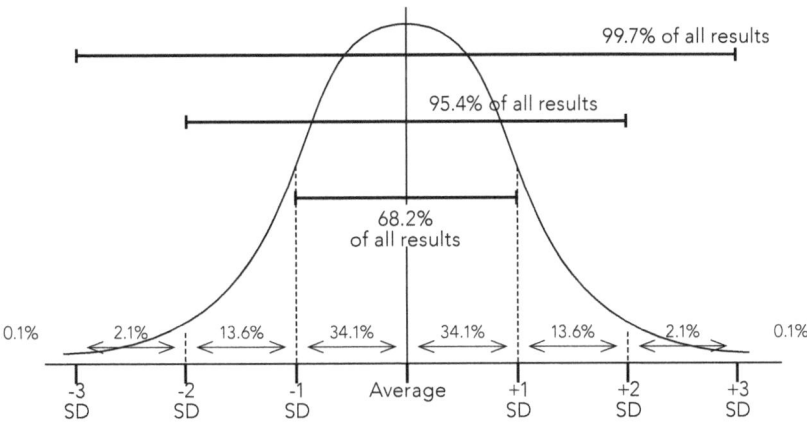

Figure 4.3. Z-score distribution

The challenge with Z-scores is that it does require a bit of mathematics to calculate – and you need to understand the idea of a standard deviation. The standard deviation is a measure of the spread of the data; the higher standard deviation, the more spread out the data is, and the lower the standard deviation, the more compressed the data is.

I will show you how Z-scores work using cumulative scores for class quizzes. Consider twenty students with the cumulative scores shown in table 4.3.

Table 4.3. Cumulative quiz scores

Student	Cumulative score
Student A	122
Student B	130
Student C	97
Student D	100
Student E	98
Student F	105
Student G	100
Student H	97
Student I	92
Student J	93
Student K	95
Student L	105
Student M	110
Student N	83
Student O	98
Student P	93
Student Q	92
Student R	93
Student S	112
Student T	98

The first thing I need to do to work out the Z-scores for each student is to calculate the average score. After entering the scores into a spreadsheet (see table 4.3), I then type the following function into the cell below (selecting the cells where the data is sitting):

=AVERAGE(B2:B21)

When I hit enter, I will see that the average score for these students is 100.65. I can scan the data to ascertain who is above and below the average, but the Z-score helps me identify more specifically how far above or below they are, relative to the spread of all the data.

The next thing needed to calculate the Z-scores is to find the standard deviation. To do this, I type the following in the cell below the average I have just calculated:

=STDEV(B2:B21)

After I hit enter, I will see that the standard deviation for the cumulative quiz scores of this group of students – this dataset – is 10.97. This means that 68.2 per cent of students' scores lie somewhere between 100.65 + 10.97 (111.62) and 100.65 – 10.97 (89.68).

Next I will calculate the Z-score for each student by entering the following function to the right of the first data point (B2 in this example):

$$=SUM((B2-\$B\$22)/\$B\$23)$$

Because I have selected the cells containing the calculated average (B22) and standard deviation (B23) as absolute values – by inserting a dollar sign ($) before their row and column coordinates ($B$22 and $B$23 respectively) – I can drag the formula down the spreadsheet calculate each student's Z-score. Now my table looks like table 4.4.

Table 4.4. Cumulative quiz scores with calculated Z-scores

Student	Cumulative score	Z-score
Student A	122	1.945
Student B	130	2.674
Student C	97	-0.333
Student D	100	-0.059
Student E	98	-0.241
Student F	105	0.396
Student G	100	-0.059
Student H	97	-0.333
Student I	92	-0.788
Student J	93	-0.697
Student K	95	-0.515
Student L	105	0.396
Student M	110	0.852
Student N	83	-1.608
Student O	98	-0.241
Student P	93	-0.697
Student Q	92	-0.788
Student R	93	-0.697
Student S	112	1.034
Student T	98	-0.241
Average	100.65	
Standard deviation	10.97	

So what's the point of all of this? In the context of the cumulative quiz results, the students who are more than 1 standard deviation below the average could be more at risk of struggling in upcoming assessment or not developing the skills they need.

Z-scores could be used for:

- conversations with students who are below about their distance from the mean
- conversations with students who are above about maintaining and improving their distance above the mean
- conversations with students in the middle about trying to hit or beat the average.

ANALYSING DATA USING COLOUR-CODING

As shown in the previous sections, NAPLAN results, ACER PAT data, GPA and Z-scores are four common types of data in our schools that can be used for noticing patterns and trends in student learning. But the trends and learnings in the data become harder to notice as we collect more data and have access to more information! Even when we understand the context behind and the meaning of individual numbers, big spreadsheets with lots of data can, quite frankly, be difficult to analyse.

This is the reason why many school learning management systems have dashboards or visualisation platforms to show student data. Sometimes these dashboards show you information you need in the way you want it, but sometimes they don't. The other limitation of many visualisation platforms is that they contain summative results and standardised testing, but they don't often provide much opportunity for displaying formative results.

If you prefer, or if you need to put together your own class dataset in a useful format, I am a huge advocate of colour-coding to help decipher the messages and patterns in the data. This usually means colouring results that are above average as green, average as yellow and below average as red. When coloured in this way, the trends become more obvious, and our analysis and the data storytelling that follows doesn't need to rely on our understanding of the numbers but is aided by the visual support of the colours. Take table 4.5, for example, which shows a set of data that has not yet been colour-coded.

Table 4.5. Data collected on three students

Student	End of semester English result	NAPLAN reading	NAPLAN writing	PAT in reading comprehension
Matthew Year 9	C	Band 9 (NMS+3)	Band 10 (NMS+4)	Stanine 9
Liane Year 9	D+	Band 5 (below NMS)	Band 6 (at NMS)	Stanine 2
Daniel Year 9	A	Band 8 (NMS+2)	Band 7 (NMS+1)	Stanine 6

How to collect and interpret the data

Even though we now know the value of stanines and the different bands for NAPLAN testing in Year 9, the trends or patterns in this data are not immediately identifiable. Of course, we could sit and analyse the individual values, but with large cohorts this becomes very time consuming!

Now compare table 4.5 with table 4.6. It is the same data, but it has been colour-coded. The colour-coding makes the trends much more easily identifiable, and the analysis and intervention slightly easier.

Table 4.6. Example of colour-coding

Student	End of semester English result	NAPLAN reading	NAPLAN writing	PAT in reading comprehension
Matthew Year 9	C	Band 9 (NMS+3)	Band 10 (NMS+4)	Stanine 9
Liane Year 9	D+	Band 5 (below NMS)	Band 6 (at NMS)	Stanine 2
Daniel Year 9	A	Band 8 (NMS+2)	Band 7 (NMS+1)	Stanine 6

By using a colour-coding system of green (above average), yellow (average) and red (below average), I can decipher messages from the data in table 4.6 quite easily. I can immediately see that Liane is finding English and literacy difficult, so something needs to be done to support her. I can also see that Matthew has performed really well in standardised testing, but not in English, and I wonder why. Conversely, Daniel has achieved really well in English, but has found standardised testing more difficult. Of course, I could have established the same things without the colour-coding, but I believe that it helps and saves a lot of time in the analysis stage.

Before you start to use colour, you need to establish a system that is consistent in everything you do – so that trying to decipher your colour-coding system is not another thing you need to remember! I have found that the easiest system is as follows.

Table 4.7. Three-colour colour-coding system example

	Below average
	Average
	Above average

Alternatively, if you would rather group the data into five categories instead of three, table 4.8 shows a more detailed version.

Table 4.8. Five-colour colour-coding system example

	Well below average
	Below average
	Average
	Above average
	Well above average

It doesn't matter whether you choose the three or five levels of colour-coding, but it does matter how you apply them. Consistency is key. Let's have a think about how you might use colours with NAPLAN bands, ACER stanines, learning area results and Z-scores. Here are examples of colour-coding for each of these types of data.

Table 4.9. Examples of colour-coding NAPLAN bands, ACER stanines, learning area results and Z-scores

NAPLAN bands	ACER stanines	Learning area results	Z-scores
NMS−1	1	E	Less than −1.5
NMS	2	D	Between −0.5 and −1.5
NMS+1	3	C	From −0.5 to 0.5
NMS+2	4	B	Above 0.5 to 1.5
NMS+3	5	A	Greater than 1.5
NMS+4	6		
	7		
	8		
	9		

Although I rely on the traffic-light system of red, yellow and green, the truth is that it does not really matter what colours you use. In fact, I have seen schools use white and different shades of blue in their colour-coding and analysis, while others use a palette more friendly to colour blindness, running from dark blue (above average) through to grey (average) and dark orange (below average). But whatever you decide, be consistent and persist with it. You will need colour-code cut-offs for each type of data that you use, but when you do it once, you can continue to use the cut-offs in the future.

To decide on the cut-offs, consider first the band of results in the assessment that you would be happy to classify as 'average'. When you establish the upper and lower limits of the average category, these are the limits of your yellow category. For example, in a quiz out of ten marks, you might decide that an average result is between four and six, and these results would be colour-coded yellow. If you are using a three-level colour-coding system, anything above your yellow category will be green (in this example, a result greater than six), and anything below will be red (a result less than four). If you prefer to use a five-level colour-coding system, find the points that separate 'well above average' and 'above average', and 'well below average' and 'well above average' results. Continuing with the quiz example, you might decide to split orange and red at two, and light green and dark green at eight.

Once you've made these decisions, store the information about your colour-coding categories somewhere that you won't lose it; you will need to refer back to these conditions in the future. There is no point changing these cut-offs in the future if you don't need to – it will make your analysis and comparison so much harder if you do! But when you apply them to future datasets you need to ensure that you remember the decisions you made. So be confident, make a decision about the categories and stick with them.

TRIANGULATING DATA

When looking for patterns, trends and stories in the data, the most important discoveries cannot necessarily be found by using a single dataset or a single number. That is where triangulation comes in (O'Neal, 2012). The term *triangulation* is mostly used to describe the corroboration of research data, but it is also highly relevant in the Australian school context. The term originally stemmed from military and navigational contexts, where multiple reference points were used to locate an object's exact position on a map. Given the basic principles of geometry, the more information provided about the object's position, the more accurate the location (Jick, 1979; Thurmond, 2001). Where one piece of data gives some indication of a person's location on a map, a second bearing provides more accurate information about where the person might be located. But a third data source confirms that neither the first nor second piece of data is incorrect, and the person's position can be located on a map. Today, the term *triangulation* is used heavily in research and defined as:

> the combination of two or more theoretical perspectives, methodological approaches, data sources, investigators, or data analysis methods. The intent of using triangulation is to decrease, negate, or counterbalance the deficiency of a single strategy, thereby increasing the ability to interpret the findings. (Thurmond, 2001, p. 253)

Using triangulation as an approach to data analysis can 'improve the accuracy of . . . judgements by collecting different kinds of data bearing on the same phenomenon' (Thurmond, 2001, p. 253). But triangulation is not merely a statistical tool – it allows for a more complete and comprehensive understanding of the phenomenon in question, and it means more confidence can be placed in the judgements. In fact, Lincoln and Guba (1985) state that no single item of information should ever be given serious consideration unless it can be triangulated. Although the terminology is not often used in education, these sentiments reflect the opinions of those in opposition to point-in-time standardised testing data because one test may not necessarily provide an accurate reflection of a student's ability. Triangulating this data with data collected from other sources or assessments means that you can ascertain its accuracy.

To triangulate data, information or data must be sought from three or more sources. In a school context, this means drawing data and information about a student from multiple sources, such as NAPLAN, PAT and learning area results. Once the data has been collected and arranged, judgements about student potential and performance are made using the majority of the data that is being analysed, rather than relying on one piece of information. For example, if two out of three pieces of data tell you a particular fact about student performance, it is fair to assume that this is probably accurate and that the third (irregular) piece of data is inaccurate. Therefore, triangulating school data means that judgements we make about a student are more accurate because they are taken from multiple sources (just like in tables 4.5 and 4.6). The process of triangulation may lead to divergent data that does not necessarily align, but it is this data that needs to be reconciled, and it is through understanding divergent data that a richer understanding is developed (Jick, 1979). Thus, triangulation helps us to better define and analyse the performance of our students.

When triangulating data, you first need to determine the types of data that you have available and choose the most relevant to triangulate. You might have access to results from NAPLAN in numeracy, reading or writing, PAT in reading, mathematics or science, ACER General Ability Tests (AGAT), DRA, sight words testing, formative or summative assessment and more. While three pieces of data are required as a minimum to triangulate, the more data we can use, the better – but the data must be relevant. Therefore, you must consider the data sources you have available and choose the ones that are going to be most useful for you to achieve the purpose of your analysis.

For example, if I wanted to triangulate data about the literacy ability of a Year 9 class, I would probably choose to use English results from the previous semester, NAPLAN reading and writing data, and PAT in reading comprehension results. I would deliberately not include PAT in mathematics, NAPLAN numeracy and other learning area results. This other data might be useful in other analyses, but in my focus on literacy it would not be relevant. To summarise, you must determine the aim of your analysis, consider the pieces of data that you have available to you and then make a decision about the most relevant data for your analysis. If your school does not have access to PAT testing, then use something else. If you teach F–Year 2 classes, you will have no NAPLAN data and so you will need to use another type of data. Determine which data will provide information that will help you evaluate your students' potential and achieve the best analysis.

Table 4.10 offers a more comprehensive example of triangulation. The results are coded using a three-colour system, from green (above average) through yellow (average) to red (below average).

How to collect and interpret the data

Table 4.10. Triangulating literacy data using learning area, NAPLAN and PAT results

Student	End of semester English result	NAPLAN reading	NAPLAN writing	PAT in reading comprehension
Matthew Year 9	C	Band 9 (NMS+3)	Band 10 (NMS+4)	Stanine 9
Liane Year 9	D+	Band 5 (–1NMS)	Band 6 (NMS)	Stanine 2
Daniel Year 9	A	Band 8 (NMS+2)	Band 7 (NMS+1)	Stanine 6
Michael Year 9	D+	Band 8 (NMS+2)	Band 6 (NMS)	Stanine 7
Emma Year 9	A–	Band 9 (NMS+3)	Band 9 (NMS+3)	Stanine 8
Shelley Year 9	B–	Band 6 (NMS)	Band 6 (NMS)	Stanine 3
Doug Year 9	B	Band 5 (–1NMS)	Band 8 (NMS+2)	Stanine 6
Carly Year 9	C+	Band 7 (NMS+1)	Band 7 (NMS+1)	Stanine 5

Although these are fictional students, now that the data is colour-coded, it is possible to analyse the data and wonder about each student's individual achievement. Some of these results tell very consistent stories about students' achievement, but others are not as easy to follow as the data is quite divergent (Jick, 1979). If these were actual students, these results may confirm what their teacher already knows about the individual student, or they might prompt questions that result in the teacher learning more about each individual and their learning needs.

Next, I'll pose some observations and hypothetical questions about the data for each of the students in table 4.10. In some cases, these questions would be easily answered if these were real students in a real school, but it is important that, when we are looking at data, we are prepared to ask the sometimes difficult questions and consider all reasons and possibilities. Sometimes we might learn that we need to take a new approach with a student or provide additional support – and that's okay! Sometimes, the learnings about the student should also be used in conversation with them. What additional observations or questions would you have about the data?

Matthew

Matthew is working at a C level in English but achieved results in bands 9 and 10 in NAPLAN reading and writing respectively and stanine 9 in the PAT in reading comprehension. Given the very promising results in NAPLAN and PAT in reading comprehension, Matthew has demonstrated that he is a bright student and has the potential to achieve good results in English. Therefore, his English result indicates that he is under-performing in this learning area and not working to the best of his ability.

Matthew or his teacher may be able to explain why this has occurred, or the teacher may not be aware that Matthew should be challenged further. Either way, this would be a good opportunity to have a conversation with Matthew highlighting his fantastic results in NAPLAN and PAT testing. Perhaps the teacher could ask Matthew what he thinks is happening. It would certainly be important for the teacher to acknowledge that Matthew has a lot of talent and has been able to demonstrate it across the external tests. By framing the conversation as one in which the teacher is trying to learn more about Matthew to help him achieve the best outcomes, Matthew should be able to explain why his results in the learning area are so different to NAPLAN and PAT results.

Liane

Liane failed English, and she is below the NMS in NAPLAN reading and at the NMS for NAPLAN writing. In the PAT in reading comprehension test, Liane was below the national average when compared with other Year 9 students across the country. The data tells us that Liane finds literacy difficult and a D+ in English is most likely commensurate with her ability. Liane or her teacher could talk more specifically about her progress, but Liane probably needs additional support and interventions to help her pass English and improve her literacy skills. Even though the data is quite consistent, there is still value in having a conversation with Liane about ways in which she could be supported and how she envisions herself improving in this learning area.

Daniel

Daniel is working at an A level in English, but achieved average results in NAPLAN Reading and Writing, and the PAT in reading comprehension. The data indicates that perhaps Daniel is of average ability, and the A in English is higher than expected, given his performance on the standardised testing. Daniel may work hard in English, submit multiple drafts or have a tutor to help develop his assignments. He may love English, but not be good at standardised tests. He might be an A student who struggles to demonstrate this in external assessment. Alternatively, Daniel's English teacher might be marking too easily, and Daniel's work might need to be cross-marked in the future. The divergent data encourages us to ask questions and try to understand what is going on for Daniel. If, as the teacher, you didn't have an answer for these questions, it would be worth having a conversation with Daniel about his results. The conversation could begin with 'Daniel, you're going so well in English at the moment, well done! Your A grade is a huge achievement! I was looking through some other results of yours recently and I've noticed though that your NAPLAN and PAT testing results were a bit lower that what you're showing me in English. Do you have any ideas why this might be?' In most cases, Daniel will be able to give you some reasons or an explanation as to why this might have occurred.

Michael

Michael has quite mixed results, which is not uncommon. He failed English and was at the NMS for NAPLAN writing, but he achieved an average result for NAPLAN reading and very high results in the PAT in reading comprehension. Assuming that it is difficult to 'fluke' those results in the reading tests, it is important to figure out what is going on here. Is Michael disengaged in English lessons? Does his behaviour affect his learning? Does he genuinely struggle with writing, or did he just have a bad day on the NAPLAN writing task? Again, the data does not give us all the answers, but it does help us build a picture about Michael's ability from which we can ask questions and have a conversation. These questions might be able to be answered by Michael's teachers, but there would be real value in asking Michael what he thinks as well.

Emma

Emma is clearly a bright student and has achieved pleasing results across all four datasets. She is classified as being in the upper two bands in NAPLAN reading and writing, and was at the top end of PAT in reading comprehension data. Her A– in English confirms that she is achieving well, and literacy is probably one of her strengths. Hopefully Emma's teacher will be looking for opportunities to extend her ability and to keep her engaged and progressing in English lessons. Even though we are not worried about Emma's performance, this data could be used in conversation with her for the teacher to learn more about the types of extension activities that she would enjoy. Tomlinson and Allan (2006) talk about having high ability students co-construct project ideas and success criteria, and for the teacher to plan 'fuzzy projects' so students have the opportunity to develop their own projects. Emma's data could be the way into this conversation with her.

Shelley

Like Daniel, Shelley has performed better in English than in the standardised testing. But her standardised testing results indicate that she is at the NMS for NAPLAN reading and writing, and below average in the PAT in reading comprehension. It would be interesting to see what her teacher reported about her ability. Does Shelley struggle with exams? Does she work slowly, and so the time pressure of NAPLAN and PAT means she finds it difficult to demonstrate her ability? Or has she been provided with modifications and scaffolding to help her achieve the B– in English? Again, the data makes us ask more questions about Shelley's progress and lead to a conversation about her progress and achievement – both with her teachers and with Shelley herself. The data does not provide all the answers, but it does start a conversation about what she needs.

Doug

Doug's data is mostly colour-coded yellow because he achieved a B in English, is in band 8 in NAPLAN writing and is in stanine 6 for PAT in reading comprehension. But Doug did not perform as well in NAPLAN reading, where he was below the NMS.

Given Doug's better performance in three out of four assessments, it is probably fair to assume that Doug did not have a great day when he did the NAPLAN reading test and infer that this result does not reflect his ability. He may have been unwell, struggled with the context of the test or just under-performed. It is worth asking Doug about how he went that day or speaking with his English teacher to see if they know why this result might have been lower. Either way, Doug is performing well and usually performs quite consistently.

Carly

Carly has achieved an average standard across all assessments. Given that she is one band above the NMS in NAPLAN reading and writing, and in the middle of the norm-referenced PAT test results, her C+ in English is possibly commensurate with her ability. Carly's teacher might be happy with her progress – she might have achieved these results with consistent effort and application. But Carly's teacher may also believe that she has not worked hard enough and has achieved these results with minimal effort and application. Again, the teacher would be able to help us understand the data better, but the data begins a conversation about Carly's progress and achievement. Like all of the previous students in this example, there is real value in having this conversation with Carly as well to learn more about her needs and preferences as a learner.

Although this example considered fictional Year 9 students and their data in a literacy analysis, this strategy can be used for students in any year level and subject area. In my experience, students at all ages can engage in a conversation about their results and data, and can talk about their strengths and weaknesses. Sure, the older they are, the more specific they might be able to be, the more self-aware they may be and the more advanced their vocabulary will be. But Foundation and Years 1, 2 and 3 students *can* engage in data-informed conversations and can sometimes blow you away with their knowledge of their strengths and weaknesses. The earlier we encourage students to build their metacognition around learning, the better!

This example showed how we can begin to translate data into questions, conversations and learnings about student progress and achievement. Using the notion of triangulation and three (or more) datasets to assist with these questions and conversations builds credibility and reliability in our assumptions about students. Further, colour-coding the data helps us more quickly formulate a picture about a student's progress as the trends become more immediately identifiable. Despite these benefits, the main downside of triangulation is that it takes time if you have to do it manually. Some school learning-management systems and data dashboards are attempting to build triangulation into their approaches, but not all. If this is your reality, the data has been prepared for you (which is great). But use these visualisations to focus on the questions and conversations that were discussed in this section so that the priority is the action you take. If you need to do so manually, I encourage you to give it a go, learn to colour-code and see what stories you can find in the data because the insights that you can gain are invaluable.

No matter whether the data is organised for you or you are developing your own spreadsheets, this process is all about the learnings in the data and the action you will take. You might identify that a student struggles in standardised tests, so you will be able to help that student improve their skills and their preparation for the next test. You may identify that a student is underperforming in your learning area, given their results in standardised testing. You may realise that a student is working consistently in your class and is achieving results commensurate with their ability, so you remember to pat them on the back and commend their work ethic. No matter what, you will learn from the data and from your conversations with your colleagues and the students themselves. These learnings will help shape your future pedagogical approaches.

Now that you understand bands, stanines, percentiles, GPAs, Z-scores, colour-coding and triangulation, the following two chapters offer practical examples of ways to use the data in your classroom (Chapter 5) and in your school (Chapter 6). These examples will draw on your understanding of the numbers and often require you to triangulate and colour-code the data. They are offered not as the only ways to use and analyse data in your classroom and school, but as a starting point from which your own ideas and approaches can develop. Have fun with it!

CHAPTER 5:
USING DATA IN YOUR CLASSROOM

For a teacher, the central purpose of analysing data is to improve the learning of one or more particular students; that is, the individual teacher and the school take the students who come to them and seek to improve the learning of those students.

(Allen, 2005, p. 87)

In my experience, Australian teachers are keen to use data in ways that will assist them and benefit their students. But despite the expectation that teachers use data, there is limited direction on how this can be done. For this reason, the following chapters consider practical ways that teachers, middle leaders and senior leaders can use data in their classrooms and schools. These strategies rely on teachers manually developing their own systems. Many schools have great dashboards that might do some of this manual work for you; however, I guarantee there will be a time where you need the data in a different way or want to organise your own. While visualisation platforms are great, they don't give the level of flexibility that our own records and electronic mark books can provide.

The focus of this particular chapter is the ways data can be used in the classroom. It features fourteen examples that have been designed specifically to support classroom teachers in using data. The skills and activities discussed here can be useful in any classroom context: primary, secondary, co-educational, single-sex, private, independent or state. Rather than talking extensively about the 'why' at this point, this chapter will embrace the 'how' and 'what'. Each example includes some discussion of the ways in which the strategy can be used in the classroom and in feedback to students, as well as tips for implementation. Of course, some examples I give here do not have a place in student feedback, but most of these data strategies can be used in conversations with students.

I have grouped the examples into three categories for classroom teachers. These three categories are:

1. preparing – using data to prepare for the beginning of a term or semester
2. differentiating – using data to differentiate teaching for different ability levels
3. tracking – using data to track performance in formative, summative and homework tasks.

The following sections will explain these categories further and provide a summary of the types of examples found in this chapter.

PREPARING

Using data before the beginning of a teaching period can help a teacher understand the ability of students coming into their class and provide a snapshot of what they should expect, how they should pitch their lessons and the differentiation that might be required. The best way to use data at the beginning of the term or semester is to triangulate the data available across three or more relevant sources to assists in formulating a picture of the strengths and weaknesses of each individual student and of the group. As a teacher, I did this at the beginning of every academic year because it showed me key information that helped me know more about my classes. Although I've used the process many times, it had the most value for me when I taught two Year 8 mathematics classes at the same time in a school that I was new to. When I triangulated their data at the beginning of the semester, I quickly learned that the two sets of class results were significantly different and that they required very different levels of scaffolding and differentiation! It meant that I walked into both classrooms prepared, knowing that they were two very different groups of young people, rather than assuming they were similar because they were both Year 8 mathematics classes in the same school. An example of how to collect, triangulate and colour-code data in this manner can be found in Example 1 (page 70).

DIFFERENTIATING

Triangulation of data can also be useful to identify the individual needs of students and the need for tailored differentiation strategies. This detail can be added to a triangulated data spreadsheet by writing individual differentiation strategies and approaches for each student or for small groups within the larger class. I began using these differentiation strategies for all of my classes when I taught in the United Kingdom because it was the expectation of my school leadership team that we had individual differentiated approaches for every student. More recently in Australia I have found the differentiation placemat (which I explore in Example 3 on page 75) has been particularly useful for documenting the adjustments made for students in all of my classes, especially so in justifying the 'extensive', 'substantial', 'supplementary', or 'quality differentiation of teacher practice' adjustments made for students in the Nationally Consistent Collection of Data (NCCD, 2018). Using data to differentiate teaching for individuals and class groups is considered in Examples 2 (page 73) and 3 (page 75).

TRACKING

Tracking can be useful throughout the academic year. It ensures that teachers know how their students are achieving and progressing and can be used in feedback to students in conversations about progress. Teachers can:

- track the class throughout the semester and year
- look for trends in elements of knowledge, skills and cognitions in assessment tasks
- track the value added for individuals and the class collectively, to measure impact
- track completed homework tasks
- track completion of competencies in certificate courses
- track class performance and monitor the GPA of the class across assessment pieces
- develop a 'rank order' to demonstrate achievement or progress using marks or grades
- show the number of As, Bs and so on in a table
- display the spread of student achievement in a box and whisker plot
- graph the progress of individual students over time.

I have used almost all of these strategies throughout my teaching career. The others I have seen used often in schools I've worked with. As a result of using data in these ways, I have known how often my students have completed homework, the spread of results in my class, and the movement of students throughout the year (progress) and at the end of the year (achievement). These data collection methods have assisted me in parent–teacher conversations about work ethic and application, provided evidence of concerns I've had about particular students, and been used in conversations with students to get them back on track or get them to aim higher. Examples 4–14 (from page 78) cover tracking performance across formative, summative and homework tasks.

This list of examples is certainly not intended to be exhaustive, nor to replace the many wonderful examples of tracking progress that are already occurring in our schools. There are also many examples of dashboards emerging that automatically display some sets of class data for you, so you might not need to manually develop the spreadsheets or you'll only need to export the page to edit and add to it. However, the tools I provide here are for teachers looking for options that they can own and modify, which will hopefully spark some interest and motivation in you to take data further. Not only are these tracking measures useful for teachers individually, but also they can also be compared and discussed across teaching teams and departments, and even be used with students to build their metacognition around themselves as learners. This chapter provides some details about using each tracking mechanism. Further, there are examples of the ways in which collecting and displaying data can lead to conversations with students and collaborative teams, and lead to data-informed conversations among teachers.

Example 1: Setting up a spreadsheet at the start of the academic year to establish the ability and potential of a class

Using data at the beginning of an academic period can assist teachers in knowing the strengths and areas of concern for the group that they will be teaching. This uses triangulation, where multiple sources of data are drawn together to develop an overall picture. Here is how you might complete this process:

1. Clearly identify the aim of your analysis or collection of data (for example, to consider the ability and potential of a Year 9 mathematics class).

2. Consider the data that you have available to triangulate in your setting. For example, you might have access to the types of data displayed in table 5.1.

Table 5.1. Available data

NAPLAN	ACER	Learning area results
Reading	PAT in reading comprehension	Mathematics
Writing	PAT in mathematics	English
Spelling	PAT in written spelling	Science
Grammar and punctuation	AGAT	
Numeracy		

3. Select the types of data that you will triangulate for your area of inquiry. For a mathematics focus, you might feel NAPLAN numeracy, PAT in mathematics and a learning area result for mathematics are the most relevant (as highlighted in table 5.2). Choose the data sources that align most closely with what you intend to investigate.

Table 5.2. Selected data

NAPLAN	ACER	Learning area results
Reading	PAT in reading comprehension	Mathematics
Writing	PAT in mathematics	English
Spelling	PAT in written spelling	Science
Grammar and punctuation	AGAT	
Numeracy		

4. Export the data so you have the three (or more) sets of data in spreadsheet software.

Table 5.3. Exported triangulated data

Student	NAPLAN numeracy scale score	PAT in mathematics stanine	Previous semester overall mathematics result
Student A	463	3	C
Student B	513	3	C–
Student C	549	3	C
Student D	554	5	D
Student E	554	5	D
Student F	549	3	C+
Student G	660	9	A
Student H	495	4	C–
Student I	Parent withdrawn	3	D–
Student J	615	5	C+
Student K	Absent	3	C–
Student L	507	3	D
Student M	559	5	C+
Student N	559	7	C+

5. Make decisions about the colour-coding structure you will use (see Chapter 4 for more information about this) and colour-code your data accordingly. (You might choose to leave the cells uncoloured if they have no data.)

USING AND ANALYSING DATA IN AUSTRALIAN SCHOOLS

Table 5.4. Colour-coded data

Student	NAPLAN numeracy scale score	PAT in mathematics stanine	Previous semester overall mathematics result
Student A	463	3	C
Student B	513	3	C–
Student C	549	3	C
Student D	554	5	D
Student E	554	5	D
Student F	549	3	C+
Student G	660	9	A
Student H	495	4	C–
Student I	Parent withdrawn	3	D–
Student J	615	5	C+
Student K	Absent	3	C–
Student L	507	3	D
Student M	559	5	C+
Student N	559	7	C+

6. Use the colour-coded data to help you consider the class collectively and to make initial decisions about students' abilities. Remember, with triangulation you should pay attention to the trend shown in the majority of the data (at least two out of three cells in this instance). Observations of this group might include:
    - There is one very high achieving student in this group.
    - The majority of the visualisation overall is yellow and orange, indicating the class is generally of average ability.
    - There are four students who failed mathematics last year (it might be a good idea to speak with the previous teacher if you don't know much about the students).

7. Further, ask yourself the following prompting questions about your data:
    - What do you notice in the data?
    - What are some areas of strength for your students?
    - What are some areas for development?
    - How could this knowledge alter the way you begin the year?
    - What strategies could you employ to ensure that you are best catering for the needs of your class?
    - What else do you need to find out about these students?
    - What formative assessment could you plan early in the term to collect some more evidence about their specific strengths and weaknesses?

Tips for implementation

I am a keen advocate of sharing data with students, but I also strongly believe that there are right and wrong ways of sharing this information. Many times, I have shared triangulated information like that collected in Example 1 with my classes, but I have shown the spreadsheet as the year progressed and as I add to the data and build the tracking spreadsheet as shown later in Example 4 (page 78). I do not believe that this information should necessarily be shared at the beginning of the year (when you may not really know the students), but it has great potential later on. See Example 4 for ideas about how to build this spreadsheet throughout the learning period and share data with students as the year progresses.

Example 2: Using data to identify individual intervention strategies

Triangulation (as performed in Example 1 on page 70) can be useful to form an overall picture of a class, and the groups and individuals within it. A further use of triangulated data is to annotate unique student needs so that you have a clearer picture of how you will support each student individually. This is one way specific adjustments for students can be documented for NCCD processes.

1. As in Example 1 (page 70), clearly identify the aim of your analysis (for example, to identify individual differentiation strategies for each student in a Year 9 mathematics class).

2. Follow Steps 2–5 of Example 1 to generate a triangulated and colour-coded dataset for the class.

3. Use the data and your own knowledge of the students to record individual intervention strategies for your class in an additional column down the right-hand side of the triangulated data. Think about each student's verified disabilities or learning difficulties, their literal position in the classroom, their relationships with others, and their ability, potential and current performance.

Table 5.5. Triangulated and colour-coded data with individual intervention strategies

Student	NAPLAN numeracy scale score	PAT in mathematics stanine	Previous semester overall mathematics result	Individual intervention strategies
Student A	463	3	C	Finds maths difficult – achieved this result with persistent effort. Sit at the front.
Student B	513	3	C–	Responds to positive encouragement – will behave poorly if she finds the work too difficult.

(continued)

Student	NAPLAN numeracy scale score	PAT in mathematics stanine	Previous semester overall mathematics result	Individual intervention strategies
Student C	549	3	C	Eager to please but finds maths difficult. Works best individually.
Student D	554	5	D	More capable than this result indicates. Makes poor behaviour choices at times. Sit with Student G perhaps? Needs regular reminders to bring all equipment to class.
Student E	554	5	D	Is capable of passing maths with consistent effort. Works well with others – pair with Student G?
Student F	549	3	C+	More capable than these results indicate – she achieved the C+ with minimal effort. Relationships (peer and teacher) are vital for success.
Student G	660	9	A	Very able student and a good support for other students. Use for peer-teaching where possible. Ensure extension activities are available at all times – negotiate these.
Student H	495	4	C–	Average ability student who works well.
Student I	Parent withdrawn	3	D–	Verified ASD, high-level OCD. Provide printed notes to maximise time on task, rather than writing notes. Requires modified assessment task.
Student J	615	5	C+	Is capable of improved results – challenge 'I'm not good at maths' mindset.
Student K	Absent	3	C–	Difficult to know potential at this stage – speak with previous teacher.
Student L	507	3	D	Verified social–emotional disorder, often inhibits learning. Use behaviour-management process consistently, focus on positives where possible. Requires modified assessment task.
Student M	559	5	C+	Learning difficulties – needs clear instructions, particularly for problem-solving.
Student N	559	7	C+	Much more capable than the C+ indicates. Show ACER result and have discussion about C+.

4. Return to this document and adjust and add to strategies throughout the year as you learn more about the students and collect more data on their performance and ability. Although the listed strategies do not provide extensive detail on the way in which you differentiate content, product and process (see Tomlinson & Allan, 2006), this exercise encourages you to start thinking about the individual shifts you will make for your students. The aim of this example is to help you create tailored plans for all of your students, drawing on your anecdotal knowledge of them as learners, as well as their standardised testing and previous results and formative tasks that you see in class. This pivots your attention to the needs of each learner, while at the same time providing evidence of the approaches you're using for each student in your class.

Tips for implementation

I would suggest that this is one of few examples in this chapter that should not be shared with students because it will possibly contain information about verifications, disabilities and student characteristics.

Example 3: Creating a differentiation placemat to identify differentiation strategies for small groups within a class

Triangulated data can be taken a step further (from Examples 1 and 2 on pages 70 and 73) to create a one-page differentiation placemat. These placemats are created in different ways in different schools, and the five-level example I provide here can be simplified to three ability groupings if necessary.

This placemat relies on teachers using triangulated data to place students in one of five differentiation categories, as displayed down the left-hand column of table 5.6. Positioning students in these categories relies on teachers considering the trends in the triangulated data of each individual student. Once all students are in one of the categories, the placemat then calls on Tomlinson and Allan's (2006) elements of differentiation to identify strategies to differentiate content, product, process and learning environment (see also, New South Wales Department of Education and Communities, 2015).

The following sample differentiation placemat provides some generic ideas of adjustments that could be made for students in a literacy-based subject. When developing your own differentiation placemat, I encourage you to add to the initial strategy suggestions in this example to tailor it to your needs and the needs of your learning area or year level. Feel free to add specific details about the adjustments made for each group of students and individuals within each group. If strategies pertain to individual students rather than the whole group, you might choose to write the student's initials after the relevant differentiation strategy in the relevant column (see an example in the 'Process' column in relation to Student H). Like in Example 2 (page 73), the information contained in this placemat can be used to outline the adjustments made (and provide evidence of these adjustments) for the NCCD.

Table 5.6. Sample differentiation placemat

Students	Content	Process	Product	Learning environment
Student G	Working above the ACARA achievement standard. Use higher-level texts where possible – at their reading age. Use a variety of reading – buddy arrangements. Exempt students from re-teaching when necessary. Use upper levels of Bloom's taxonomy and Marzano's thinking skills. Reflect on form and content.	Use high-tiered activities that have high complexity, challenge and little support. Co-create personal task lists so students move on to an appropriate task if finished. Encourage depth in an investigation. Explicit teaching: 'I do, we do, you do.'	Allow students to help design assessment tasks around learning intentions and success criteria. Give extension tasks. Use more 'fuzzy' projects.	Use independent/inquiry learning space. Encourage collaborative learning. Offer praise and encouragement.
Student N	Working at/above the ACARA achievement standard. Use higher-level texts where possible – at their reading age. Use a variety of reading-buddy arrangements. Exempt students from re-teaching when necessary. Use upper levels of Bloom's taxonomy and Marzano's thinking skills. Reflect on form and content.	Use high-tiered activities that have high complexity, challenge and little support. Co-create personal task lists so students move on to an appropriate task if finished. Encourage depth in an investigation. Explicit teaching: 'I do, we do, you do.'	Allow students to help design assessment tasks around learning intentions and success criteria. Use more 'fuzzy' projects.	Use independent/inquiry learning space. Encourage collaborative learning. Offer praise and encouragement.

Using data in your classroom

Student C Student H Student J Student M	Working at/around the ACARA achievement standard. Use standard-level texts where possible – at their reading age. Use a variety of reading – buddy arrangements. Re-teach/exempt from re-teaching where necessary. Challenge to progress up Bloom's taxonomy and Marzano's thinking skills.	Use activities that have some complexity, challenge and some support when needed. Give standard time to complete the task. Explicit teaching – 'I do, we do, you do.' Allow student to work in a pair with Student N where possible (Student H only).	Provide different options for students to convey understanding. Use clearly defined projects.	Encourage students to use independent/inquiry learning space. Encourage collaborative learning. Offer praise and encouragement.
Student D Student E Student F Student K	Working at/below the ACARA achievement standard. Use texts that match their reading age. Use hands-on activities to help with understanding. Use a variety of reading-buddy arrangements. Re-teach where necessary. Challenge to progress up Bloom's taxonomy and Marzano's thinking skills.	Use activities that have less complexity, challenge and some scaffolding. Some additional support/guidance may be required. Give more time to complete the task. Develop activities that cater for learning styles.	Provide different options for students to convey understanding. Provide less complexity in tasks. Use clearly defined projects. Teacher aides to support assessment process. Use scaffolding to support assessment.	With support staff, encourage students to use independent/inquiry spaces. Sit at front of room. Encourage collaborative learning. Offer praise and encouragement.
Student A Student B Student I Student L	Working below/off the ACARA achievement standard. Use texts that match their reading age. Use hands-on activities to help with understanding. Use a variety of reading-buddy arrangements. Re-teach where necessary. Focus on lower levels of Bloom's taxonomy and Marzano's thinking skills. Focus on decoding, fluency.	Use activities that are well scaffolded and provide support when needed. Teacher aides to provide additional support and guidance. Give more time to complete the task. Develop activities that cater for learning styles. Use visual prompts.	Provide different options for students to convey understanding. Use modified language in task sheets. Lower complexity in tasks. Use clearly defined projects. Teacher aides to support assessment process. Use scaffolding to support assessment.	With support staff, encourage students to use independent/inquiry spaces. Sit at front of room. Encourage collaborative learning. Offer praise and encouragement.

Tips for implementation

As with Example 2 (page 73), this example is mostly used for teacher and teacher-aide planning and potentially contains information that should not be shared with students.

Example 4: Tracking class performance throughout a semester or year

It may be useful for you to develop a tracking spreadsheet that collects data throughout the term, semester or year, including standardised testing data, previous achievement in the learning area, a target grade for the current academic period, homework completion, formative and summative assessment results, and overall results for the academic period.

There is no right or wrong way to collate this data, but table 5.7 is an example of how a spreadsheet like this could look. In this example, you will see I started the spreadsheet at the beginning of the academic year with standardised testing data relevant to the subject I was teaching (it was a humanities subject, so reading comprehension and writing are particularly important) and each student's previous semester result. At the beginning of the year, I worked through having conversations with students to set a target grade for Semester 1. Students set their goals based on their previous performance and their strengths and weaknesses in the skills needed in the subject. I then started tracking the completion of their homework tasks (red: incomplete, yellow: at least half completed, and green: completed). These were key formative tasks that I planned to support students in developing the skills they needed to succeed. Following this, there were five in-class assessments that I recorded, then the final assignment and overall grades for the semester. This spreadsheet was really beneficial for me because it helped me stay organised, but the real power in recording the data in this way was the strength of the conversations I could have with students about their progress, particularly towards their individual goals.

I have always used spreadsheets such as the one given in this example in conversations with students and their parents, as it provides specific and quantifiable information about the student's progress and learning. However, in the senior secondary school classes I have taught, I have projected this spreadsheet onto the whiteboard during lesson time and have discussed the data with students as a class. I wouldn't always recommend you do this, and if you do plan to, it is so important that you think about your strategy and that you ease into it gently. Your students value what you value, so if you are able to show them the benefit in being transparent about their results and build a collaborative culture of 'we're in this together' you are more likely to succeed.

Using data in your classroom

Table 5.7. Tracking class performance

Student	Student A	Student B	Student C	Student D	Student E	Student F	Student G	Student H	Student I	Student J	Student K	Student L	Student M	Student N	Student O	Student P
Year 9 NAPLAN reading	461	541	DNS	534	548	479	DNS	DNS	511	519	576	DNS	569	555	461	461
Year 9 NAPLAN writing	372	547	DNS	DNS	522	445	DNS	DNS	472	497	497	DNS	535	458	497	445
Previous learning area grade	C	C-	N/A	C	B+	B-	C	A-	C+	B-	B-	B	B-	A	C-	C+
Target this year	C+	C	C	B	A	B	C+	A-	B	A	B	B	B	A	C	B-
Homework 1																
Homework 2																
Homework 3																
Homework 4																
Class task 1 (out of 10)	4.5	2.5	4	5	7.5	6	2	8.5	9	6.5	6	6	5	8.5	5	7.5
Class task 2 (out of 10)	4.5	2.5	6	6.5	9	0	6	7	7	7.5	4.5	5	7	7	6	6
Class task 3 (out of 10)	5.5	6.5	4	9	8.5	2.5	4.5	8	8.5	9	4.5	4	7.5	9	6.5	8
Class task 4 (out of 10)	6.5	7	5	8	7.5	6.5	7	7.5	8	8	6	6.5	6.5	8	0	6.5
Class task 5 (out of 10)	0	6	6.5	6.5	0	0	5	8.5	7	8	0	6.5	8	0	7	
Average	4.2	4.9	5.1	7.0	6.5	3.0	4.9	7.9	7.9	7.8	4.2	4.3	6.5	8.1	3.5	7.0
Grade in-class assessment	D+	C-	C	B-	B-	D-	C-	B+	B+	B+	D+	D+	B-	B+	D	B-
Assignment knowledge grade	D+	C+	E	B-	B-	E	C	A-	B	B	B-	C-	C-	A-	B-	B-
Assignment skills grade	D+	C+	E	C+	B-	E	C	B+	B-	B	B-	C-	C-	A-	B-	C
Term 1 overall knowledge grade	D+	C	D	B-	B-	E+	C	A-	B+	B+	C	C-	C+	A-	C	B-
Term 1 overall skills grade	D+	C+	E	C+	B-	E	C	B+	B-	B	B-	C-	C-	A-	C	C
Overall term result	D+	C+	D-	B-	B-	E+	C	A-	B	B+	C+	C-	C	A-	C	B-

NOTE: 'DNS' stands for 'Did not sit the test'.

Tips for implementation

Example 4 has a lot of potential with students, and I have seen this type of tracking spreadsheet positively affect student achievement on many occasions. The way you introduce this data and tracking to students will determine whether or not it is ultimately successful. If framed in the context of helping the class achieve their goals and that everyone has skills in different areas, this tracking sheet can be used, and will be received, positively.

When I use spreadsheets like this with students, I introduce the idea about a week before I share it with a deidentified example of other data to show students what it will look like. Following this, I speak to every student individually to show them their data so they know what will be shown, if and when I share it. During those conversations I encourage students to let me know if they would like me to hide their results, and I give them a few days to think about it and either follow up with me directly or let me know via email if they are not comfortable with it. Showing students in a one-on-one conversation removes some of the uncertainty about their results, and it gives them a chance to ask me questions about it. It is also an opportunity for me to reassure students that this is about supporting them and their learning.

Here is an example of the way that I introduce this tracking sheet to students:

> *I have a spreadsheet that contains all of your recent results on NAPLAN and PAT, your previous semester's result for this learning area, and your homework completion and assessment results. I would like to share this with you in the next few days – not as something to point out differences in our ability, but so we know where our strengths are and we know what we have to work on. You know that we are all good at different things. These numbers are only a small part of who you are and what you can do. But by knowing our strengths and areas for growth in this learning area, we can build on our strengths and can work on the things we aren't so good at. This is a sample of what the spreadsheet will look like.*
>
> *[Display an example spreadsheet on the board.]*
>
> *During this lesson, I will come around to each of you and show you the data that I have for you that would go up on the spreadsheet for this class. If you would prefer that I do not show your data, please tell me and I'll leave yours out. That's totally okay – it is your data after all . . . You own it! If you have a think about it after class today or tomorrow and decide you would rather I leave your data out, just send me an email or come and see me. That's okay too.*
>
> *I won't put this up for the class for a few days. But the reason I'm asking you about this is because I have seen this type of tracking work before and knowing more about our ability helps us improve in the future. By making the marking and our strengths more transparent, we can all ask better questions of ourselves and others, and it will hopefully provide you with an*

idea of who in the class might either benefit from your support or be able to help you out a bit. There's nothing stopping us all doing really well in this subject – let's use the wisdom in the room and support one another.

You will notice here that the focus is on improving as a group. I use collaborative language such as *we* and *us*, to build the notion of a team that is working together to achieve success. When positively framed like this, you are more likely to have buy-in from students. I am yet to have any student email or tell me that they do not want their data shown. I have no doubt that there are right and wrong ways to approach this with students (and I know that I can be genuine and more convincing because I have seen this work numerous times), but it is important that you focus on the class improving together.

I know the impact that this practice has had on some of my students because I was there, in the room, having the conversations with them. For the purpose of highlighting the impact it can have on students, I decided to contact some of my previous students to ask them what they thought. One shared the following feedback:

I found it very helpful when my results were projected on the board. I knew how I was going and I wasn't in the dark. If the results I got were not the ones I wanted to achieve in the end of the semester it would give me a boost to work even harder to pick up my grades. But if I hadn't known my results as I went along, I would have thought I was doing fine and not put in that extra bit of work. (personal communication, December 11, 2017)

Although it is a slightly different context, I used a similar approach with a Year 12 cohort to track students and predict grades in the Queensland Core Skills (QCS) test. One student that I worked with in improving QCS results stated:

I think sharing the data and predictions was crucial and played a big role in our terrific QCS score. We could see where we were weakest and what needed improving, and also what we did really well. For some it was a pleasant surprise, and others got a bit of a shock. Then with the overall cohort data, it was really good that we all got to see it because it gave us more drive to do it for one another and to not let the team down.

I'd definitely recommend doing this for other teachers. It gives students a clear understanding of where they're currently sitting, allowing them to adjust their study habits accordingly. It allows for students to really realise that it is a team effort and everyone matters in the team, inspiring all to lift for each other. And finally, it's really rewarding if and when students do well to be celebrated by everyone in the team, because ultimately by improving their score they're improving everyone else's. (personal communication, December 12, 2017)

Sharing this data with students works, but how you sell it to your students will ultimately determine the level of impact. Remember, the focus is on helping students thrive and achieve good results, and it is about 'us' as a team of learners who work together and support each other. The more students know about their performance and the more transparent we can be with their data, the greater impact these strategies will have.

Example 5: Investigating strengths and gaps in assessment tasks

While tracking students longitudinally or comparing their learning area results with standardised assessment results is useful, it is also important to look more closely at the elements of specific tasks that your class may be finding difficult. This can be done with formative or summative assessments and can consider specific skills, content or cognitions that are being assessed. This specific investigation into the elements of assessment tasks allows us to develop a better understanding of the specific interventions and assistance required by our students. Although there will be unique differences between students and some will have different needs than others, this process allows you to identify overall trends for your class. If you have access to the ACER Online Assessment and Reporting System (OARS) platform you can do a similar analysis in strands and questions. Similarly, after NAPLAN results are returned you will also be able to do an analysis of criteria and or question types.

1. Organise the data in your spreadsheet according to the aim of your analysis (for example, specific skills, content or cognitions). This will be reflected in the column headings shown across the top of your spreadsheet as in table 5.8. The data must be displayed in a way that is comparable. If each skill, content area or cognition has a different number of marks allocated to it, this means you will need to convert these marks to percentages.

Table 5.8. Student results in assessment criteria

Student	Comprehending	Analysing	Evaluating	Synthesising	Total
Student A	85	50	54	69	65
Student B	90	94	90	90	91
Student C	87	77	77	79	80
Student D	85	77	85	85	83
Student E	75	59	72	65	68
Student F	88	69	78	80	79

2. Average the scores at the bottom of each column. Do this by typing the following function (selecting the cells where the data is sitting):

=AVERAGE(B2:B7)

Using data in your classroom

Table 5.9 Student results in assessment criteria with averages

Student	Comprehending	Analysing	Evaluating	Synthesising	Total
Student A	85	50	54	69	65
Student B	90	94	90	90	91
Student C	87	77	77	79	80
Student D	85	77	85	85	83
Student E	75	59	72	65	68
Student F	88	69	78	80	79
Average	85	71	76	78	77

3. Use the averages to create a line graph. The easiest way is to highlight the heading row and the averages you've just calculated (the top and bottom rows) and select the line graph option from the charts menu.

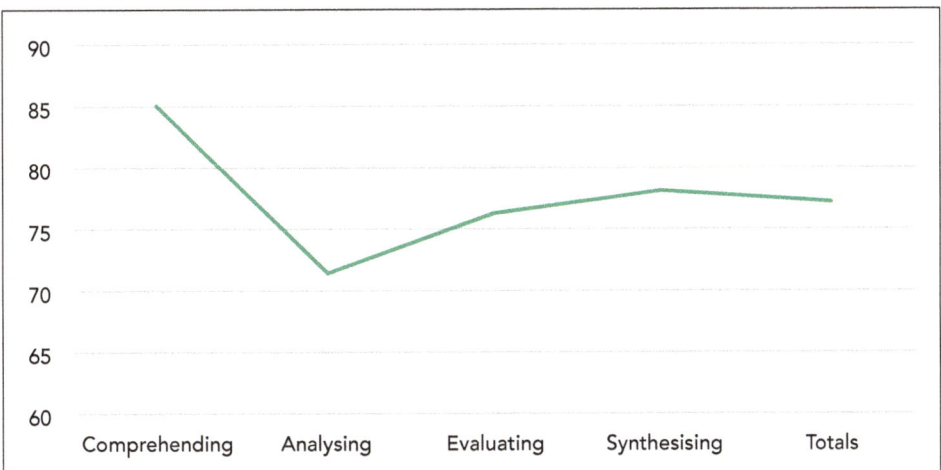

Figure 5.1. Average percentage results for each assessment criteria

If you run similar assessments at different times through the learning period, you can show more than one task on the same graph. To do this, follow the process from Steps 1 and 2, then build your summary table of the different tasks underneath one another, like in table 5.10.

Table 5.10. Average result for each assessment criteria across three assessments

	Comprehending	Analysing	Evaluating	Synthesising	Total
Average: Assessment 1	85	71	76	78	77
Average: Assessment 2	81	71	76	75	78
Average: Assessment 3	96	87	71	81	81

83

4. In the same way as you did in Step 3, highlight the table and insert a line graph.

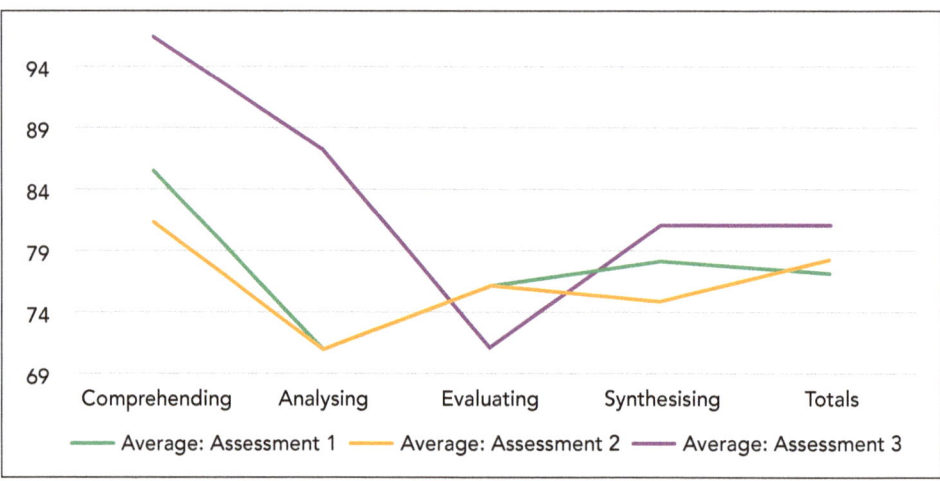

Figure 5.2. Average results for each assessment criteria in Assessments 1–3

5. Consider what the visualisation is telling you. If I saw figure 5.2, I would notice that the Assessment 3 percentage total has improved, so whatever interventions or steps I put in place after the second assessment have generally worked. As a part of this improvement, the comprehending, analysing and synthesising scores have increased quite a bit. I have questions about the evaluation score though. What happened in this task to cause the significant drop in performance? What were the common errors that students made? What structured, direct teaching might students benefit from, or how can I give them more opportunities to practice this cognition? You will know the answers to some of these questions, but it should start a process of reflection and generate questions that lead to further assistance for students.

Tips for implementation

This analysis is particularly useful for helping teachers identify the particular cognitions, skills or types of questions that their students are finding challenging. It is important to consider the areas that students are performing best in, those that are they performing the lowest in, and those in between. The benefit of looking at the success stories is that it provides something for us to celebrate with students; it can also be an opportunity to consider what has worked that is potentially transferable to other areas.

This is a relatively simple example in that it only considers four cognitions and the total score; however, this approach can be used for much larger datasets and assessments. The graph you generate can also be used with your class in discussion about the areas they could benefit from focusing on. Don't be afraid to show them and ask what they see and what help they think they might need to improve.

Example 6: Calculating the value added for students based on previous achievement

As John Hattie (2017) stated, 'we do not send our students to schools to maintain the average; we do not ask teachers to teach to the average. But we do expect schools to add value to what students bring to school' (para. 4). One of the ways that we can track this is by measuring the value that we have added to individual students and classes by using the fifteen-point scale from A+ to E– to show the number of points a student has moved up or down. This can be done to track movement in formative or summative tasks, or in end of semester results. It can also be done using the five-point scale from A to E if you don't use pluses and minuses. Some ways in which this information can be used with students can be found in the tips for implementation at the end of this example.

1. Download learning area data from the two tasks or periods that you would like to compare (perhaps two semester results).

Table 5.11. Student results for two reporting periods

Student	Previous semester	Current semester
Student A	B+	A–
Student B	C	C
Student C	C–	C+
Student D	A–	A+
Student E	A–	A–
Student F	B+	B–
Student G	C+	C+
Student H	C+	B–
Student I	D+	D
Student J	C	C
Student K	B	B–
Student L	C+	B–

2. Enter in a new column the number of sub-levels each student has moved from the first data point to the second. It is possible to set up a VLOOKUP formula that does this for you (and I cover this in more detail in Example 9 on page 92), but depending on the size of your class and your tech proficiency it is possibly just as quick to type these numbers in yourself. To do this, you need to calculate the number of steps students have moved from the first to second measure. The number will be positive if the results have improved (a move from B+ to A– is +1, C+ to B+ is +3, and so on), zero if the student achieves the same result (for example, from B– to B–), or negative if their second result is lower (from A– to B+ is –1, B+ to C+ is –3, and so on).

You can either colour-code these manually or set a conditional format.

Table 5.12. Student movement from one reporting period to the next

Student	Previous semester	Current semester	Movement
Student A	B+	A–	+1
Student B	C	C	0
Student C	C–	C+	+2
Student D	A–	A+	+2
Student E	A–	A–	0
Student F	B+	B–	–2
Student G	C+	C+	0
Student H	C+	B–	+1
Student I	D+	D	–1
Student J	C	C	0
Student K	B	B–	–1
Student L	C+	B–	+1

3. Once you have a movement score for each student, you can generate a general picture of your class performance by using the following formula at the bottom of the table (selecting the relevant cells) to see the overall movement:

=AVERAGE(D2:D13)

Table 5.13. Average student movement from one reporting period to the next

	Previous semester	Current semester	Movement
Student A	B+	A–	+1
Student B	C	C	0
Student C	C–	C+	+2
Student D	A–	A+	+2
Student E	A–	A–	0
Student F	B+	B–	–2
Student G	C+	C+	0
Student H	C+	B–	+1
Student I	D+	D	–1
Student J	C	C	0
Student K	B	B–	–1
Student L	C+	B–	+1
		Average	0.25

4. You can use this average to track the class progress over time. Anything above zero means that generally, the class is making progress; if they reach the number one, then every student (on average) has improved by one sub-level. An average of zero means that students generally performed as they had previously. An average under zero (a negative number) means that the class, on average, did not achieve as well as they did in the previous task or period. This is not to say that individual students did not improve – this is average for the class.

Tips for implementation

Value added is a measure of the impact you have had as a teacher on your students. One of the easiest ways to calculate the value added is by using the fifteen-point scale to measure the number of sub-levels a student has moved. Another way of doing this – particularly if you want to compare task results and there is a numerical score – is to calculate and compare the percentage result:

percentage result = student's score ÷ total number of marks available × 100

The use of percentages rather than raw scores is really important because not all of the formative and summative tasks in your classroom will add up to the same number of marks. Percentages mean that you can compare the values more easily.

In Example 6, the value added is calculated for individual students and for the whole class. This information is useful for teachers, but it is also worth discussing with students. If the overall class value-added score is positive, show the class (even if you only show the movement column or the overall score) and congratulate them on achieving better results than they did last semester or year. If the value added is zero, this is also worth talking about – particularly framed in the context of 'we can always get better at what we do and we should never settle for what we've achieved before'. Alternatively, if the value-added score is negative, it is again worth discussing with students the reasons they achieved lower grades than last time. Is there a new strategy that you could all try? Why do students think they performed at a lower standard? Hear the students' perceptions on how they think they can achieve better in the future and then set goals to improve in the next assessment.

Having individual conversations with students about their movement is also a really good opportunity to discuss their progress, rather than solely achievement. Susan Brookhart (2011, 2017) discusses the three types of feedback that students can receive: comparison to a criterion, comparison to their own previous performance or comparison relative to their peers. A quantifiable conversation where you discuss how a student has grown (or not) over time can be a really powerful conversation, particularly because not all students may be able to achieve the highest marks, but all students can make progress. Remember to focus on the importance of learning behaviours and dispositions – being persistent, gritty and asking questions – and celebrate when students are showing growth.

Example 7: Tracking homework

Homework completion can be tracked electronically. In the following example, the dates and exercises across the top row are homework tasks that were checked. Cells are coloured green if completed, yellow if more than half was completed or red if less than half was completed. When I used this tracking process recently in a senior mathematics class, I allowed students to catch up on their homework and convert the colours from red or yellow to green as we progressed. I did this because many of my students worked different nights during the week, so I allowed them to finish the work when they next had a night at home. In this example, the asterisks represent homework that was originally incomplete on the day I checked (so I marked it red at the time and wrote a note in the student's diary). If the cell is also green, the student completed the task at a later date. Putting an asterisk in the cell meant I could keep a record of how often this happened and how often I had written notes in diaries.

Using data in your classroom

Table 5.14. Homework tracking sheet

Student	Year 10 result	Year 11 target	Skills check	Ex 4A	Ex 4B	Ex 4D	Ex 5D	Ex 5B	Ex 5F	Chapter review	Quiz	Ex 9C	Ex 9D	Ex 9E	Ex 9F
Student A	C	C+							*	*	absent		*	*	*
Student B	B−	B			absent						D−		*	*	
Student C	D+	C−	absent		absent	absent	absent			absent	C+		*	*	*
Student D	D+	C−									D				
Student E	C+	B−		*		*					D				*
Student F	B	B+	absent							*	absent				*
Student G	B−	B					*				B−				
Student H	C	C+							*		absent				
Student I	D+	C−		*		*	*	absent	*	*	absent				absent
Student J	C	C+					absent	absent		absent	B−	absent	absent	absent	
Student K	B	B+			absent				*		B−				
Student L	D+	C−				absent	absent	absent			D	absent	absent	absent	absent
Student M	D+	C−				absent	absent				D				
Student N	D+	C−		*		*	*				D−		*		
Student O	B−	B				*	*				B				
Student P	C	C+		*		*		*			C−				
Student Q	N/A	C		*		*	absent	absent			D−	absent	*	absent	*
Student R	D+	C−					*	absent			D+	absent		absent	absent
Student S	C	C+					absent				D			*	*

Tips for implementation

You could build this type of spreadsheet throughout a unit, first basing it on triangulated data as shown in Example 1 (page 70). Although this example doesn't show standardised testing data, it can be a good starting point and aid conversations with students about homework completion. Either way, I have had real success tracking homework in this way and displaying the tracking sheet on the whiteboard during lessons.

In one school I taught in, we were expected to issue a forty-five-minute after-school detention to students who did not complete homework three times in a term. This spreadsheet helped me track their progress and then work with students to avoid the use of the detention system. I told students that when they had three red boxes, they would be given a detention, but also that they were welcome to catch up on homework and convert red or yellow boxes to green ones to avoid detention. It was a useful, completely transparent deterrent and I was able to say to students, 'You now have two red boxes; one more set of incomplete homework and you will get a detention. What can you catch up on first to avoid this?' I found this system worked for me, and students often caught up on homework that they had not been able to complete due to night-time work, assignments or sports training. There were certainly students who played the game – only doing half the homework so it was yellow, not red, to avoid detentions. But given that many of these students told me that they did not normally do mathematics homework at all, I was satisfied that at least half of the homework was completed on a regular basis.

Another school I taught in used a Responsible Thinking Classroom® model, which excluded the option of after-school or lunchtime detentions from classroom teachers to focus on restorative practices rather than punitive measures. I was worried that my homework tracking system would not work, so I had to re-think my approach. I decided that my strategy in this school should be that three red boxes means an email to parents about incomplete homework. Despite my initial reservations, this worked just as well as the threat of detention had – even with Year 12 students, who again informed me that they rarely completed mathematics homework. After I left the school, I asked students their thoughts on the homework tracking sheet. One of my students said:

> *The homework tracking sheet helped me stay motivated and alert throughout my studies, and it allowed me to easily see what I had or hadn't completed. It also made sure that I wasn't left behind throughout the classwork. (personal communication, December 11, 2017)*

I believe that students are competitive, they aim to please, they want to succeed, they value when teachers invest time in conversations about their progress and achievement, and they do not want teachers contacting parents or issuing detentions for incomplete work. All of these factors work in your favour with this tracking sheet, and you can show them that you're on their side and trying to help them avoid consequences.

Example 8: Tracking competencies and module completion

Some learning areas – particularly in the senior years – may be competency based, and so the A–E tracking sheet shown so far may not be the best fit. The following is an example of tracking task completion in a competency-based learning area, with three major assessments and five or six competency tasks per assessment.

The red squares are incomplete competencies, yellow has been started, and green represents completion and achievement at a pass, merit or distinction level (the letters in the green boxes). The black rectangles indicate the student completed the whole assignment and to which standard.

Table 5.15. Module completion tracking sheet

Student	Target grade	Current grade	Assignment 1					Assignment 2						Assignment 3					
			Local	National	Table	National organisations	Report	Characteristic	Risk assess	Posters	Warm up	Injuries/illnesses	Appropriate equipment	Leaflet	Officiating	Coaching 1	Coaching 2	Evaluation 1	Evaluation 2
Student A	Pass	P	Pass						M	P					2				
Student B	Pass	P	Pass												2				
Student C	Pass	P	Pass					P	M	M					P				
Student D	Merit	M	Merit					Merit						P	M				
Student E	Pass	P	Pass						P	P					D				
Student F	Merit	M	Merit					Merit						M	M				
Student G	Pass	P	Pass					P	P	M		M			M				
Student H	Pass	P	P		P		P			P					M				
Student I	Merit	M	Pass					Merit						P	D				
Student J	Merit	M	Merit					Merit						P	M				
Student K	Pass	P	P	P	P		P			P					2				
Student L	Pass	P			P		P								M				
Student M	Pass	P	P	P	P	P	P								2				
Student N	Merit	M	Merit						M	D	M				M				
Student O	Pass	P	Pass					Pass						M	2				
Student P	Pass	P	Pass					Merit						M	D				

Tips for implementation

I used this tracking system when I taught in the United Kingdom to track competencies in a senior sport and recreation learning area. The learning area was divided into three modules, each made up of smaller tasks. In many lessons, students worked through the tasks at their own pace and, when completed, I would colour the cell green and enter *P, M* or *D* to show whether the work was at the pass, merit or distinction standard, respectively. When students completed all the tasks in a module, I merged the cells, coloured them black and entered the overall achievement level for the module.

In the lessons in which students were working through the tasks, I had the spreadsheet on the board at all times. This reminded students of how they were progressing, showed me which students I needed to follow up with and helped with my recording of student results. Again, this was a way for me to collect data on my students that directly informed conversations with them about ways I could help them improve. Students who were disappointed in their grade for individual tasks often went back and improved their work to move into the merit or distinction categories. Like in previous examples, I told my students that me sharing this information was for their benefit, and to ensure that we all achieved our goals together and passed the course. I offered students the option to have their name removed from the spreadsheet shown in class, but in the multiple groups that I used this system with I never once had a student ask for their name to be removed.

Example 9: Tracking progress of students in assessment using the GPA system

The GPA system can be used to measure the average performance of a class, and then to track class performance in different assessment tasks and over time. This can be used in group verbal feedback to the class about the progress (or lack thereof) that they are making. An example of a conversation that you might have with students using this data can be found in the tips for implementation following this example.

1. Download the learning area result data from the two academic periods that you would like to compare (perhaps two semester results).

Table 5.16. Student results for two reporting periods

Student	Previous semester	Current semester
Student A	B+	A–
Student B	C	C
Student C	C–	C+
Student D	A	A
Student E	A–	A–
Student F	B+	B–
Student G	C+	C+
Student H	C+	B–
Student I	D	D+
Student J	C	C
Student K	B	B–
Student L	C+	B–

2. Create a table converting grades from A+ to E– to numerical values along the fifteen-point scale in a second sheet.

Table 5.17. Numerical values of grades from A+ to E– using a fifteen-point scale

Grade	Numerical value
A+	15
A	14
A–	13
B+	12
B	11
B–	10
C+	9
C	8
C–	7
D+	6
D	5
D–	4
E+	3
E	2
E–	1

3. Insert a column to the right of the grades given in each learning period and use the VLOOKUP function to allocate a numerical score, a mark out of fifteen, to each grade in these columns. For this example, I entered the following formula in the cell to the right of the first grade to be allocated a value (here, B2):

=VLOOKUP(B2,Sheet2!$A$2:$B$16,2,0)

I then dragged that formula down the length of the column to encompass all the grades given in the first reporting period. To allocate numerical values to the remaining grades, I repeated the process in the second new column, updating the initial cell reference in the given formula from B2 to D2.

Table 5.18. Student results for two reporting periods (grades and numerical scores)

Student	Previous semester	Numerical score	Current semester	Numerical score
Student A	B+	12	A−	13
Student B	C	8	C	8
Student C	C−	7	C+	9
Student D	A	14	A	14
Student E	A−	13	A−	13
Student F	B+	12	B−	10
Student G	C+	9	C+	9
Student H	C+	9	B−	10
Student I	D	5	D+	6
Student J	C	8	C	8
Student K	B	11	B−	10
Student L	C+	9	B−	10

4. Calculate the average score for the class, the GPA, at the bottom of these columns with the following formula (selecting the relevant cells in each instance):

$$=AVERAGE(C2:C13)$$

You can then use the fifteen-point scale to convert this GPA back into a grade. The spreadsheet will then look like table 5.19.

Table 5.19. Student results for two reporting periods including GPA and average grade calculations

Student	Previous semester	Numerical score	Current semester	Numerical score
Student A	B+	12	A−	13
Student B	C	8	C	8
Student C	C−	7	C+	9
Student D	A	14	A	14
Student E	A−	13	A−	13
Student F	B+	12	B−	10
Student G	C+	9	C+	9
Student H	C+	9	B−	10
Student I	D	5	D+	6
Student J	C	8	C	8
Student K	B	11	B−	10
Student L	C+	9	B−	10
GPA		9.75		10
Average grade	C+		B−	

It can be seen here that the class has improved from the previous semester to the current semester, moving from a C+ average to a B− average. Again, some students have made good improvement, while others have not. This is based on an average of the whole class, and therefore does not necessarily recognise individual improvement.

Tips for implementation

Calculating a GPA for the class after an assessment task or unit helps answer those questions from students such as 'What was the average mark?' or 'How did everyone else do?' Like the measure of value added, tracking the GPA provides an overall picture of how a class is achieving. I have found that students often want to know how they achieved relative to the group, and the GPA system is one way to do this. In a way, this is students attempting to put a context and an understanding around their grade. They want to know whether they performed better than most, they topped the class or everyone else performed better than they did.

The way I have introduced this in junior school classes in the past has been to talk to them about the 'average grade'. I've said things like this:

> *I decided to calculate the average grade for this last piece of assessment and compare it to your previous assessment. As you know, I believe we can always do better and make progress, so I think the average grade is a good way of comparing what we achieved this time to last time. Last time, our class average was a B− for the extended experimental investigation, but this time, our average rose to a B. Well done! That means that on average, everyone achieved one sub-level higher than last time.*
>
> *That's awesome work, and it shows that when we put in the effort and put our minds to it we can do better and achieve better results than we have before. I have seen many of you work really hard on this task: you asked good questions, spent time reviewing and improving your work, and worked hard to analyse your data to provide important insights about what you found. Good job!*

Example 10a: Developing a rank order of student achievement using grades

In my doctoral research, students indicated that they like knowing how their performance compares with their peers (Fisk, 2017). Specifically, a rank order of position in the class was something that many students in my study discussed positively. Although the students in my study acknowledged that this type of feedback does not provide specific information about how to improve in a learning area, they reported that the rank order data motivates them to work harder and provides more context around their achievement. In my experience teaching in secondary schools, my students responded in the same way – many believe a rank order allows them to see their performance compared to the performance of others and how far away they are from others. I have used a rank order in the classroom on the whiteboard and in some cases (for Year 12 results, for example) I've printed it out and put it on the wall.

The following is an example of how you can arrange this data.

1. Organise the data you would like to rank in a spreadsheet as in table 5.20.

Table 5.20. Student results for one assessment

Student	Result
Student A	C
Student B	B
Student C	A–
Student D	D
Student E	C+
Student F	B
Student G	C–
Student H	C–
Student I	C–
Student J	B–
Student K	A
Student L	C+
Student M	B+
Student N	A
Student O	C+
Student P	C
Student Q	C–
Student R	D+
Student S	B–
Student T	C+
Student U	C

2. Use spreadsheet software to sort the right-hand column. Although it is not perfect, sorting the data in this manner will assist you.

Table 5.21. Sorted student results

Student	Result
Student K	A
Student N	A
Student C	A–
Student B	B
Student F	B
Student J	B–
Student S	B–
Student M	B+
Student A	C
Student P	C
Student U	C
Student G	C–
Student H	C–
Student I	C–
Student Q	C–
Student E	C+
Student L	C+
Student O	C+
Student T	C+
Student D	D
Student R	D+

3. After the data is organised in this way, construct a template that shows every grade possible (from A+ to E–).
4. Manually input the student names.

Table 5.22. Spread of student results per grade category

Possible grades	Students
A+	
A	Student K, Student N
A–	Student C
B+	Student M
B	Student B, Student F
B–	Student J, Student S
C+	Student E, Student L, Student O, Student T
C	Student A, Student P, Student U
C–	Student G, Student H, Student I, Student Q
D+	Student R
D	Student D
D–	
E+	
E	
E–	

5. Ask students whether they would like to see the ranking (particularly speak to the lower-ranked students to gauge their perspectives) and even *how* they would like it used in class. If students are unsure about the reaction of their peers, you might like to replace their names with codes, animals or colours, so they know who they are and can still see the spread of the results.

Tips for implementation

Many schools that I have worked at used rank order in different ways, although none were as confronting as my school in London, which ranked the entire cohort of Year 9 science students in the main corridor all year round. The research that I completed for my doctorate showed me that the secondary students I interviewed wanted to know their position in their cohort, and that students usually have the emotional intelligence to know that they all have strengths and weaknesses in different areas and do better in some learning areas than others (Fisk, 2017). To introduce the idea of a rank order with a class or cohort, I usually say something like:

> *Later in the lesson I am going to show you the rank order of everyone in our class from the recent assessment task. The purpose of me showing you this is to help you all develop a better understanding of your performance, and*

to help you set goals for the future. We all know that there are some learning areas (and, in fact, things in life) that we are better at than others, and some that we find harder. That is life, and it is absolutely okay.

I would hate to think that this information would ever be used to give someone a hard time or to remind anyone that one person achieved a better mark than someone else. It is purely to show you how you are going and help you in the future. If you really do not feel comfortable with me putting your name up, please let me know in the next few minutes before I display the rank order. If you would like to have a look individually before it goes up on the board, come and let me know.

Again, I recently asked past Year 12 students about the impact of using the rank order in class. One student said:

The rank order was another key motivating tool for me as I wanted to stay on top of the class throughout the whole year. The rank order clearly indicated my level of achievement and compared my achievement with my goals.

I would definitely recommend the homework tracking sheet as well as the rank order because they develop motivation within students and also create a bit of a competitive vibe, which allows students to consistently improve their knowledge and capabilities. (personal communication, December 11, 2017)

Talking through and introducing the rank order in a way that is framed to support both learning and an understanding of grades works. Students want to know how they are performing compared with others and will appreciate the information if you use it as a way for the class to work towards achieving their goals. However, if you don't love this idea (and that's absolutely okay!), there are other ways that you may already do this, without the numerical data and spreadsheets.

In a school in north Queensland, Sylvia, a Year 3/4 teacher, showed me how she tracks her students in learning their times tables. Times tables might be a rote learning exercise, but any primary school teacher or maths teacher knows how important number facts are in building numeracy and mathematical skills. Sylvia built a wall of times tables ninjas on her wall. Students had their own ninja; they wrote their name on them and placed them on the wall when they could recite their 1× tables. As they built their proficiency in higher levels, they moved their ninja up the wall. To cater for the different expectations for Years 3 and Year 4 students in her composite class, the Year 4 students had additional levels added to the right-hand side (4×, 6× and 7×), while Year 3 students only had to move up 1×, 2×, 3× and 5×.

USING AND ANALYSING DATA IN AUSTRALIAN SCHOOLS

Figure 5.3. Sample data wall showing student achievement in learning times tables

Example 10b: Developing a rank order of student achievement using marks

At times, it may be more useful to rank students using marks rather than grades. This can be beneficial in assessments where marks are used to determine overall achievement. The doctoral research that I undertook indicated that marks are used regularly, but that students do not always know what is classified as 'good' or 'average' (Fisk, 2017). Providing some context around how other students in the class or cohort performed can help with this understanding, and students that I have used this process with have appreciated the additional feedback. In my doctoral research, one of the teachers that I interviewed raised a good point. She said that if a student got fifteen out of twenty-five and was disappointed but could see that most other students got between ten and sixteen out of twenty-five, the rank order would provide valuable feedback. On the other hand, if a student achieved seventeen out of twenty-five and was happy with the result, it would also be worth them knowing if their result was at the bottom end of the class.

1. Organise the data you would like to rank in a spreadsheet as in table 5.23.

Table 5.23. Student results for one assessment

Student	Result
Student A	18
Student B	7
Student C	12
Student D	11
Student E	9
Student F	18
Student G	20
Student H	12
Student I	14
Student J	6
Student K	10
Student L	12
Student M	10
Student N	18
Student O	18
Student P	11
Student Q	15
Student R	14
Student S	15
Student T	11
Student U	12

2. Use spreadsheet software to sort the right-hand column from highest to lowest.

Table 5.24. Sorted student results

Student	Result
Student G	20
Student A	18
Student F	18
Student N	18
Student O	18
Student Q	15
Student S	15
Student I	14
Student R	14
Student C	12
Student H	12
Student L	12
Student U	12
Student D	11
Student P	11
Student T	11
Student K	10
Student M	10
Student E	9
Student B	7
Student J	6

3. After the data is sorted, construct a template for the mark categories, being sure to include all the mark possibilities (20–0 in this case).
4. Manually input the student names.

Table 5.25. Spread of student results per mark

Possible marks	Students
20	Student G
19	
18	Student A, Student F, Student N, Student O
17	
16	
15	Student Q, Student S
14	Student I, Student R
13	
12	Student C, Student H, Student L, Student U
11	Student D, Student P, Student T
10	Student K, Student M
9	Student E
8	
7	Student B
6	Student J
5	
4	
3	
2	
1	
0	

5. Ask students whether they would like to see the data (particularly speak to the students who have achieved lower marks to gauge their perspectives) used in class. As stated in the previous example, if there is hesitation around sharing this data, you can replace students' names with codes, colours or animals, so that students know which one they are and can see how everyone else performed.

Tips for implementation

This example is very similar to the previous one and thus does not require much further commentary. Once again, you can share this type of data and feedback with your students to help them improve, particularly when results are in the format of marks rather than A–E grades.

Example 11a: Developing a rank order of student progress using grades

All teachers know that despite the amount of effort, scaffolding and guidance provided, some students will find it challenging to ever achieve an A grade or arrive at the top of the rank order for achievement. For this reason, it is just as important to recognise the progress that students make because any improvement, irrespective of where it is from or to, represents a shift in mindset, approach or effort. The following is a way you can measure and celebrate progress. An example of the way you can share this data with students can be found in the tips for implementation.

1. Collect the two sets of data in a spreadsheet that shows the information you would like to compare, as in table 5.26.

Table 5.26. Student results for two assessments

Student	Assessment 1	Assessment 2
Student A	C	C+
Student B	B	B
Student C	A–	B+
Student D	D	D+
Student E	C+	B–
Student F	B	C+
Student G	C–	C+
Student H	C–	B–
Student I	C–	C–
Student J	B–	B+
Student K	A	A–

2. Record in a new column the number of sub-levels each student has moved. As in Example 6 (page 85), positive and negative numbers indicate upward and downward movement respectively, while a zero indicates no movement. You could also use a VLOOKUP formula, as I did in Example 9 (page 92), to first allocate a mark to each grade and then subtract the first value from the second to calculate movement.

Table 5.27. Student movement from Assessment 1 to Assessment 2

Student	Assessment 1	Assessment 2	Movement
Student A	C	C+	1
Student B	B	B	0
Student C	A–	B+	–1
Student D	D	D+	1
Student E	C+	B–	1
Student F	B	C+	–2
Student G	C–	C+	2
Student H	C–	B–	3
Student I	C–	C–	0
Student J	B–	B+	2
Student K	A	A–	–1

3. Use the sorting function in your spreadsheet software to sort the movement column from largest to smallest.

Table 5.28. Sorted student movement from Assessment 1 to Assessment 2

Student	Assessment 1	Assessment 2	Movement
Student H	C–	B–	3
Student G	C–	C+	2
Student J	B–	B+	2
Student A	C	C+	1
Student D	D	D+	1
Student E	C+	B–	1
Student B	B	B	0
Student I	C–	C–	0
Student C	A–	B+	–1
Student K	A	A–	–1
Student F	B	C+	–2

You can display this progress data in this very format – simply hide the 'Assessment 1' and 'Assessment 2' columns if you do not want to show the individual grades. Like the previous two examples, you can also replace student names with codes, colours or animals to represent each student so that the data remains anonymous. You even might take it step further and colour-code the results.

Tips for implementation

Example 11a differs slightly from Example 10a (page 95) because it shows the progress that students have made from their previous achievement and celebrates improvement rather than the highest achievers. Of course, students who are already achieving in the A category have less opportunity to improve than students who regularly achieve Bs and Cs, but they are recognised and celebrated as being at the top of achievement rank orders and simply in achieving an A for their work. The benefit of this type of data and feedback is that it celebrates students who have worked hard – from whatever their starting point was – to achieve improved results.

Therefore, I would strongly encourage you to share progress feedback with students and to have conversations with them about their growth over time. Sometimes your students who make significant progress may be students who rarely, if at all, receive academic recognition throughout their schooling career. In Chapter 3 I shared Angela Duckworth's (2016) theory of moving from talent to achievement and showed that effort counts twice in her formula for success. This type of progress feedback can provide information on the amount of effort that a student has put in, can positively impact their mindset and self-belief, and can lead to development of skills and achievement. Why wouldn't you want to share that with students?

I have shared this information with students in the following way:

> *In this class we always talk about how important it is to be making progress, as well as celebrating students who achieve great marks. But some of us don't find this content easy, and I know some of you work tirelessly in class time and at home to make improvements. Although I am so proud of the students who got As in the novel-study task, I just want to take a moment to celebrate two students in particular.*
>
> *Chris achieved his best result ever in English in this task, getting a whole grade higher than he did in the last task. I've seen how hard Chris has worked on this: he asked for lots of feedback, did a lot of work at home and has given his absolute best during class. Congratulations Chris. I am so proud of you. Let's give him a round of applause.*
>
> *The second person I'd like to acknowledge today is Victoria. She has been trying so hard to crack into the B grade all year and she got there with this task. In fact, she didn't just scrape it in; she got a B+! Again, Victoria has worked so hard to achieve this. She set herself a goal at the beginning of the year and she has achieved it. I know she's pretty happy, and we're all very proud of her! Let's give her a round of applause too!*

Carol Dweck (2006) talks about the importance of rewarding and celebrating effort, and the impact that it has on students developing their growth mindset. Examples such as these show not only the students you single out but also every student in the class that with hard work and effort, it is possible to improve, and that intelligence is not fixed.

Example 11b: Developing a rank order of student progress using marks

This is an example of a way you can celebrate progress using marks rather than grades. It is very similar to the previous example and should likewise be shared with students where possible.

1. Collect the two sets of data in a spreadsheet that shows the information you would like to compare, as in table 5.29.

Table 5.29. Student results for two quizzes

Student	Quiz 1	Quiz 2
Student A	15	15
Student B	14	16
Student C	11	12
Student D	19	18
Student E	8	12
Student F	17	19
Student G	16	20
Student H	16	16
Student I	11	14
Student J	15	14
Student K	12	13

2. Select the cell to the right of the first student's marks and enter the following SUM function to calculate the movement from Quiz 1 (B2) to Quiz 2 (C2):

=SUM(C2-B2)

Hover over the bottom right-hand corner of this cell and drag the formula down the column to calculate each student's movement.

Table 5.30. Student movement from Quiz 1 to Quiz 2

Student	Quiz 1	Quiz 2	Movement
Student A	15	15	0
Student B	14	16	2
Student C	11	12	1
Student D	19	18	−1
Student E	8	12	4
Student F	17	19	2
Student G	16	20	4
Student H	16	16	0
Student I	11	14	3
Student J	15	14	−1
Student K	12	13	1

3. Use the sorting function in your spreadsheet software to sort the movement column from largest to smallest.

Table 5.31. Sorted student movement from Quiz 1 to Quiz 2

Student	Quiz 1	Quiz 2	Movement
Student E	8	12	4
Student G	16	20	4
Student I	11	14	3
Student B	14	16	2
Student F	17	19	2
Student C	11	12	1
Student K	12	13	1
Student A	15	15	0
Student H	16	16	0
Student D	19	18	−1
Student J	15	14	−1

To display this progress data, you can leave it in this format or hide the 'Quiz 1' and 'Quiz 2' columns to avoid showing individual marks.

Tips for implementation

Again, Example 11b is very similar to Example 11a (page 104) and thus requires little further commentary. The only thing to note here is that if the tasks or activities that you are comparing have different totals, it is important to convert these results to a percentage first so you can compare like-for-like (percentage result = student's score ÷

total number of marks available × 100). Knowing the power of feedback and moving from talent to achievement, go and put this data to work for your students when you use marks instead of A–E grades.

Example 12: Developing a table of values to show the number of As, Bs, Cs and so on

Example 10a (page 95) showed the use of a rank order of student achievement from A+ to E–. If you are not comfortable doing this, another way of providing feedback to students on the achievement of the group is to publish a table of values to show the number of students who achieved each grade. This can be done in either five grade categories or using the fifteen-point scale from A+ to E–. A school that I previously taught in had a similar table on reports at the end of semester showing the number of students in the cohort who achieved each grade overall. Although this example sits in the chapter on using data in classes, it can be used for individual assessment tasks, overall grades, on reports and to compare students to the spread of results across their cohort.

1. Collect the data you would like to group in a spreadsheet, as in table 5.32.

Table 5.32. Student results for one assessment

Student	Result
Student A	C
Student B	B
Student C	A–
Student D	D
Student E	C+
Student F	B
Student G	C–
Student H	C–
Student I	C–
Student J	B–
Student K	A
Student L	C+
Student M	B+
Student N	A
Student O	C+
Student P	C
Student Q	C–
Student R	D+
Student S	B–
Student T	C+
Student U	C

2. Use spreadsheet software to sort the right-hand column. Although it is not perfect, sorting it in this manner will assist you.

Table 5.33. Sorted student results

Student	Result
Student K	A
Student N	A
Student C	A–
Student B	B
Student F	B
Student J	B–
Student S	B–
Student M	B+
Student A	C
Student P	C
Student U	C
Student G	C–
Student H	C–
Student I	C–
Student Q	C–
Student E	C+
Student L	C+
Student O	C+
Student T	C+
Student D	D
Student R	D+

3. After the data is organised in this way, construct a template that displays the grade categories you want to show – whether that's every grade possible from A+ to E– (using a fifteen-point scale, table 5.34) or from A to E (using a five-point scale, table 5.35).

Table 5.34. Spread of student results per grade category (fifteen-point scale)

Possible grades	Number of students
A+	0
A	2
A–	1
B+	1
B	2
B–	2
C+	4
C	3
C–	4
D+	1
D	1
D–	0
E+	0
E	0
E–	0

Table 5.35. Spread of student results per grade category (five-point scale)

Possible grades	Number of students
A	3
B	5
C	11
D	2
E	0

4. Either manually count and enter or use the count function in your spreadsheet software to input the number of students who have achieved each grade category.

5. If your students are visual learners, you may also like to generate a graph of the class achievement, as in figure 5.4, by highlighting this data and selecting the column graph option from the charts menu.

USING AND ANALYSING DATA IN AUSTRALIAN SCHOOLS

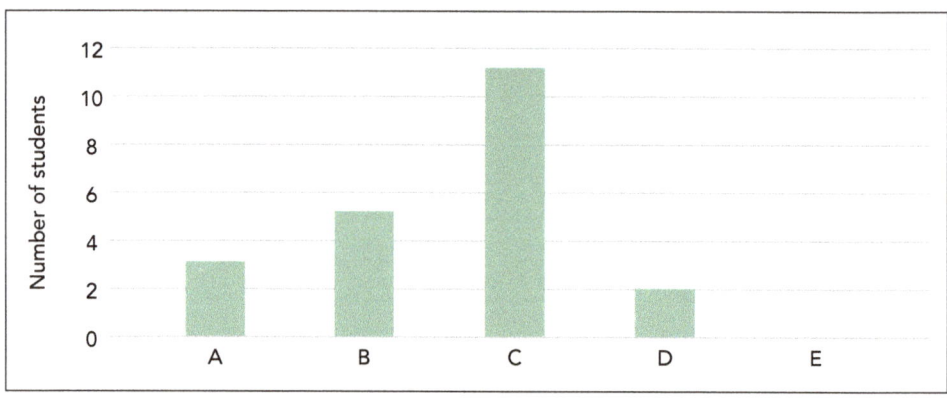

Figure 5.4. Spread of student results per grade category (five-point scale)

Tips for implementation

Sharing this type of feedback with students should not require you to discuss the information with your students first because it is completely anonymous and deidentified.

Like the rank orders, students in my doctoral study reported that they liked knowing the number of students who achieved As, Bs, Cs and so on in an assessment piece because they perceived that this information is beneficial in a few ways (Fisk, 2017). If a student achieves a B and is disappointed with their grade but sees that only one student achieved an A, it may make the student feel better about their performance. On the other hand, if a student achieves a C and is content, it is also useful to know if no student achieved less that the C grade because this would indicate that their performance was at the bottom of the group.

It is up to you whether you use the table of values with the fifteen-point scale from A+ to E– or the five-point scale from A to E, but the former offers more specific information and is particularly useful when you have a large cohort of students or students' results are close together. It helps students understand the difference between the number of B+s, Bs and B–s in the cohort (for example) and provides more information about where their performance was situated.

Example 13: Displaying the spread of student achievement in a box and whisker plot

A common way that I see student data represented in schools (and occasionally on reports) is in box and whisker plots; however, I also know that there are plenty of educators who don't understand how to read and interpret them. This concerns me a little, because if we aren't sure what they tell us, there's a good chance that students and parents have no idea!

Despite the ambiguity around the messages they convey, box and whisker plots can be a really useful tool to show the spread of data in a class or cohort. They allow you identify the overall trends and where student results are grouped, and consider your highest and lowest results as well as outliers. There are several fundamental points that you should know about this type of visualisation:

- Box and whisker plots show the spread of the data.
- Exactly 25 per cent of the data sits in each of the four sections – the top whisker (the top 25 per cent of the data), the top half of the box (50–75 per cent), the bottom half of the box (25–50 per cent), and the bottom whisker (the bottom 25 per cent).
- The ends of the whiskers represent the highest and the lowest scores in the data (unless there are outliers – see the final point in this list).
- The line in the middle of the box represents the median, which is the middle score if they were all lined up in numerical order (not the average – this is a common misunderstanding).
- The shorter the box or whisker, the closer together the data sits. The longer the box or whisker, the more spread out the data is.
- The middle 50 per cent of the data is represented in the large box in the middle of the two whiskers (meaning the two boxes show the data from 25 per cent to 75 per cent).
- If you have any in your dataset, outliers – numbers that are significantly higher or lower than the majority of the data – will be shown as single dots above or below the end of the whisker.

Thankfully, box and whisker plots are increasingly being generated for us in learning management systems, so we don't have to go through the manual process – plus Excel now allows you to draw one relatively easily (particularly compared to how difficult it used to be). To get started on generating your own box and whisker plots, follow these instructions.

1. Collect the data that you would like to show in a box and whisker plot in your spreadsheet as in table 5.36.

Table 5.36. Student scores

Student	Score
Student A	12
Student B	8
Student C	7
Student D	14
Student E	13
Student F	12
Student G	9
Student H	9
Student I	5
Student J	8
Student K	11
Student L	9

2. Highlight the column showing the scores and insert a graph, selecting the box and whisker option. If you are not happy with the axis values, double click the axis and the menu should open which allows you to manually set the maximum and minimum values. You can also change the name of the visualisation, colour, size and so on.

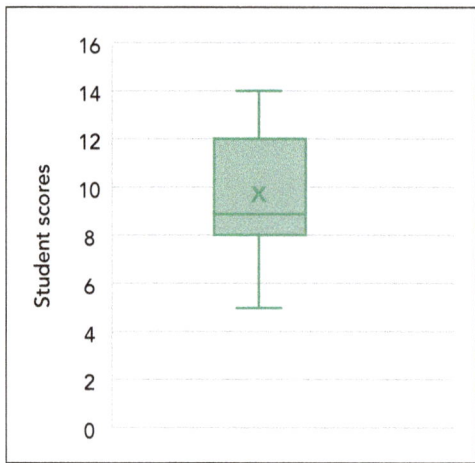

Figure 5.5. Spread of student scores

3. A box and whisker plot can also be generated easily to compare multiple tasks side by side (assuming the totals are the same or the results are in

percentages). To do this, organise your data into one table where the information is side by side as in table 5.37.

Table 5.37. Student scores in two assessment tasks

Student	Assessment 1 score	Assessment 2 score
Student A	12	12
Student B	8	8
Student C	7	14
Student D	14	20
Student E	13	13
Student F	12	20
Student G	9	9
Student H	9	9
Student I	5	5
Student J	8	3
Student K	11	11
Student L	9	12

4. Follow the same process as in Step 2, highlighting the two columns showing the scores, to insert a box and whisker plot.

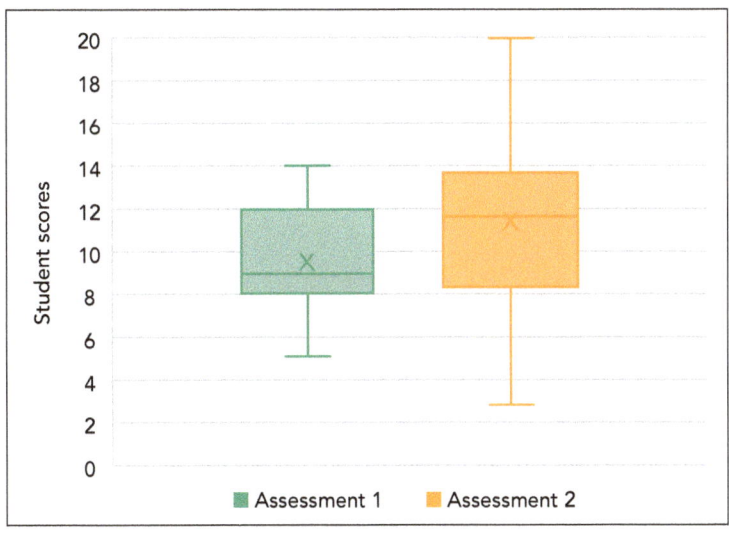

Figure 5.6. Spread of student scores in two assessment tasks

Tips for implementation

You can use of this method of displaying data in a number of ways: for your own reflection and comparison, in conversation with other teachers in your teaching team or department, and with students or parents.

When I use box and whisker visualisations to compare results across two or more tasks for the same group of students, these are some the things that I look for straight away:

- the position of the medians (In this example, the middle score was higher in the second task, which means there was general improvement.)
- the height of the maximums (The highest score in the second task was much higher than the first, meaning that top students performed better in the second task.)
- the position of the minimums (The lowest score was in the second test, so although students generally improved there was at least one student with a very low result.)
- the position of the quartiles, the five horizontal lines (In this example, I notice that the top fifty per cent of students in the second task performed about the same or higher than the top twenty-five per cent of students in the first task. I know this because the middle line in the orange box is at about the same position as the top of the blue box.).

If your learning management system generates these for you, it will probably also generate box and whisker plots that represent each student's position in the spread of results. These can be really useful in conversations with students to show whether they're improving, above or below the median, or generally achieving similar results in each task.

Example 14a: Graphing progress of individual students over time using line graphs

As noted in the earlier sections of this book, there is much discussion in Australian schools and policy around the expectation that teachers will track progress as well as achievement. Historically, this hasn't been done all that well; we are far better at talking about and reporting on achievement than on progress.

Several examples in this chapter include ways to look at progress for students across tasks or semesters as well as overall progress for a class. However, to do progress-tracking well, each student needs their own tracking profile so their progress can be shown over time.

Here are three different strategies for using line graphs to show progress – involving a free Google template, a school visualisation dashboard and students tracking their own performance – and corresponding tips for implementation.

Strategy 1: Google template

To make this task easier for teachers, Google has designed a 'Grade book' template that allows teachers to collect student results on one page, calculate average results for different tasks, automatically calculate overall grades and view student results relative to the rest of the group. To access the template, log into your Google account, select Google Sheets in the top right-hand menu, and expand the templates gallery so you can see them all. Scroll down to the education section and open the 'Grade book' template.

There are a couple of reasons why I really like this template and the three tabs of visualisation it generates. It allows you to customise your A–E result cut-offs on the first tab, meaning you can set different parameters and adjust for your specific context. It also shows you an overall view of your class's performance in terms of grade distribution across all tasks as well as average scores in each task (see figure 5.7). This is really helpful for analysing class or cohort performance and gives you a great snapshot of the spread of results and differences in different tasks.

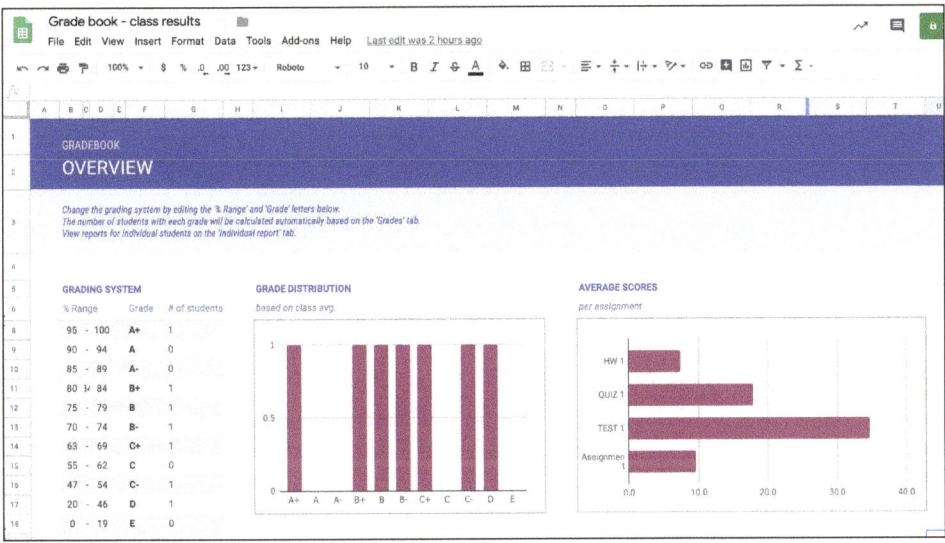

Figure 5.7. Sample view of the first tab in the Google 'Grade book' template

In the second tab, you can enter results for a range of tasks for each student in your class (see figure 5.8). It doesn't matter whether these results are from standardised tests, subject marks, formative assessments or summative assessments because the template converts each to percentages, no matter what the total marks were. Essentially, you can enter the names of the tasks and the total marks, and it will calculate each student's overall percentage in the subject and their associated grade.

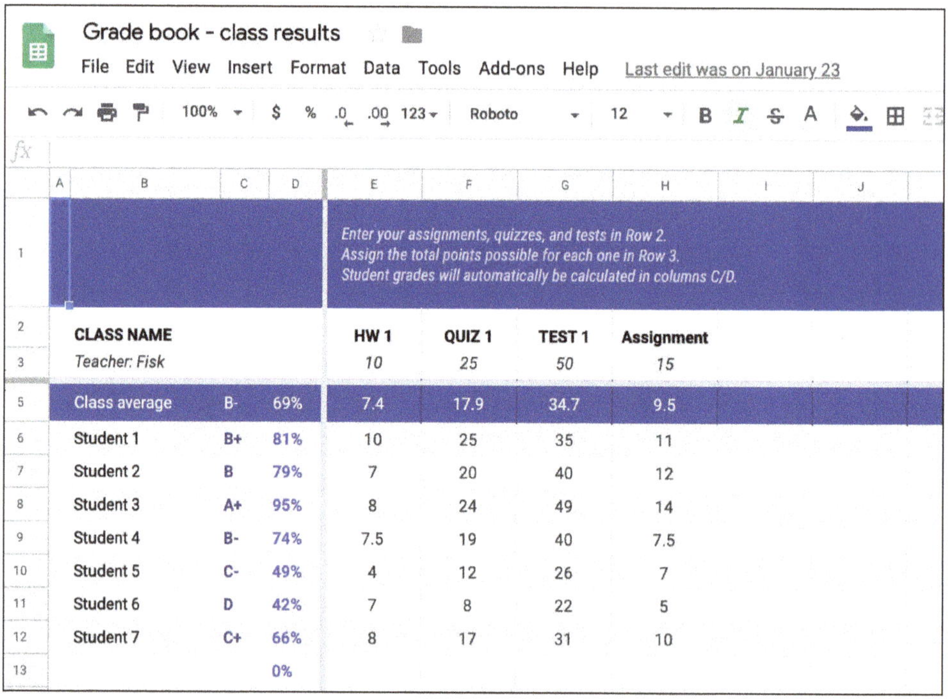

USING AND ANALYSING DATA IN AUSTRALIAN SCHOOLS

	A	B	C	D	E	F	G	H	I	J
		Grade book - class results								
		File Edit View Insert Format Data Tools Add-ons Help						Last edit was on January 23		
1					Enter your assignments, quizzes, and tests in Row 2. Assign the total points possible for each one in Row 3. Student grades will automatically be calculated in columns C/D.					
2		CLASS NAME			HW 1	QUIZ 1	TEST 1	Assignment		
3		Teacher: Fisk			10	25	50	15		
5		Class average	B-	69%	7.4	17.9	34.7	9.5		
6		Student 1	B+	81%	10	25	35	11		
7		Student 2	B	79%	7	20	40	12		
8		Student 3	A+	95%	8	24	49	14		
9		Student 4	B-	74%	7.5	19	40	7.5		
10		Student 5	C-	49%	4	12	26	7		
11		Student 6	D	42%	7	8	22	5		
12		Student 7	C+	66%	8	17	31	10		
13				0%						

Figure 5.8. Sample view of the second tab in the Google 'Grade book' template

My favourite feature of this template is in the third tab, where you can track a student's progress over time relative to the class average. This visualisation is generated automatically from the data entered in the second tab, and you'll notice that the visualisation is for individual students (see figure 5.9). It compares their results (the dark-blue line in the figure 5.9 example) for each task to the class average (the light-purple line). This can be a really useful representation of the progress a student is making and can be used in conversations with students and parents.

Using data in your classroom

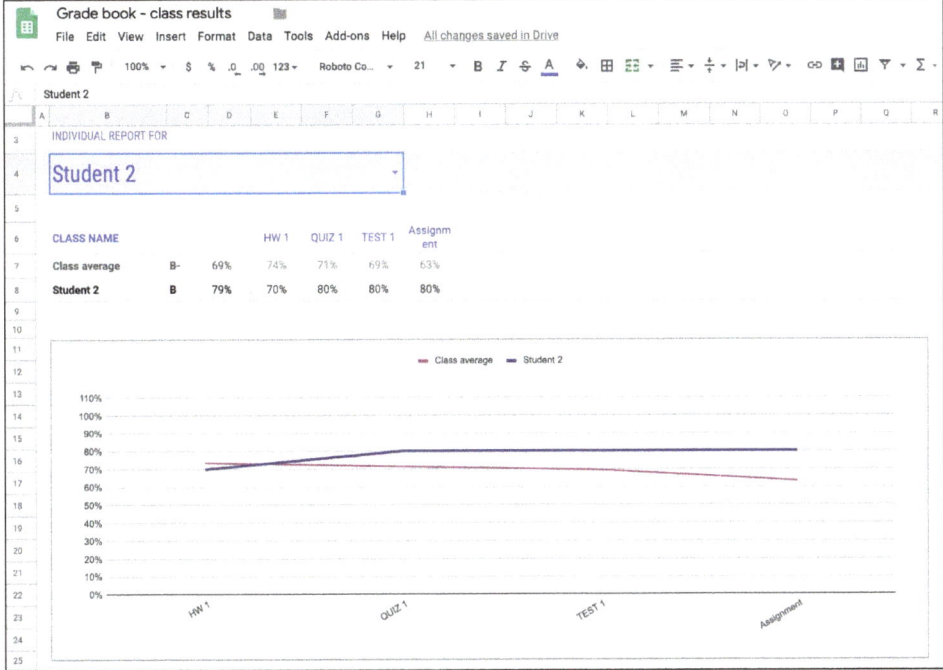

Figure 5.9. Sample view of the third tab in the Google 'Grade book' template

Tips for implementation

I have used the third tab of this spreadsheet to monitor the progress of individual students and have referred to it in conversations with students and occasionally in parent–teacher interviews. While student performance relative to their peers isn't very important, it does provide contextual information for students who may benefit from it. For example, if a student usually performs above the average result but drops below, it would be a good time to check in with them to see how they are. If a student is often below the class average but achieves above the class average, it would be a great opportunity to recognise their achievement, celebrate with them and possibly even send an email home. If a student is consistently low but not putting in satisfactory effort, this visualisation could help the conversation.

Strategy 2: Visualisation dashboard

Learning management systems visualise data in many different ways, but a common longitudinal representation found in many visualisation dashboards is subject results over time (see figure 5.10). Typically appearing as a trend graph of summative results that are often six months apart, this deals with overall results and averages rather than tracking individual tasks as we did in the previous strategy. Although this uses summative results, when it is viewed over time it shows progress (remembering that progress is the incremental steps and movement forward).

Subject average: B									Semester 1, 2020	Unit 2 Year 11, 2019	Unit 1 Year 11, 2019
Student details						Subject results					
Student	Class	Sex	House	Age	Time at school	Trend	Subject result – semester 1, 2020	Previous subject result	Subject history	Core	Core	Core
A	B	M	F	17y 4m	3y 8m	↓	C+	B–		9.2 (C+)	8 (C)	9.2 (C+)
B	A	F	C	18y 2m	5y 8m	→	B	B+		11.33 (B)	10.83 (B)	9.4 (C+)
C	A	M	C	18y 2m	5y 8m	↑	C+	D+		8 (C)	7 (C–)	7.25 (C+)
DS	A	M	F	18y 0m	5y 8m	↓	C+	B–		10.4 (B–)	9.8 (B–)	10.22 (B–)
E	A	F	F	17y 5m	5y 8m	→	B	B		11.5 (B+)	10.17 (B–)	10.67 (B)
F	A	M	K	18y 11m	1y 8m	↑	B+	C		7.75 (C)	7.75 (C)	7 (C–)

Note: the first column "Student" header spans the student icon/letter column. Columns shown left-to-right under Student details are: Student, Class, Sex, House, Age, Time at school. Under Subject results: Trend, Subject result – semester 1, 2020, Previous subject result, Subject history. Then Semester 1, 2020 (Core), Unit 2 Year 11, 2019 (Core), Unit 1 Year 11, 2019 (Core).

Figure 5.10. Sample view of student summative subject results taken from the TrackOne visualisation dashboard

Tips for implementation

As in the visualisation in the third tab of the Google template, these line graphs can be used by teachers to build an overall understanding of the progress their class has made over time, but also in conversation with students and their parents. The conversation with the first student in this diagram (where the line was high for three semesters and is starting to drop), will be very different to the third student (up-and-down performance, but generally heading upwards) and very different again to the sixth (consistently improving over time). But none are more important than the other and using the data as a prompt can lead to great conversations with young people.

Strategy 3: Students track their own performance

The final strategy for tracking progress of students over time involves students themselves. When I was in Year 6, I had a graph in the back of my maths book and each week after our quiz we had to record our score out of twenty and draw the next section of the line graph. I've seen this strategy used in a number of primary and secondary schools and it can be really effective. Not only does it track and collect data on progress over time but also students are involved in the process! These graphs might show a score out of a consistent total (if you run the same sized quiz regularly, for example) or a percentage correct, or it might have the scale from A+ to E– on the y-axis. If you're going to give this strategy a go, choose units that work across the range of tasks that

Using data in your classroom

you would like to use it for, but ensure that you create opportunities for students to reflect on their progress.

I saw an extension of this idea in a Year 6 classroom recently. Students were tracking their progress in spelling tests on individual line graphs on the wall of their classroom (see figure 5.11). Before he set up the board, the teacher talked to his students about the benefits of setting goals and not trying to compete against others but instead hit their own personal bests. He also talked about the fact that they wouldn't improve every week necessarily, but they were making progress if their graphs were generally trending upwards. He followed this up by awarding students who achieved full marks, made good progress and hit personal bests. Consequently, he said, his students were really engaged in the process and found it a really positive experience.

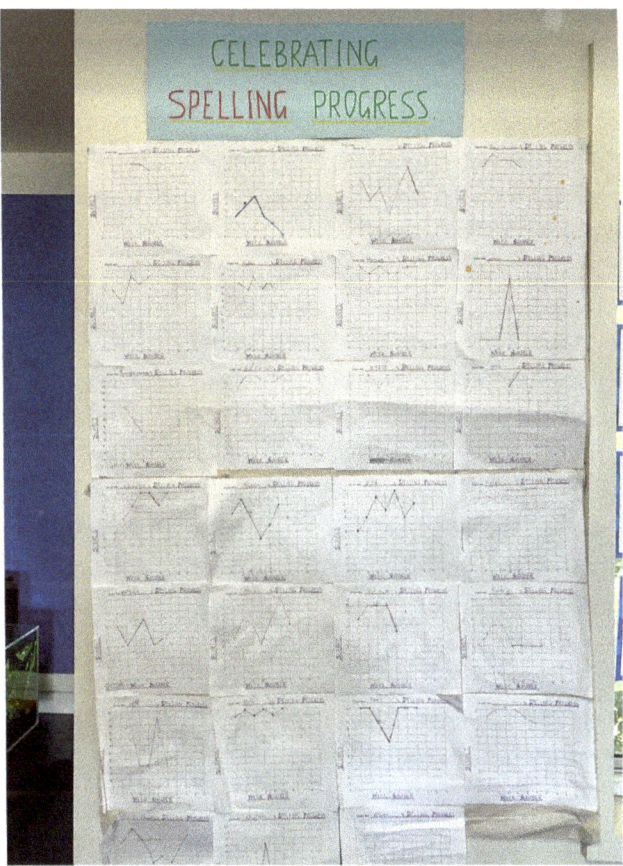

Figure 5.11. Student tracking line graphs on the wall in a Year 6 classroom

Tips for implementation

Before you introduce this to your class, think about the way you will explain it to them – particularly if they haven't done this type of tracking in front of others before. Remember, students will value what you value. If you 'sell' this strategy as an activity that allows them to grow together and emphasise that progress and improvement won't happen every week – and that's okay – then students are more likely to use it well and be motivated by it.

Example 14b: Graphing progress of individual students over time using colour-coded spreadsheets

Sometimes the data you collect is not quantitative in nature, meaning that you're unable to graph it longitudinally in a line or bar graph. Another way of looking at progress, particularly if it relates to criterion-based assessment, is to record the elements of the descriptors a student has not achieved, is on their way to achieving or has already achieved. A benefit of doing this is that rather than only reporting on large summative tasks at the end of semester, you will be able to see the smaller incremental steps that students make towards demonstrating the achievement standard, selected skills or understanding.

There are a couple of different ways to do this. This example shows some of the descriptors for the numeracy continuum provided by ACARA at Level 1a, which is a pre-Foundation level of numeracy. A similar process could also be used for the literacy continuum, the larger literacy and numeracy progressions, and the Australian Curriculum content descriptors and elaborations. As shown in table 5.38, cells are coloured for each student to represent whether they have demonstrated a particular skill, are on their way towards demonstrating proficiency, or are yet to demonstrate proficiency. What this does is generate a visualisation of the progress a student is making and shows what each student can do at the current point in time. It is also possible to transfer this information to the next teacher, who can build on this visualisation as students improve.

If you want to consider students' growth over a particular learning period, you can compare this spreadsheet to the version given at the beginning of the learning period. Assuming that your students came to you with the previous teacher's completed data, you could compare the number of elements attained by each student during the time in your class with how many they attained in the previous period. This can be used in conversation with parents and students, and the comments that you can make are very specific. For example, you would be able to say things like:

> *Last year, [Student A] was working towards being able to recognise 'a whole' and 'parts of a whole' within everyday contexts. This year, [Student A] has demonstrated that they are able to do this.*

If you have students working off-level, on the general capabilities or towards the year-level achievement standard, this can be a useful tool to help you know whether or not individual students are demonstrating relevant skills and understanding, and should or could be progressed to the next level.

Using data in your classroom

Table 5.38. Example tracking sheet for numeracy progressions along Level 1a of the Learning Continuum of Numeracy

Element	Estimating and calculating with whole numbers			Recognising and using patterns and relationships	Using fractions, decimals, percentages, ratios and rates	Using spatial reasoning		Interpreting statistical information
Criteria	Demonstrate concepts of counting using everyday experiences	Recognise the effects of adding to and taking away from a collection of objects	Identify situations that involve the use of money	Recognise simple patterns in everyday contexts	Recognise a 'whole' and 'parts of a whole' within everyday contexts	Sort or match objects according to their features	Demonstrate awareness of position of self and objects in relation to everyday contexts	Display information using real objects or photographs and respond to questions about the information displayed
Student A	G	R	R	R	R	R	R	Y
Student B	G	G	G	G	G	R	G	Y
Student C	G	G	G	G	G	R	G	Y
Student D	G	Y	Y	Y	Y	R	Y	Y
Student E	G	G	G	G	R	R	G	Y
Student F	G	G	G	G	R	R	G	Y
Student G	G	G	G	G	R	R	G	G
Student H	G	G	G	R	R	R	R	Y
Student I	G	G	G	G	R	R	G	Y
Student J	G	G	G	G	R	R	G	Y
Student K	G	G	G	G	R	R	G	G
Student L	G	G	G	G	R	R	G	Y
Student M	R	R	R	R	R	R	R	R

SOURCE: Adapted from ACARA, n.d.

Another way that you can make the progress tracking a little more obvious is by recording the date or the school term each element was achieved or demonstrated (see table 5.39). This allows you to see the elements achieved in a reporting period and compare this to where students were at the end of the previous reporting period. To make this even clearer, you can change the text from the previous period to one colour (for example, black) and show any progress or edits to the spreadsheet in a different colour (white). What that would mean is that when reporting on progress and discussing progress the teacher could talk really specifically and could see quite easily which elements of the criteria or which skills or understandings had been demonstrated in that specific assessment period.

Table 5.39. Example tracking sheet for numeracy progressions along Level 1a of the Learning Continuum of Numeracy showing the term in which the skill or understanding was demonstrated

Element	Estimating and calculating with whole numbers			Recognising and using patterns and relationships	Using fractions, decimals, percentages, ratios and rates	Using spatial reasoning		Interpreting statistical information
Criteria	Demonstrate concepts of counting using everyday experiences	Recognise the effects of adding to and taking away from a collection of objects	Identify situations that involve the use of money	Recognise simple patterns in everyday contexts	Recognise a 'whole' and 'parts of a whole' within everyday contexts	Sort or match objects according to their features	Demonstrate awareness of position of self and objects in relation to everyday contexts	Display information using real objects or photographs and respond to questions about the information displayed
Student A	Term 1							
Student B	Term 1	Term 2	Term 2	Term 3	Term 3		Term 3	
Student C	Term 1	Term 1	Term 2	Term 2	Term 3		Term 3	
Student D	Term 1							
Student E	Term 1	Term 1	Term 2	Term 3	Term 3		Term 3	
Student F	Term 1	Term 1	Term 2	Term 3	Term 3		Term 3	
Student G	Term 1	Term 1	Term 2	Term 2	Term 3		Term 3	Term 3
Student H	Term 1	Term 1	Term 3		Term 3			
Student I	Term 1	Term 2	Term 2	Term 2	Term 3		Term 3	
Student J	Term 1	Term 1	Term 1	Term 1	Term 2		Term 3	
Student K	Term 1	Term 2	Term 2	Term 1	Term 1		Term 3	Term 3
Student L	Term 1	Term 1	Term 1	Term 2	Term 2		Term 3	
Student M	Term 1							

SOURCE: Adapted from ACARA, n.d.

Tips for implementation

There are a couple of different ways that this spreadsheet can be used. Primarily this is a great tool for a teacher to assess the progress (or lack thereof) that their students are making. If, for example, you can see that a student had achieved quite a few green boxes throughout the semester then you know that they are progressing well and you can see what elements to work on next. On the other hand, if a student is making slow progress or hasn't added any green cells spreadsheet at an appropriate time in the assessment period, it indicates that it may be necessary to go back and have a conversation with the student and their parents about what might be hindering progress.

As I've already stated, if we believe that all progress is good progress and that students will progress and improve at different rates, then we just need to use a tracking mechanism like this to keep an eye on how they are going. This type of system prevents students from flying under the radar or going through a semester without achieving or experiencing the progress that we expect. It also allows us to move students on once they have demonstrated all of the curriculum at that level.

CHAPTER 6

USING DATA IN YOUR SCHOOL

Data are not information; information is that which results from the interpretation of data.

(Mitroff & Sagasti, 1973, p. 123)

This chapter discusses the 'what' of data (Sinek, 2009, 2017): the ways middle and senior leaders can use data for large groups or cohorts. There are a multitude of ways data can be used for cohorts and schools, but for the purpose of this discussion the uses of data at these levels have been categorised as follows:

- identifying groups in a cohort for intervention, extension or class streaming
- measuring and comparing academic growth in learning areas
- reviewing NAPLAN data
- reviewing ACER PAT data
- creating data walls
- implementing other school data measures, including wellbeing.

Depending on the aims and use of the data and the school context, the methods of analysis will differ. The examples provided in this chapter are intended to illustrate how data might be used at a school or cohort level, as well as provide insight into how these ideas can be expanded on in the future. Many of the examples provided in this chapter can be modified and used by classroom teachers – they should not be limited to cohort and school use. As in the previous chapter, the examples provided here are certainly not exhaustive, and it is my hope that this will inspire many new and improved, contextually appropriate data systems in Australian schools.

IDENTIFYING GROUPS WITHIN A COHORT FOR INTERVENTION, EXTENSION OR CLASS STREAMING

As stated in Chapter 4, triangulation in the school context is the process of combining different sources of data to form a more accurate picture of a student's ability and challenges. Triangulation requires at least three pieces of data, and in the first section of this chapter you will use your triangulation skills to assist in identifying key groups of students. Identifying and grouping students can be used to:

1. identify students for extension programs
2. identify students for intervention programs
3. stream students into class groups based on ability.

Throughout my career, I have used triangulated data for all three of these purposes. I identified students for a gifted and talented program in the same year in which I had a group of students come out of class for additional numeracy support. I am a huge believer in streaming class groups, as I have witnessed increased engagement of students due to more effective differentiation from teachers. Interestingly, triangulated data led to an interesting conversation in one school I worked in, where a student achieved exceptional results in PAT in reading comprehension and NAPLAN reading and writing while only achieving Cs in English. The English teacher argued against the student being in the extension class because he hadn't looked at the standardised testing results and only knew him as a C student! Despite the argument from the teacher, the student went into the extension group and thrived. Samples of this type of data use are available in Examples 15–17 (from page 130).

MEASURING AND COMPARING ACADEMIC GROWTH IN LEARNING AREAS

There may be some occasions where it is necessary and beneficial to compare student performance in learning areas and to track their growth. This might be useful for academic mentoring purposes, for teachers, to identify students who are making significant or very little progress, or to award high achievers at awards nights. This can be done by:

1. tracking class performance and measuring growth by GPA
2. calculating individual student GPAs across learning areas
3. comparing the value added for different classes in the same learning area.

When I was teaching in the United Kingdom, standardised reporting associated a value-added result to each student and, consequently, to each teacher. Although I do not advocate for using value-added measures to check up on teachers, I learned a lot about my impact as a teacher from having this data. I really did find it useful because I could see the impact that I was having on individual students compared with their previous teachers and on the class as a whole. Further, GPA can be used to track students individually and for awards. I know of a school in Brisbane that recognises students at their annual awards night who improve their GPA by 0.5 or more each year. Models of these comparisons can be found in Examples 18–20 (from page 139).

REVIEWING NAPLAN DATA

Australian teachers hear a lot about NAPLAN. As a data source NAPLAN can provide useful information for teachers and schools, but I believe it is currently under-used. NAPLAN data can be used for cohorts and schools in a number of ways, including:

- using raw data to compare NAPLAN scale scores across year levels and cohorts
- using the My School website to compare NAPLAN growth to the rest of Australia
- using the My School website to compare NAPLAN growth to similar schools in Australia
- using the My School website to compare NAPLAN growth to students who started with the same starting score in other Australian schools.

Analysis of NAPLAN data should be part and parcel of what we do as teachers. I have found real value in this process: in working with curriculum leaders to modify programs, talking to the parent body about school improvement, writing a school renewal plan, setting goals for the school, talking to cohorts of students about areas for development and so on. The list is endless! Demonstrations of NAPLAN data use and analysis can be found in Examples 21 (page 146), 22 (page 153) and 27 (page 167).

REVIEWING ACER PAT DATA

ACER PAT assesses student ability across a range of skills and abilities. Using and analysing this type of data for the school or a cohort can be done by:

- measuring the progress in scale scores from year to year
- creating a scatterplot to track achievement versus question difficulty.

As with NAPLAN data, I have used PAT data to modify school programs, inform school renewal plans, set school goals, implement intervention programs for particular cohorts and groups, and more. Again, there are so many uses for this data! Some of these can be found in Examples 23 (page 158), 24 (page 161) and 26 (page 164).

CREATING DATA WALLS

Data walls are considered to be a high-yield strategy and are increasingly being used in Australian schools (Bishop & Bishop, 2017). The data walls demonstrated in this chapter show:

- PAT progress and achievement data
- NAPLAN progress and achievement data
- attendance
- behaviour entries
- literacy and numeracy data
- other types of progress.

Most of the schools that I have visited in Australia have some sort of data wall, and this is for good reason. I have developed all of these types of data walls in schools that I've worked in and at times I've been able to combine some of different types of data. For example, the data wall at my most recent school showed writing scores, PAT reading comprehension results, NAPLAN reading and writing results as well as progress in the writing scores from their previous attempt. Data walls can be found in Examples 26–30 (from page 164).

IMPLEMENTING OTHER SCHOOL DATA MEASURES, INCLUDING WELLBEING

In addition to the examples already provided in this chapter, there are many other instances when data analysis is useful. These include:

- graphing results
- tracking qualitative data from classroom walk-through
- tracking student wellbeing.

To end this chapter, these other school data measures can be found in Examples 25 (page 163), 31 (page 177) and 32 (page 180).

Example 15: Using cohort data to identify top performers

This example outlines the process used to identify high-achieving students – perhaps (as in this example) to identify students for an extension English class. As mentioned in the introduction to this chapter, I once had an unforgettable conversation with a teacher who was trying to stop a student moving into the extension class. The triangulated data helped prove it was the right place for them. Remember, trust the trend in the majority of the data.

1. Identify the aim of your analysis (for example, to identify students for an extension English class).
2. Consider the data that you have available and select the most relevant to triangulate. For this group, for example, you might select NAPLAN reading and writing, PAT in reading comprehension and English learning area results as shown in table 6.1.

Table 6.1. Available and selected data

NAPLAN	ACER	Learning area results
Reading	PAT in reading comprehension	Mathematics
Writing	PAT in mathematics	English
Spelling	PAT in written spelling	Science
Grammar and punctuation	PAT – general ability testing	
Numeracy		

3. Export the data so you have the three (or more) sets available in your spreadsheet software.

Table 6.2. Exported triangulated data

Student	PAT in reading stanine	NAPLAN reading scale score	NAPLAN writing scale score	Previous semester overall English result
Student A	DNS	605	573	B–
Student B	4	584	497	B–
Student C	DNS	584	560	B–
Student D	7	584	547	B–
Student E	6	628	560	B+
Student F	7	628	497	A–
Student G	4	584	522	C–
Student H	4	576	597	A
Student I	DNS	636	573	A
Student J	DNS	DNS	DNS	DNS
Student K	5	584	643	B+
Student L	4	548	510	B
Student M	5	584	485	B+
Student N	5	DNS	547	C+
Student O	5	584	445	B
Student P	8	652	654	B+
Student Q	5	534	522	A
Student R	2	526	472	C+
Student S	7	691	547	C–

4. Make decisions about the colour-coding structure you will use (see Chapter 4). In this example, I have chosen to use the five-level colour-coding system.

5. Colour-code your spreadsheet – either manually or using conditional formatting – to indicate 'well above average', 'above average', 'around average', 'below average' and 'well below average'.

Table 6.3. Colour-coded data

Student	PAT in reading stanine	Year 9 NAPLAN reading scale score	Year 9 NAPLAN writing scale score	Previous semester overall English result
Student A	DNS	605	573	B–
Student B	4	584	497	B–
Student C	DNS	584	560	B–
Student D	7	584	547	B–
Student E	6	628	560	B+
Student F	7	628	497	A–
Student G	4	584	522	C–
Student H	4	576	597	A
Student I	DNS	636	573	A
Student J	DNS	DNS	DNS	DNS
Student K	5	584	643	B+
Student L	4	548	510	B
Student M	5	584	485	B+
Student N	5	DNS	547	C+
Student O	5	584	445	B
Student P	8	652	654	B+
Student Q	5	534	522	A
Student R	2	526	472	C+
Student S	7	691	547	C–

6. View the triangulated results and decide what the visible trends indicate. In this example, that means deciding which students should be included in the extension English class based on the majority of the data.

If seven students were required for this extension class, consider who you would choose. Some are easily identifiable from the data above, for example Students F, I, K, P and S. But who would be your next two?

Students D, E, H, M and Q are all potential inclusions in this extension class because they have performed above the average in one assessment °type. Your first-hand knowledge of the students will help you with this decision, but if you look at the data only, you could argue to include Student E because their NAPLAN reading result is particularly high, or Student D because they were one of the highest performers in the PAT in reading comprehension.

What is the correct answer? There isn't one! Consider the data, consult your teaching staff and use what you know qualitatively about students' ability and potential to make the final decision. Remember, data is wonderful, but it can never tell us everything or have all the answers.

Tips for implementation

The purpose of using data in this particular manner is to identify high-achieving students or students with potential who could enter an extension class. For that reason, sharing this information with students is not necessary because it is purely used as a means by which students are organised. Students may question their inclusion (or exclusion) in the program, so there may be an opportunity to show students this data if they have questions about the selection process. However, it is probably not going to be necessary.

Example 16: Using cohort data to identify at-risk students

This example identifies the other end of the scale: students 'at risk' (in this case, in mathematics). This process might be necessary for allocating students to numeracy groups or identifying key students to be put into a numeracy intervention program. Again, I have used this process many times to identify students who would be best suited to modified classes or programs. In some cases, when class sizes changed through the year, I used triangulated data to identify which students were best suited for the move to a modified class.

1. Clearly identify the aim of your analysis (for example, to identify students for numeracy intervention).

2. Consider the data that you have available and select the most relevant to triangulate. For this group, for example, you might select NAPLAN numeracy, PAT mathematics and mathematics learning area results as shown in table 6.4.

Table 6.4. Available and selected data

NAPLAN	ACER	Learning area results
Reading	PAT in reading comprehension	Mathematics
Writing	PAT in mathematics	English
Spelling	PAT in written spelling	Science
Grammar and punctuation	PAT – general ability testing	
Numeracy		

3. Like we did in previous examples, export the data so you have the three (or more) datasets in your spreadsheet software.

Table 6.5. Exported triangulated data

Student	NAPLAN numeracy scale score	PAT in mathematics stanine	Previous semester overall mathematics result
Student A	463	3	C
Student B	513	3	C−
Student C	549	3	C
Student D	554	5	D
Student E	554	5	D
Student F	549	3	C+
Student G	660	9	A
Student H	495	4	C−
Student I	Parent withdrawn	3	D−
Student J	615	5	C+
Student K	Absent	3	C−
Student L	507	3	D
Student M	559	5	C+
Student N	559	7	C+

4. Make decisions about the colour-coding structure you will use (see Chapter 4). In this example, I have once again chosen to use the five-level colour-coding system.

5. Colour-code your data either manually or using conditional formatting.

Table 6.6. Colour-coded data

Student	NAPLAN numeracy scale score	PAT in mathematics stanine	Previous semester overall mathematics result
Student A	463	3	C
Student B	513	3	C−
Student C	549	3	C
Student D	554	5	D
Student E	554	5	D
Student F	549	3	C+
Student G	660	9	A
Student H	495	4	C−
Student I	Parent withdrawn	3	D−
Student J	615	5	C+
Student K	Absent	3	C−
Student L	507	3	D
Student M	559	5	C+
Student N	559	7	C+

6. Consider each student individually and make a decision about which students should be included in the intervention program based on what two or three pieces of the data – that is, the overall trend – indicate. Generate your list of students for the intervention program.

In this case, the students you would choose for a numeracy intervention program are definitely students A, I and L. Who else would you add? In this colour-coding system, orange indicates 'At the national minimum standard' in NAPLAN. For this reason, I would argue that Student B should be in the intervention list, but not Student H because the latter achieved stanine 4 on the PAT and are currently passing mathematics. Again, your first-hand knowledge of the students will help you to make these decisions.

Tips for implementation

Example 16 assists teachers in sorting students requiring additional assistance. For that reason, it is unlikely that you will need to use this data in feedback to students, unless of course they are questioning why they are involved (or not involved) in the program.

Example 17: Using data to assist with streaming classes and timetabling

If there is a significant variation in the ability of students in a cohort, it might be beneficial to stream classes according to their literacy or numeracy ability. Streaming can be beneficial because it groups students of similar ability together so that some students' learning can be extended and others can receive more intensive or structured learning. Although it is important for all teachers to be able to differentiate, sometimes streaming can lead to improved outcomes for a range of ability groups.

In a school I recently worked in, I began my first year there with a wide range of abilities in my Year 9 class – from a student working at the Year 2 achievement standard, to others that were aspiring to go to university to study engineering. Now, I am a strong advocate for targeted and effective differentiation, but there is no way I was truly catering to all the needs of the students in that class. The following year we streamed the cohort, and I strongly believe that students at all ability levels were better off for the changes we made to the class groups. It also allowed us to target teacher aide support in the classes that had higher needs and to extend the students who loved and were good at mathematics.

This example explores triangulating data to stream English classes based on literacy skills:

1. Consider the data that you have available and select the most relevant to triangulate. To stream English classes, you might select NAPLAN reading, writing, spelling, and grammar and punctuation, PAT reading comprehension, and English learning area results as shown in table 6.7.

USING AND ANALYSING DATA IN AUSTRALIAN SCHOOLS

Table 6.7. Available and selected data

NAPLAN	ACER	Learning area results
Reading	PAT in reading comprehension	Mathematics
Writing	PAT in mathematics	English
Spelling	PAT in written spelling	Science
Grammar and punctuation	PAT – general ability testing	
Numeracy		

2. As in the previous two examples, export and colour-code the data for the students you would like to stream.

Table 6.8. Colour-coded data

Student	NAPLAN reading scale score	NAPLAN writing scale score	NAPLAN spelling scale score	NAPLAN grammar and punctuation scale score	PAT in reading stanine	English result
Student 1	500	445	507	518	2	C
Student 2	394	289	339	428	DNS	D+
Student 3	Absent	510	450	518	3	C
Student 4	434	276	387	475	1	D
Student 5	537	560	542	575	4	C+
Student 6	434	372	414	475	1	C–
Student 7	461	276	477	460	1	D+
Student 8	485	431	533	490	1	B–
Student 9	113	620	593	560	5	A–
Student 10	591	510	477	504	6	A–
Student 11	545	510	567	590	5	B+
Student 12	405	510	464	460	2	C+
Student 13	452	431	464	428	1	C
Student 14	625	458	464	560	6	A
Student 15	425	358	414	428	1	C–
Student 16	434	344	533	475	3	B–
Student 17	545	372	507	475	3	C
Student 18	607	535	516	560	6	B+
Student 19	545	497	488	475	5	B+
Student 20	Absent	316	533	460	3	C
Student 21	405	358	414	410	3	D
Student 22	537	485	558	475	1	C–
Student 23	452	387	387	504	DNS	B–
Student 24	443	401	450	475	1	C+
Student 25	425	358	498	444	DNS	C

Student 26	599	416	498	490	8	A
Student 27	382	344	387	370	3	D–
Student 28	515	510	507	532	4	B
Student 29	425	387	414	428	1	D
Student 30	500	485	450	444	3	C+
Student 31	425	458	550	428	2	C+
Student 32	537	458	414	546	DNS	B–
Student 33	530	431	507	391	3	C
Student 34	552	445	603	490	5	B–
Student 35	415	330	450	444	1	B–
Student 36	485	547	645	518	3	B
Student 37	575	458	584	546	5	B
Student 38	508	445	488	546	4	C+
Student 39	500	485	450	504	2	C
Student 40	530	472	575	590	4	B
Student 41	500	445	498	428	3	C
Student 42	477	416	464	532	3	D+

3. Using the sort function in your spreadsheet software, sort the data by the dataset you would like to pay most attention to. You should then be able to sort by the next most important data column, and so on.

4. Add a new column and begin to allocate students to each class. Number the students in the top class (Class 1) and the lowest class (Class 3) first. They will be most obvious because they will be at either end of your spreadsheet. Then work through the middle to ensure each student has been allocated to a class.

Table 6.9. Colour-coded data sorted by the class number

Student	NAPLAN reading scale score	NAPLAN writing scale score	NAPLAN spelling scale score	NAPLAN grammar and punctuation scale score	PAT in reading stanine	English result	Class number
Student 9	113	620	593	560	5	A–	1
Student 10	591	510	477	504	6	A–	1
Student 11	545	510	567	590	5	B+	1
Student 14	625	458	464	560	6	A	1
Student 18	607	535	516	560	6	B+	1
Student 26	599	416	498	490	8	A	1
Student 19	545	497	488	475	5	B+	1
Student 34	552	445	603	490	5	B–	1
Student 36	485	547	645	518	3	B	1
Student 37	575	458	584	546	5	B	1

(continued)

Student	NAPLAN reading scale score	NAPLAN writing scale score	NAPLAN spelling scale score	NAPLAN grammar and punctuation scale score	PAT in reading stanine	English result	Class number
Student 40	530	472	575	590	4	B	1
Student 1	500	445	507	518	2	C	2
Student 16	434	344	533	475	3	B–	2
Student 23	452	387	387	504	DNS	B–	2
Student 39	500	485	450	504	2	C	2
Student 41	500	445	498	428	3	C	2
Student 3	Absent	510	450	518	3	C	2
Student 5	537	560	542	575	4	C+	2
Student 35	415	330	450	444	1	B–	2
Student 38	508	445	488	546	4	C+	2
Student 8	485	431	533	490	1	B–	2
Student 13	452	431	464	428	1	C	2
Student 20	Absent	316	533	460	3	C	2
Student 25	425	358	498	444	DNS	C	2
Student 28	515	510	507	532	4	B	2
Student 30	500	485	450	444	3	C+	2
Student 31	425	458	550	428	2	C+	2
Student 32	537	458	414	546	DNS	B–	2
Student 2	394	289	339	428	DNS	D+	3
Student 4	434	276	387	475	1	D	3
Student 7	461	276	477	460	1	D+	3
Student 21	405	358	414	410	3	D	3
Student 27	382	344	387	370	3	D–	3
Student 29	425	387	414	428	1	D	3
Student 42	477	416	464	532	3	D+	3
Student 6	434	372	414	475	1	C–	3
Student 12	405	510	464	460	2	C+	3
Student 15	425	358	414	428	1	C–	3
Student 17	545	372	507	475	3	C	3
Student 22	537	485	558	475	1	C–	3
Student 24	443	401	450	475	1	C+	3
Student 33	530	431	507	391	3	C	3

5. Consider the class allocation across the whole cohort to ensure class sizes are appropriate (if anything, Class 3 could be a little smaller and Class 1 could be a little larger). Remember to consult the teachers of this year group to ensure combinations of students are appropriate.

Tips for implementation

This example covers the process of using data to help with sorting students into the most appropriate streamed classes. It is unlikely that this data would be used in feedback to students, other than if they were questioning the class they were placed in. But it is important to point out at this stage that, when streaming, a big risk you face is a lot of 'naughty kids' ending up in the lower classes. Some people approach streaming by putting the 'good students' in the top class and then stacking the lowest classes with the most challenging students. This is not how streaming is meant to be done. Streaming according to data and ability often spreads these students out – and in the cohorts that I have streamed using data, I haven't had an overly difficult class compared to the others (the one time we came close, we shuffled the classes after we had a bit more information on the students). The reason for this is that some of our most disruptive students can actually be some of our brightest.

In the cohorts I've streamed in this way, the students in the lowest class were genuinely great kids that found learning really challenging. But streaming meant that they were able to access curriculum pitched at their level, in a smaller group, with teacher aide support. The disruptive students were spread among all classes, so they did not impact one class more than others, but most importantly, they were placed in classes that were pitched at their ability level. I really wonder how much of the poor behaviour in classrooms comes from either content being too difficult for students to engage with or students not being challenged enough!

The other thing I have done is put some of the 'hardest', yet brightest, students in the extension class. In 2018 there were two students in particular – one in Year 9 and one in Year 10 – who were well known for being disruptive. Having them in the extension class showed them (and I also regularly told them) that I knew they had potential and they absolutely deserved to be there. It also worked in my favour because their friends weren't in the class with them, meaning they were not as disruptive as they had been in the past. It also meant that other teachers were not trying to teach the other classes with these key players in them. That placement worked better for one of the students than the other, but I am glad I put both of them in the extension class.

Example 18: Comparing the performance of different classes

It is possible to compare the achievement of multiple classes within year levels and learning areas. This kind of analysis allows us to identify strategies that might have worked well for a particular group of students or identify a class that is struggling more than others. In Example 9 (page 92) we looked at comparing the GPAs of a single class for different tasks throughout the year. This example is similar, instead comparing one class's progress against that of another class. While this example uses data for only two classes, this can be done for all classes in a year level, regardless of the number. It is also possible to analyse overall task results, semester results and even individual criteria results using this method.

1. Download the results data that you would like to compare (for example, two sets of data for the same assessment task from different classes).

Table 6.10. Assessment results for two different classes

Class 1 assessment results	Class 2 assessment results
B+	A–
C	C
C–	C+
A	A
A–	A–
B+	B–
C+	C+
C+	B–
D	D+
C	C
B	B–
C+	B–

2. Create a table converting grades from A+ to E– to numerical values along the fifteen-point scale (I usually do this on the second sheet in the spreadsheet).

Table 6.11. Numerical values of grades from A+ to E– using a fifteen-point scale

Grade	Numerical value
A+	15
A	14
A–	13
B+	12
B	11
B–	10
C+	9
C	8
C–	7
D+	6
D	5
D–	4
E+	3
E	2
E–	1

3. As in Example 9 (page 92), add a new column to the right of each class's results and use the VLOOKUP function to allocate a numerical value to each grade.
4. Calculate the average score (the GPA) for each class at the bottom of these new columns using the AVERAGE formula.
5. Finally, use the VLOOKUP function or manually convert each class's GPA to a grade.

Table 6.12. Assessment results for two different classes including GPA calculation

Class 1 assessment results	Class 1 numerical scores	Class 2 assessment results	Class 2 numerical scores
B+	12	A–	13
C	8	C	8
C–	7	C+	9
A	14	A	14
A–	13	A–	13
B+	12	B–	10
C+	9	C+	9
C+	9	B–	10
D	5	D+	6
C	8	C	8
B	11	B–	10
C+	9	B–	10
GPA	9.75	GPA	10
Average grade	C+	Average grade	B–

It can be seen here that Class 2 outperformed Class 1 in this task because their average result was a B– compared with a C+. This data should be shared and celebrated with the Class 2. This data might also lead to a formative conversation with the students in Class 1 about what they can do in the next term or semester to try and raise their results and beat the class next door.

Tips for implementation

Example 18 demonstrates how GPA can be used to measure the achievement of a class and compare their performance with other classes. This feedback, which distils individual performance into overall results, can be used with the classes in question. For example, you might say something like:

Our class average for this assessment task was a B– and the other class's average was a C+. Well done! That means that on average, everyone in

this class achieved one sub-level higher than the class next door. That's awesome work. I hope you are proud of your efforts.

Example 19: Calculating individual student grade point averages across learning areas

Many learning management systems have a manual GPA function, but some do not. This is one way of manually calculating individual student GPA.

In this example I compare GPAs for two students, across two different assessment periods. As stated in the introduction to this chapter, I know of schools (and some learning management systems) that generate a GPA for all students, and indeed students are well-versed in their GPA and progress over the years. One school I know uses this information to recognise the students who make the most progress at their annual awards night.

1. Download the learning area data from the two academic periods that you would like to compare (for example, two semester results).

Table 6.13. Student results for two reporting periods

Student	Learning area	Semester 1	Semester 2
Student A	English	B+	A–
	Mathematics	C	C
	Science	C–	C+
	History	A	A
	Geography	A–	A–
	Health and physical education	B+	B–
Student B	English	C+	C+
	Mathematics	C+	B–
	Science	D	D+
	History	C	C
	Geography	B	B–
	Health and physical education	C+	B–

2. Use the VLOOKUP function to calculate a numerical score for each grade in a new column to the right of each reporting period's data. (See Example 9 on page 92 for more information about using VLOOKUP to convert grades to numerical values.)

3. Add a new row beneath each student's results and, selecting the numerical scores you've just calculated, use the AVERAGE formula to establish GPA for each student in each semester.

Table 6.14. Student results for two assessment periods including GPA calculation

Student	Learning area	Semester 1	Numerical score	Semester 2	Numerical score
Student A	English	B+	12	A–	13
	Mathematics	C	8	C	8
	Science	C–	7	C+	9
	History	A	14	A	14
	Geography	A–	13	A–	13
	Health and physical education	B+	12	B–	10
		AVERAGE	11		11.17
Student B	English	C+	9	C+	9
	Mathematics	C+	9	B–	10
	Science	D	5	D+	6
	History	C	8	C	8
	Geography	B	11	B–	10
	Health and physical education	C+	9	B–	10
		AVERAGE	8.5		8.83

4. What do you notice about the data? Ask yourself the following questions:
   - Which student had a higher GPA?
   - Did both students improve?
   - Which student improved more? How do you know this?

Tips for implementation

Using the GPA system to calculate GPAs for students is useful feedback for students to receive. A GPA might be useful at the following times:

- learning area selection for Years 11 and 12
- academic mentoring at any age group
- goal-setting – having students set goals to raise their GPA
- intervention groups
- awards night – awarding the students with the highest GPA or GPA of 13 and higher (A– and above) or measuring progress to award students who have made the greatest improvements to their GPA throughout the year.

Again, the power lies in feeding this information back to students and having them develop a better understanding of their strengths and performance, so that they can set goals for improvement in the future.

Example 20: Comparing growth across classes – value added

As seen in Chapter 5, value added can be used by teachers to track the progress of a class. In addition, value added can be used to compare the outcomes of two or more classes. But a downside of this method is that high-performing classes have less room for growth, meaning it is not always the most relevant comparison. This is similar to the process covered in Example 6 (page 85), the key difference being that the comparison is across classes and not the assessment results for each individual student.

1. Download the learning area result data from the two classes that you would like to compare as in table 6.15 (for example, two classes with the same teacher).

Table 6.15. Student results in two classes for two reporting periods

Class 1	Semester 1	Semester 2	Class 2	Semester 1	Semester 2
Student A	B+	A–	Student M	C	B
Student B	C	C	Student N	B	B
Student C	C–	C+	Student O	D	D+
Student D	A–	A+	Student P	D	C
Student E	A–	A–	Student Q	B+	B
Student F	B+	B–	Student R	A	A
Student G	C+	C+	Student S	B–	B+
Student H	C+	B–	Student T	C+	C+
Student I	D+	D	Student U	C–	C+
Student J	C	C	Student V	B	C
Student K	B	B–	Student W	B–	B–
Student L	C+	B–	Student X	A	B+

2. Measure the number of sub-levels the students have moved as we did in Example 6 (page 85). You could do this either manually or by assigning the fifteen-point scale using the VLOOKUP function and subtracting the first result from the second to calculate the movement. Further, colour-code the movement either manually or by setting a conditional format for the cells to change automatically, if you prefer (green, positive movement; yellow, no movement; red, downwards movement).

Using data in your school

Table 6.16. Student movement in two classes from one reporting period to the next

Class 1	Semester 1	Semester 2	Movement	Class 2	Semester 1	Semester 2	Movement
Student A	B+	A–	+1	Student M	C	B	+3
Student B	C	C	0	Student N	B	B	0
Student C	C–	C+	+2	Student O	D	D+	+1
Student D	A–	A+	+2	Student P	D	C	+3
Student E	A–	A–	0	Student Q	B+	B	–1
Student F	B+	B–	–2	Student R	A	A	0
Student G	C+	C+	0	Student S	B–	B+	+2
Student H	C+	B–	+1	Student T	C+	C+	0
Student I	D+	D	–1	Student U	C–	C+	+2
Student J	C	C	0	Student V	B	C	–3
Student K	B	B–	–1	Student W	B–	B–	0
Student L	C+	B–	+1	Student X	A	B+	–2

3. To truly get an overall picture of the movement of the two classes, generate a score for each class's performance by using the AVERAGE formula at the bottom of the table. Colour-code the score in the same way in which you colour-coded the individual movement (green, positive numbers; yellow, zeros; red, negative numbers).

Table 6.17. Average student movement in two classes from one reporting period to the next

Class 1	Semester 1	Semester 2	Movement	Class 2	Semester 1	Semester 2	Movement
Student A	B+	A–	+1	Student M	C	B	+3
Student B	C	C	0	Student N	B	B	0
Student C	C–	C+	+2	Student O	D	D+	+1
Student D	A–	A+	+2	Student P	D	C	+3
Student E	A–	A–	0	Student Q	B+	B	–1
Student F	B+	B–	–2	Student R	A	A	0
Student G	C+	C+	0	Student S	B–	B+	+2
Student H	C+	B–	+1	Student T	C+	C+	0
Student I	D+	D	–1	Student U	C–	C+	+2
Student J	C	C	0	Student V	B	C	–3
Student K	B	B–	–1	Student W	B–	B–	0
Student L	C+	B–	+1	Student X	A	B+	–2
		Value added	0.25			Value added	0.42

4. In this example, as both of the value-added scores are positive numbers, both classes made progress on the whole. Given that Class 2's value-added score is slightly higher than that of Class 1, it could be said that Class 2 made more progress than Class 1. Though the value-added score does not tell us everything about the two classes (Class 1 should still be celebrating that they had three students achieve As overall), it is another measure that might be useful in your school. I actually used this to keep track of my own teaching: to measure whether I am moving my classes on and to compare my classes to see where I have had most impact. This encouraged me to reflect on the processes that were working in one classroom compared to where they maybe weren't as successful in others.

Tips for implementation

Calculating the value added for an entire class is useful data for teachers and middle leaders to evaluate the impact of a particular program, or to measure student learning. But value-added data can also be useful information to share with students. You might say something like:

> I've been tracking how we've been going in all of the assessment tasks so far. I use a measurement called value added to see whether as a group we're moving forward and progressing. A positive value-added score means that as a group we're making progress, a score of 0 means we achieved the same as last time and a negative score means that collectively our results dropped a little from the previous assessment. As you know, I believe that we can always do better and achieve better results if we work hard and persist. I'm pleased to say that our value-added score from last assessment to this assessment is 0.54. This means that collectively we're improving our work and getting better at what we do. Well done!

Example 21a: Considering NAPLAN scale scores over time – tracking a cohort

A cohort can be tracked over time to see how they are progressing compared with the Australian averages for NAPLAN. I use this information to track the number of points the cohort is away from the national average for the test, and then work out the percentage difference. As NAPLAN grades change over time and across year levels, I believe calculating percentage change is the most appropriate way to track a cohort. On the other hand, it is possible to track, say, Year 5 NAPLAN results each year; this is beneficial, but it will show some variation due to the strengths and differences in the cohorts as they progress through the school. Tracking a cohort and their results over time allows you to instead compare the students against their own performance the last time they took the test.

As can be seen in table 6.18, the cohort in this example is tracked from their first NAPLAN test in Year 3, through Years 5 and 7, and into Year 9. A few things to note:

- No data was harmed in the development of this spreadsheet!
- The NAPLAN mean scores change each year. This example uses the 2017 estimated national averages for all year levels.
- The percentage difference from the national mean is important, as is the percentage change for where the cohort were two years ago. I used the SUM formula to determine the change in scores, and then for the first year calculated the percentage difference using this formula:

    percentage difference = change in score ÷ previous score × 100

For each subsequent year, subtract the previous percentage distance from the mean from the new percentage distance from the mean.

- The benefit of comparing the percentage change across year levels is that it doesn't matter whether the student results are hovering around the mean, always below it or always above it. Instead it provides a measure from which you can compare how your students performed against their previous results. It helps you answer questions such as:
    - Did this cohort perform better than they did last time?
    - What areas should we focus on in the lead-up to the next test?
    - What progress have they made (or not made), and why might this be the case?
- You can use a formatting function to automatically colour-code positive numbers (green), zeros (yellow) and negative numbers (red).
- Given that there were no NAPLAN tests undertaken in 2020, there will be a gap for the year levels who had been scheduled to do the tests. This strategy is still useful and possible; it will just be a (long!) four-year gap between collection points for affected cohorts.

USING AND ANALYSING DATA IN AUSTRALIAN SCHOOLS

Table 6.18. Tracking a cohort's performance in NAPLAN from Year 3 to Year 9

	National reading mean score	National writing mean score	National spelling mean score	National grammar and punctuation mean score	National numeracy mean score
Year 3	431.3	413.6	416.2	439.3	409.4
	School mean	School mean	School mean	School mean	School mean
	410	390	415	430	410
	Difference from mean	Difference from mean	Difference from mean	Difference from mean	Difference from mean
	−21.3	−23.6	−1.2	−9.3	0.6
	Percentage difference	Percentage difference	Percentage difference	Percentage difference	Percentage difference
	-4.94%	-5.71%	-0.29%	-2.12%	0.15%
Year 5	National reading mean score	National writing mean score	National spelling mean score	National grammar and punctuation mean score	National numeracy mean score
	505.6	472.5	500.9	499.3	493.8
	School mean	School mean	School mean	School mean	School mean
	500	465	485	502	500
	Difference from mean	Difference from mean	Difference from mean	Difference from mean	Difference from mean
	−5.6	−7.5	−15.9	2.7	6.2
	Percentage difference	Percentage difference	Percentage difference	Percentage difference	Percentage difference
	−1.11%	−1.59%	−3.17%	0.54%	1.26%
	Percentage change from Year 3	Percentage change from Year 3	Percentage change from Year 3	Percentage change from Year 3	Percentage change from Year 3
	3.83%	4.12%	−2.89%	2.66%	1.11%

Using data in your school

	National reading mean score	National writing mean score	National spelling mean score	National grammar and punctuation mean score	National numeracy mean score
Year 7	544.7	513	549.6	541.6	553.8
	School mean	School mean	School mean	School mean	School mean
	545	510	530	545	556
	Difference from mean	Difference from mean	Difference from mean	Difference from mean	Difference from mean
	0.3	–3	–19.6	3.4	2.2
	Percentage difference	Percentage difference	Percentage difference	Percentage difference	Percentage difference
	0.06%	–0.58%	–3.57%	0.63%	0.40%
	Percentage change from Year 5	Percentage change from Year 5	Percentage change from Year 5	Percentage change from Year 5	Percentage change from Year 5
	1.16%	1.00%	–0.39%	0.09%	–0.86%
Year 9	National reading mean score	National writing mean score	National spelling mean score	National grammar and punctuation mean score	National numeracy mean score
	580.9	551.9	581.5	574.1	592
	School mean	School mean	School mean	School mean	School mean
	581	555	588	590	600
	Difference from mean	Difference from mean	Difference from mean	Difference from mean	Difference from mean
	0.1	3.1	6.5	15.9	8
	Percentage difference	Percentage difference	Percentage difference	Percentage difference	Percentage difference
	0.02%	0.56%	1.12%	2.77%	1.35%
	Percentage change from Year 7	Percentage change from Year 7	Percentage change from Year 7	Percentage change from Year 7	Percentage change from Year 7
	–1.15%	–0.44%	1.51%	2.68%	2.21%

Tips for implementation

Tracking NAPLAN scores over time might be useful predominantly for teachers, middle leaders and senior leaders, but what we learn can also be used in conversation with students. Students interviewed in my study stated that they wanted to know more about their strengths and weaknesses – individually and collectively as a group – and I believe that longitudinal NAPLAN scores compared with the national averages can form the basis of an engaging, formative discussion with students. This data can be used to highlight areas in which a cohort achieved well and identify the areas that they need to work on as a group. It can be used to justify spending more time on a particular skill or revising a particular topic. The good thing about dealing with average scale scores is that no individual is singled out and a conversation can be had about the entire group working harder to improve in some areas, rather than speaking only to (or about) selected students.

Example 21b: Considering NAPLAN scale scores over time – tracking a program

As well as tracking a cohort across year levels and multiple NAPLAN tests, there is also value in tracking a year level longitudinally as a way to evaluate your programs. Where the previous example might be useful in identifying specific areas of attention required for a particular cohort, tracking a year level every year enables you to see whether there are gaps or areas of excellence in your teaching teams or programs. In a primary school that I worked with recently, the NAPLAN results in Year 5 reading were consistently improving. The NAPLAN results provided quantifiable data to show that their Years 2–4 reading program was having an impact. When there is an investment in time and resources in a particular improvement strategy, this is important affirmation that it is working. On the other hand, the writing results for Year 5 were slowly dropping off, due to there being less of a focus on this aspect of literacy. Recognising this gap meant we were able to celebrate the reading program, while also thinking about ways that teaching and developing students' writing could be prioritised.

As can be seen in table 6.19, the achievement of Year 7 students has been tracked in this example across 2016, 2017, 2018 and 2019. A few things to note:

- The NAPLAN means change each year. The 2017 estimated national averages were used in this table for the final comparison, and estimated means were used for other years.

- In many instances, the average national score for writing decreased from year to year; however, there was some improvement in some year levels in the 2019 tests.

- The percentage difference from the mean is important, as is the percentage change from the previous year. As in the previous example, I used the SUM formula to determine the percentage change.

- As noted in Example 21a (page 146), a benefit of comparing the percentage change across years is that it doesn't matter whether your students' results are hovering around the mean, always below it or always above it. Instead it provides a measure from which you can compare how your students performed in relation to previous cohorts. In this example, it helps you answer questions such as:
    - Did they do better than the students last year?
    - What areas are students in our school consistently finding difficult, and what can we do about it?
    - What are areas of strength for our students, and why is this the case?

Using data in your school

- ◆ What are we doing that is working, and what can we learn from?
- You can use a formatting function to automatically colour-code positive numbers (green), zeros (yellow) and negative numbers (red).
- Given that no NAPLAN tests were completed in 2020, there will be a gap for the year levels who had been scheduled to do the tests in that year. This strategy is still useful and possible; you will just have a gap in your data and your analysis will jump from 2019 to 2021.

Table 6.19. Tracking Year 7 NAPLAN results 2016–2019

	National reading mean score	National writing mean score	National spelling mean score	National grammar and punctuation mean score	National numeracy mean score
Year 7 (2016)	536	525	539	530	545
	School mean	School mean	School mean	School mean	School mean
	538	522	540	530	550
	Difference from mean	Difference from mean	Difference from mean	Difference from mean	Difference from mean
	2	−3	1	0	5
	Percentage difference	Percentage difference	Percentage difference	Percentage difference	Percentage difference
	0.37%	−0.57%	0.19%	0.00%	0.92%
Year 7 (2017)	National reading mean score	National writing mean score	National spelling mean score	National grammar and punctuation mean score	National numeracy mean score
	538	518	541	534	547
	School mean	School mean	School mean	School mean	School mean
	537	515	545	534	550
	Difference from mean	Difference from mean	Difference from mean	Difference from mean	Difference from mean
	−1	−3	4	0	3
	Percentage difference	Percentage difference	Percentage difference	Percentage difference	Percentage difference
	−0.19%	−0.58%	0.74%	0.00%	0.55%
	Percentage change from last year	Percentage change from last year	Percentage change from last year	Percentage change from last year	Percentage change from last year
	−0.56%	−0.01%	0.55%	0.00%	−0.37%

(continued)

USING AND ANALYSING DATA IN AUSTRALIAN SCHOOLS

	National reading mean score	National writing mean score	National spelling mean score	National grammar and punctuation mean score	National numeracy mean score
Year 7 (2018)	540	515	545	538	548
	School mean	School mean	School mean	School mean	School mean
	541	513	550	538	550
	Difference from mean	Difference from mean	Difference from mean	Difference from mean	Difference from mean
	1	−2	5	0	2
	Percentage difference	Percentage difference	Percentage difference	Percentage difference	Percentage difference
	0.19%	−0.39%	0.92%	0.00%	0.36%
	Percentage change from last year	Percentage change from last year	Percentage change from last year	Percentage change from last year	Percentage change from last year
	0.37%	0.19%	0.18%	0.00%	−0.18%
Year 7 (2019)	National reading mean score	National writing mean score	National spelling mean score	National grammar and punctuation mean score	National numeracy mean score
	544.7	513	549.6	541.6	553.8
	School mean	School mean	School mean	School mean	School mean
	544	511	555	541.6	555
	Difference from mean	Difference from mean	Difference from mean	Difference from mean	Difference from mean
	−0.7	−2	5.4	0	1.2
	Percentage difference	Percentage difference	Percentage difference	Percentage difference	Percentage difference
	−0.13%	−0.39%	0.98%	0.00%	0.22%
	Percentage change from last year	Percentage change from last year	Percentage change from last year	Percentage change from last year	Percentage change from last year
	−0.50%	−0.58%	0.80%	0.00%	0.40%

Tips for implementation

Tracking NAPLAN performance is great feedback for teachers, but it is also potentially useful information for students. In this context, the conversation that you could have with students about their NAPLAN performance would be relative to the cohort who sat the test the previous year. Many students are competitive, and most would like to know if they beat the previous year group and achieved a higher average scale score. Students also like to know if they were close to or beat the national mean, particularly if you're in a school where this doesn't happen often.

I used a similar strategy when working with a group of students to improve their performance in the QCS test. Like with NAPLAN, Year 12 cohorts can be compared to previous cohorts who have moved through the school, and when the QCS test was in place we could compare students with the QCS state average. This is also possible with ATARs both for learning areas and for overall cohort results. The conversations that we had around the formative assessments and students' goals were relative to the previous year groups' achievement and the state averages. The students even set their own target of a school score that was above the state average, and they created a hashtag for social media posts leading up to the test (as only teenagers could). Guess what? They achieved their goal and the highest QCS mean in the school's history.

Example 22a: My School NAPLAN achievement compared to national averages

Other than tracking the school's NAPLAN scale scores and achievement over time, it is also possible to use the My School website to measure your school's achievement against the national average. The national average provides an indication of how other schools across the country performed and can be a potentially useful comparison for schools that are trying to reach, meet, or beat the average.

1. Go to the My School website and search for your school.
2. Click on 'View school profile' and then select 'NAPLAN'.
3. Select 'Numbers' from the drop-down menu.
4. NAPLAN test averages in each year level are compared with 'Schools with similar students' and 'All Australian students', so select which you would like to compare against or hover over the scale score. For each comparison, the results are colour-coded green, white or red, depending on whether the results are above, close to or below the average, respectively.
5. Consider your school data compared to schools with similar students and all Australian students. What is your immediate reaction to the colours?
6. Look more closely at the data and answer the following questions:
    - What are your areas of strength? Has a particular year level performed well, or have students performed well on a particular test?
    - What are your school's overall gaps? Has a particular year level underperformed, or do your students find one type of test particularly difficult?
    - If you change the year the data is drawn from, are the red areas in the same places? What does this tell you?
    - Can you identify any trends in red, white and green areas?
    - What does this data tell you about your programs, and what might be done to make improvements?

Tips for implementation

Using the My School website to analyse NAPLAN results is useful for teachers, middle leaders and senior leaders. This is data that can be shared with students, particularly if your cohort improves or achieves higher results than the previous year. If your results indicate that your students have achieved at the national average (and previous cohorts had not) or beat the national average, this is absolutely worth sharing with your students. Use this an opportunity to congratulate them and celebrate their good work.

Example 22b: My School NAPLAN growth compared to national averages

It is also possible to compare NAPLAN growth to national averages using a graphing function on the My School website.

1. Go to the My School website and search for your school.
2. Click on 'View school profile' and then select 'NAPLAN'.
3. Select 'Student gain' from the drop-down menu.
4. Select the desired year-level range, test type, time span, and average or median. Select 'All schools' from the categories below the graph.
5. Compare the line that represents your school (maroon) with the line that represents all schools (black). If your line moves below the black line (as in figure 6.1), it means your students made less progress than the national average. If your maroon line moves up and away from the black, it means that you made more progress than the national average.
6. Consider your school data compared with all Australian schools. What is your immediate reaction to the movement of the lines?
7. Look more closely at the data and answer the following questions:
    - Where did your school start compared to all other schools in the country?
    - Where did you end up compared to all schools in Australia?
    - Have you made more progress than Australian schools? (Is your line steeper? Does your maroon line move above, below or closer to the black line?) Or have you made less progress than other schools? (Is your line flatter?)
    - What is happening in your school to create this progress or lack thereof? What is working well with your programs? Where are the gaps?
    - How can you share this progress or lack thereof with staff and middle leaders?
    - What could you implement in your school to address the areas of concern?

Using data in your school

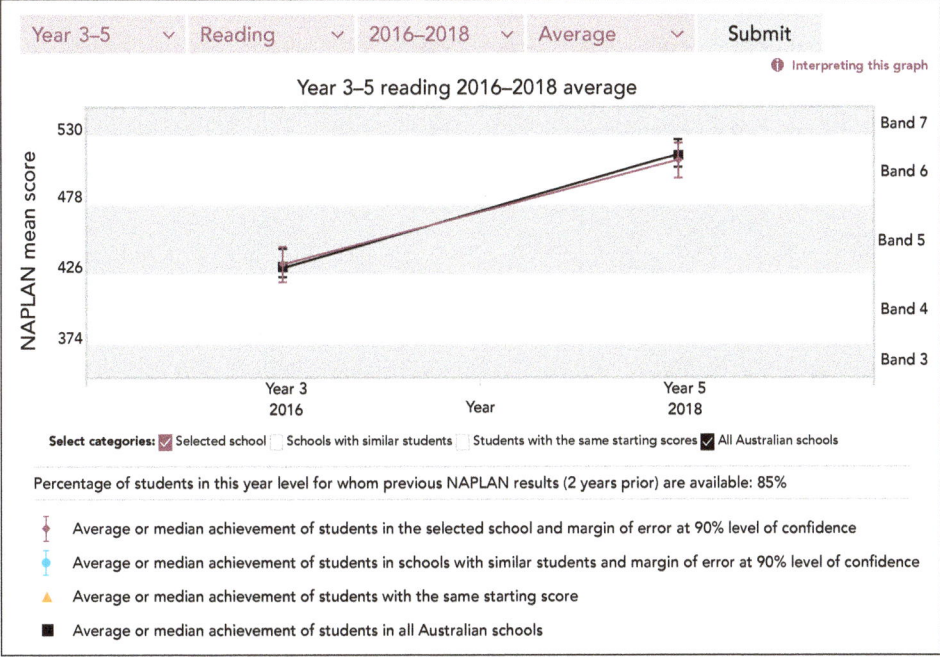

Figure 6.1. Sample view of a My School visualisation comparing a school's student gain with the national average

Tips for implementation

The graphed version of growth compared with the national averages is useful for educators, but it should absolutely be shared with students if you have reason to celebrate!

Example 22c: My School NAPLAN growth compared to schools with similar students

It is also possible to compare your school's NAPLAN growth to schools with similar students using a graphing function on the My School website. Schools and students are deemed to be similar if their Index of Community Socio-Educational Advantage (ICSEA) score is similar. Being able to compare your school results against schools that are more like you is particularly useful at either end of the socio-economic spectrum. I worked with a school recently that was justifying low results with their socio-economic status. The comparison of their results to those of schools with similar ICSEA scores was a good introduction to my conversation with the leadership team. For them, it turned out that, even though they were going to find it hard to hit the national averages year after year across all five tests, schools with similar ICSEA scores were performing at a higher level.

1. Go to the My School website and search for your school.
2. Click on 'View school profile' and then select 'NAPLAN'.
3. Select 'Student gain' under the drop-down menu.

USING AND ANALYSING DATA IN AUSTRALIAN SCHOOLS

4. Select the desired year-level range, test type, time span, and average or median. Select 'Schools with similar students' from the categories below the graph.

5. Compare the line that represents your school (maroon) with the line that represents similar schools (light blue).

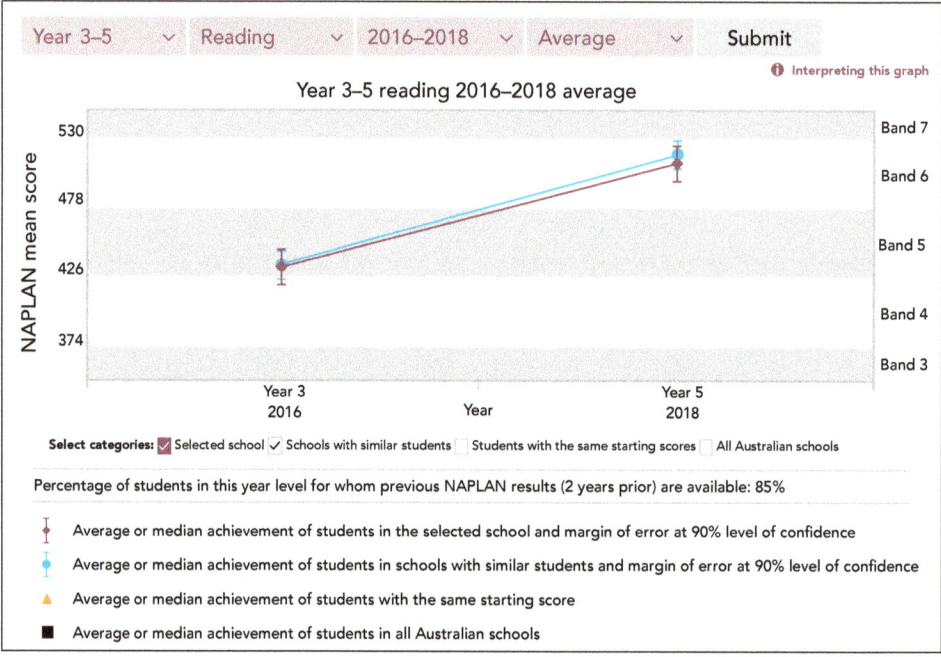

Figure 6.2. Sample view of a My School visualisation comparing a school's student gain with similar schools

6. Consider your school data compared with schools with similar students. What is your immediate reaction to the movement of the lines?

7. Look more closely at the image and answer the following questions:
    ◆ Where did your school start compared to schools with similar students?
    ◆ Where did you end up compared to schools with similar students?
    ◆ Have you made more progress than schools with similar students? (Is your line steeper? Does your maroon line move further away from or get closer to the light-blue line?) Or have you made less progress than other schools with similar students? (Is your line flatter?)
    ◆ What is happening in your school to create this progress or lack thereof? What impact are your programs having?

Tips for implementation

Comparing your school's NAPLAN performance to schools with similar students might be really great feedback to give students, particularly if they achieved pleasing results. This measure compares your performance to schools with a similar ICSEA value and shows your students' achievement compared to these 'like' schools and students. Again, if you do not normally achieve at this level, or your students have outperformed similar schools, celebrate this with students and congratulate them – they would love to hear this feedback!

Example 22d: My School NAPLAN growth compared to students with the same starting score

It is also possible to compare NAPLAN growth with students who achieved the same starting score in the previous test, using a graphing function on the My School website. Some people argue against the use of the ICSEA comparison as, after all, it is an averagef representation of the school and doesn't reflect the broad spectrum of individuals in the school. However, comparing results with students who achieved a similar score two years prior removes the impact of socio-economic factors and only looks at students who were at the same level to consider how much progress they made.

1. Go to the My School website and search for your school.
2. Click on 'View school profile' and then select 'NAPLAN'.
3. Click on 'Student gain' under the drop-down menu.
4. Select the desired year-level range, test type, time span, and average or median. Select 'Students with the same starting scores' from the categories below the graph.
5. Compare the line that represents your school (maroon) with the line that represents students who achieved the same starting score in the previous test (yellow).
6. Consider your school data compared with students of the same starting scores. What is your immediate reaction to the movement of the lines?
7. Look more closely at the data and answer the following questions:
    ◆ Where did your students finish, relative to students across Australia with the same starting score?
    ◆ Have your students made more or less progress than students on the same starting score? (Does your maroon line move above or below the yellow line?) Or have your students made less progress than other schools? (Is your line flatter?)
    ◆ What is happening in your school to create this progress or lack thereof? What are the strengths and gaps in your programs that might be attributed to this difference?
    ◆ How do you share this progress or lack thereof with staff and middle leaders?

USING AND ANALYSING DATA IN AUSTRALIAN SCHOOLS

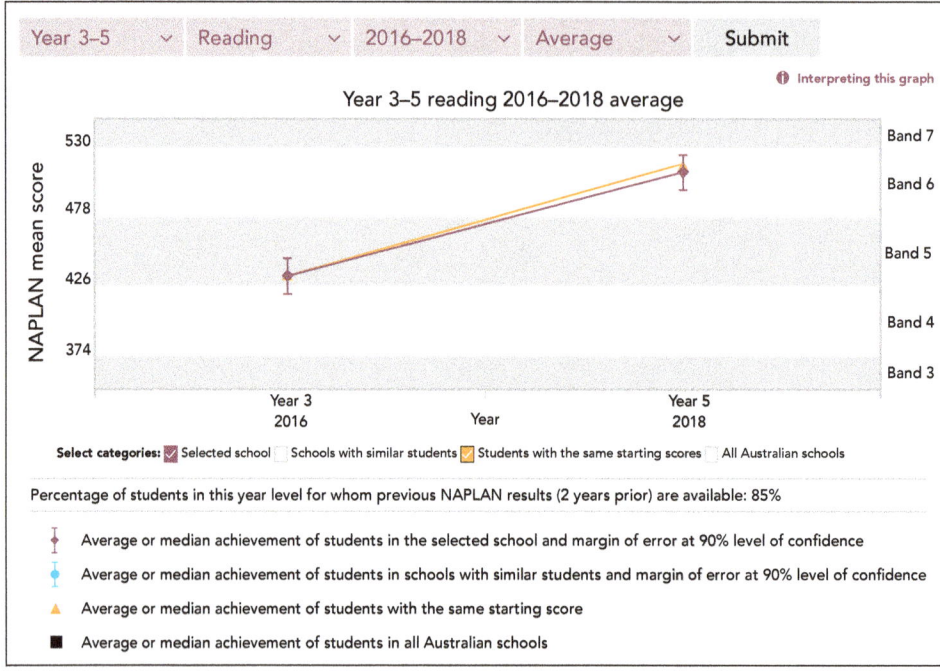

Figure 6.3. Sample view of a My School visualisation comparing a school's student gain with students with the same starting score

Tips for implementation

Again, sharing NAPLAN data with students can be good feedback for them, particularly if they achieved better than students with the same starting score. I believe this comparison is more useful than comparisons to schools with similar students because it compares your students' performance with students who achieved similar results in the test two years prior, irrespective of their ICSEA score and socio-economic status. Again, if your students have outperformed other students with the same starting score, let them know!

Example 23: Using ACER scale scores to measure progress

Irrespective of the ACER test that the students undertake, an improvement in a student's scale score should be evident at each testing point. As an ACER staff member once said to me, 'Any growth is good growth.' There is no expected level of progress, but the higher the numbers and progress from the previous test, and the more green cells, the better! PAT scale score data provides good information about the impact of your programs, but I also used it recently to celebrate students who had made the most progress in literacy and numeracy. The school I was in recognised students who demonstrated the highest growth in the cohort at an assembly and presented the top five students in each test with a certificate. Again, this recognition was irrespective of how high or low the student achievement was, and the focus was on developing growth mindsets and celebrating students who made great progress.

1. Export the previous year's PAT data from the ACER OARS website (or school dashboard if it has already been downloaded).
2. Delete all of the question information so you only have the student names and the scale score column.
3. Export the current year's PAT data from the ACER OARS website (or school dashboard if it has already been downloaded).
4. Delete the question information for the current period, so that you only have student names and the scale score column.
5. Merge these datasets into one spreadsheet, as shown in table 6.20.

Table 6.20. Student scale score results for two standardised tests

Student	Scale score Year 9	Scale score Year 10
Student A	126.2	130.1
Student B	126.2	133.2
Student C	131.8	131.7
Student D	126.2	122.3
Student E	131.8	141
Student F	133.1	142.2
Student G	141	143.4
Student H	129.1	139.7
Student I	131.8	137.2
Student J	159.1	154.1
Student K	115.4	128.5

6. Add a fourth column and calculate the difference between the scale scores. You can colour-code the difference (as positive, green, and negative, red) if you would like to.

Table 6.21. The difference between student achievement in two standardised assessments

Student	Scale score Year 9	Scale score Year 10	Difference
Student A	126.2	130.1	3.9
Student B	126.2	133.2	7
Student C	131.8	131.7	−0.1
Student D	126.2	122.3	−3.9
Student E	131.8	141	9.2
Student F	133.1	142.2	9.1
Student G	141	143.4	2.4
Student H	129.1	139.7	10.6
Student I	131.8	137.2	5.4
Student J	159.1	154.1	−5
Student K	115.4	128.5	13.1

7. Although all growth is good in terms of the number of scale score points, the percentage growth is a more accurate measure of how much the student has grown. For this, use the following formula (selecting the relevant cells):

=SUM(D2/B2*100)

You can also colour-code these cells to indicate whether progress was positive (green) or negative (red).

Table 6.22. The percentage difference between two standardised assessments

Student	Scale score Year 9	Scale score Year 10	Difference	Percentage difference
Student A	126.2	130.1	3.9	3.09%
Student B	126.2	133.2	7	5.55%
Student C	131.8	131.7	−0.1	−0.08%
Student D	126.2	122.3	−3.9	−3.09%
Student E	131.8	141	9.2	6.98%
Student F	133.1	142.2	9.1	6.84%
Student G	141	143.4	2.4	1.70%
Student H	129.1	139.7	10.6	8.21%
Student I	131.8	137.2	5.4	4.10%
Student J	159.1	154.1	−5	−3.14%
Student K	115.4	128.5	13.1	11.35%

Tips for implementation

As stated in Chapter 3, providing feedback and data on progress and growth can potentially feed into the 'effort' component of Angela Duckworth's equations for moving from talent to achievement. Measuring growth with ACER scale scores is one way of celebrating improvement with your students. In theory, all students should improve their scale score as they progress through the tests, but we know that students will make different amounts of progress at different times. This data strategy can be used to identify the students who have made the most progress in the year group. In the past, I have shown students their movement in ACER testing and then awarded the top five achievers as well as the five students who made the most progress at an assembly, and a school I'm working with (as I'm writing this) is about to do the same thing. Awarding progress in this manner starts an entirely different conversation about progress rather than achievement, and it may lead to you recognising the efforts of students who do not ordinarily receive academic praise when awards are focused on achievement only.

Example 24: Creating an ACER difficulty versus percentage correct scatterplot

This example demonstrates how to use the ACER PAT scale score and question difficulty to identify areas in which your students performed particularly well, or particularly poorly. It is important to note that the accuracy of the trend line and your interpretation will increase when using the full thirty-six to forty questions for the test. The tips for implementation section that follows the example provides a discussion of the ways in which I have used this strategy in the past.

1. Log into the ACER OARS platform, run a report for the test you are analysing and export the data to a spreadsheet.

2. Once the data has been exported, delete all information in the sheet, other than the difficulty level and percentage correct, as in table 6.23.

Table 6.23. Sample dataset

Scale score difficulty level	246	246	270	266	254	268	258	276	244	272
Percentage correct within this group	60%	50%	45%	65%	65%	65%	55%	35%	80%	55%

3. Using the scatterplot function in your spreadsheet software, create a scatterplot of the data. To do this, highlight the columns containing the data, go to the 'Insert' tab, select 'Recommended charts' and select the scatterplot.

4. Insert a trendline on the graph (select the 'Chart design' tab, click 'Add chart element', then select 'Trendline' and the linear option). You will notice in the

USING AND ANALYSING DATA IN AUSTRALIAN SCHOOLS

example shown in figure 6.4 that as the difficulty increases, the percentage of students who answered the question correctly decreases.

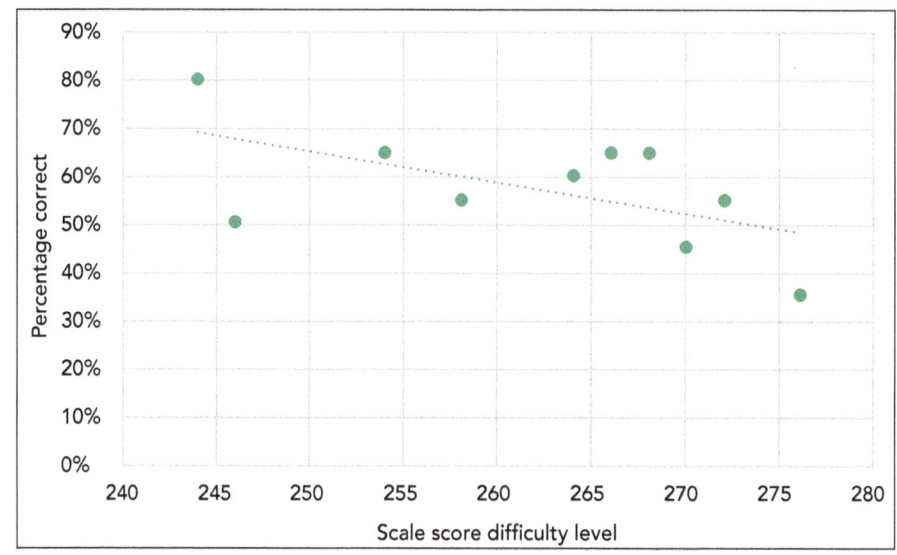

Figure 6.4. Scatterplot showing percentage correct versus question difficulty

5. Use the trendline to identify questions where your students have either significantly underperformed (a long way below the trendline) or significantly overperformed (a long way above the trendline) according to the level of difficulty. If you hover over a point in the graph, it will show the data point from which it was formed. For example, students significantly underperformed in Question 2 (difficulty 246, 50 per cent correct), and performed well in Question 9 (difficulty 244, 80 per cent correct).

Tips for implementation

The ACER scatterplot has the most value for educators because it indicates the areas of strength and weakness in a particular cohort. Although this will most commonly be used by teachers, it is possible that this information can be fed back to students, accompanied by a conversation about areas that they achieved well in and areas that require further attention. If strategies to address gaps are shared with students, this will increase their understanding of the test, orient them towards the benefits of this type of feedback and direct their attention to areas that require it.

Once you have identified the areas that are noticeably different from the trend line, go further in your investigation by using the ACER OARS platform to look at the question specifically. Ask yourself some of the following questions:

- What strand did the question assess?
- What particular skill did it assess?

- For PAT reading, what text type did it use?
- Why might this be a particular gap or area of strength?
- For low results, what was a common error made by students? How can you address the common error that is being made?

At a previous school, we analysed our PAT results to identify areas of strength and weakness in our programs across the school. While we were able to identify that 'interpreting implied information' was a weakness for our students in reading comprehension across the college, a clear issue for our Year 6 cohort was adding and subtracting large numbers without using a calculator. As it was such an issue across the year group, the head of mathematics and the maths teachers implemented a short, intensive program to improve this particular skill. Teachers explained to students the reason they were spending time on developing this skill and, consequently, students improved. We filled a gap that we did not realise we had prior to the analysis of the data, without significantly impacting the already planned mathematics program.

Example 25: Graphing numerical data

Graphing numerical data is a way of keeping track of progress of a class or cohort, and at other times it is great way to provide feedback to students to show them how they performed compared with their peers. I have seen this method used in the classroom to show the number of students who achieved particular scores in an assessment task or overall grades for a semester or year of study. I've also seen column graphs on reports, showing the number of students who achieved each grade and the spread of the cohort. These are not the only two options, though. There are many more uses for graphed data!

1. Take a set of raw scores and enter them in a spreadsheet as in table 6.24.

Table 6.24. Student results

| 15 | 16 | 17 | 11 | 20 | 18 | 9 | 11 | 12 | 17 |

2. Select the scores, click on the 'Insert' tab, then on 'Recommended charts' and then on 'Clustered column'. You will need to adjust the heading and add axis labels, but it will look something like figure 6.5.

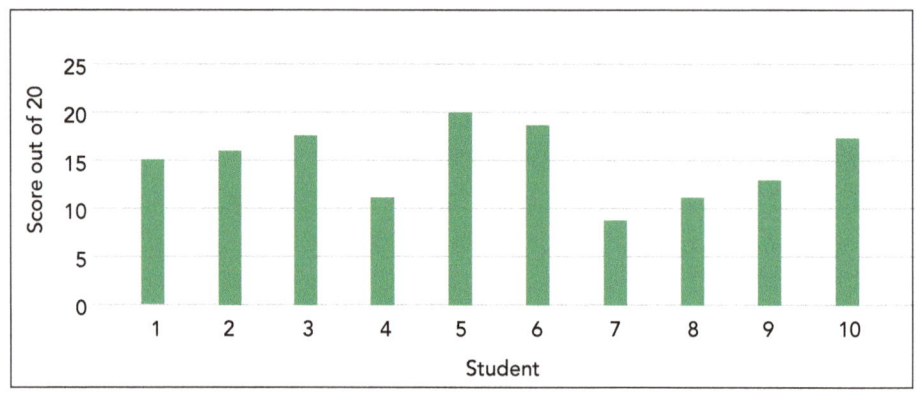

Figure 6.5. Clustered column graph showing students' scores

Tips for implementation

Graphing numerical data and results has the most use when the data is fed back to students. Students in my doctoral study reported that they valued this type of feedback and appreciated knowing how they had performed compared to other students in the cohort (Fisk, 2017). This information can stay anonymous like in the example shown in figure 6.5, or it can be labelled with each student's name. In my experience, even when you choose to make it anonymous, it will not take long for students to share which number they are and compare themselves with their friends. This type of tracking might also be useful for a teacher when planning their next steps with a class or cohort, but remember to use the power of feedback with students to maximise its impact.

Example 26a: Data wall showing PAT achievement data

A data wall for PAT data is best organised using stanines. Stanines are an easy comparison of student achievement because students can be organised into one of nine categories. Using Sharratt and Fullan's (2012) notion of putting faces on the data, images of each student should be used to personalise the data wall. I find data walls incredibly useful because they are a great way to get data off our laptops and into a format that is easy to interpret. By looking at a PAT data wall showing attainment, I can see the faces of my students who are above average, average and below average. It gives me information that can be used in data-informed conversations with students about their challenges in the learning area, or their successes. In teaching teams, beginning meetings at the data wall (particularly in short cycles of planning meetings or PLCs) orients the conversation to the young people who are ultimately affected by our teaching, and encourages us to ask questions about what more our students need us to do for them. The tips for implementation below include an example of a recent conversation that I witnessed between a principal and a student at a data wall. Your data wall for PAT attainment data might look something like figure 6.6.

Figure 6.6. Data wall showing PAT achievement data

Tips for implementation

Data walls are a high-yield strategy, meaning that they have a significant impact on achievement. Data walls, although usually positioned in staffrooms and out of direct student access, can be used with and for students. After a recent series of PAT, the data wall at my school was updated. A student who is very able, but often disengaged, performed poorly and her face was positioned below many students in her year level. Of course, this is useful information for her teachers to know, but when the principal ran into the student at lunchtime one day, he took her into the office to look at the data wall. He showed her the position of her achievement compared with her peers. She immediately responded by saying, 'That's because I didn't take the test seriously. I'll try harder next time.' The student had no idea where and how the data was used, but as soon as she found out, and could see her performance relative to her peers, she was determined to do better next time.

Example 26b: Data wall showing PAT progress data

Although the previous data wall example focusing on student achievement in PAT has merit, another way of visually representing PAT data is to show progress. As stated in Chapter 4, in PAT students usually remain in the same stanine from year to year. This indicates that they are making progress in line with Australian norms and are roughly positioned in the same place as the previous time they took the test. But we do not want students going backward, and with intervention some students will improve. Figure 6.7 is an example of a data wall that demonstrates movement and progress in PAT, rather than achievement only.

I find this representation of student data really useful as a class teacher. I can quickly and easily see who has made the expected amount of progress, who has moved ahead quite rapidly, and who hasn't made the expected progress. Knowing the data and the faces of the students encourages me to adjust my strategies and pedagogy, engage in conversations with students on both ends, and differentiate where I need to.

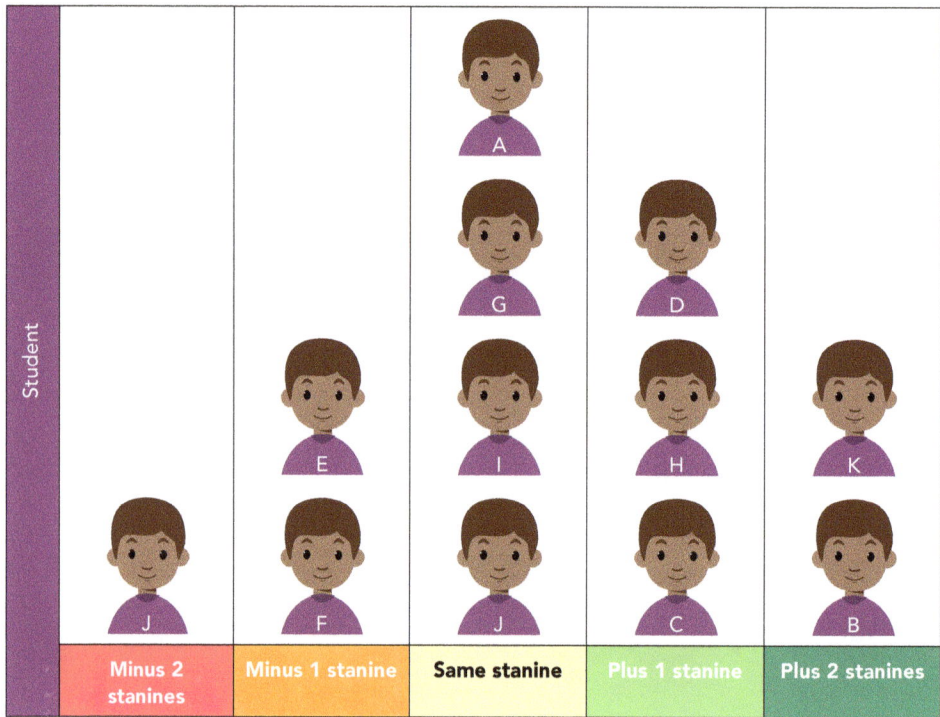

Figure 6.7. Data wall showing PAT progress data

Tips for implementation

Like the previous examples that demonstrate growth rather than achievement, this data wall should be shared with students to celebrate progress. It is particularly useful if you have a large number of students who have shown progress and if you have students who would not normally be recognised for academic achievement but have made good progress. Again, capitalise on the power of feedback and share this information with your students – they will no doubt be happy to see how they achieved compared to the previous year. It will hopefully also increase their motivation to do well when they take the test in the future.

Using data in your school

Example 27a: Data wall showing NAPLAN achievement data

NAPLAN data can be placed on a data wall to graphically represent the performance of students in your school. NAPLAN bands are more user-friendly than scale scores and bands are easier to use when described relative to the national minimum standard (NMS). As stated in Chapter 4, the bands in each year level are often referred to as: below NMS, at NMS, NMS+1, NMS+2, NMS+3 and NMS+4. Like in Example 26a (page 164), a data wall of NAPLAN achievement data provides a quick and easy way to personalise the data for your classes. It helps a class teacher identify groups and individuals in the group and their associated attainment. Your data wall for NAPLAN achievement could look something like the sample given in figure 6.8.

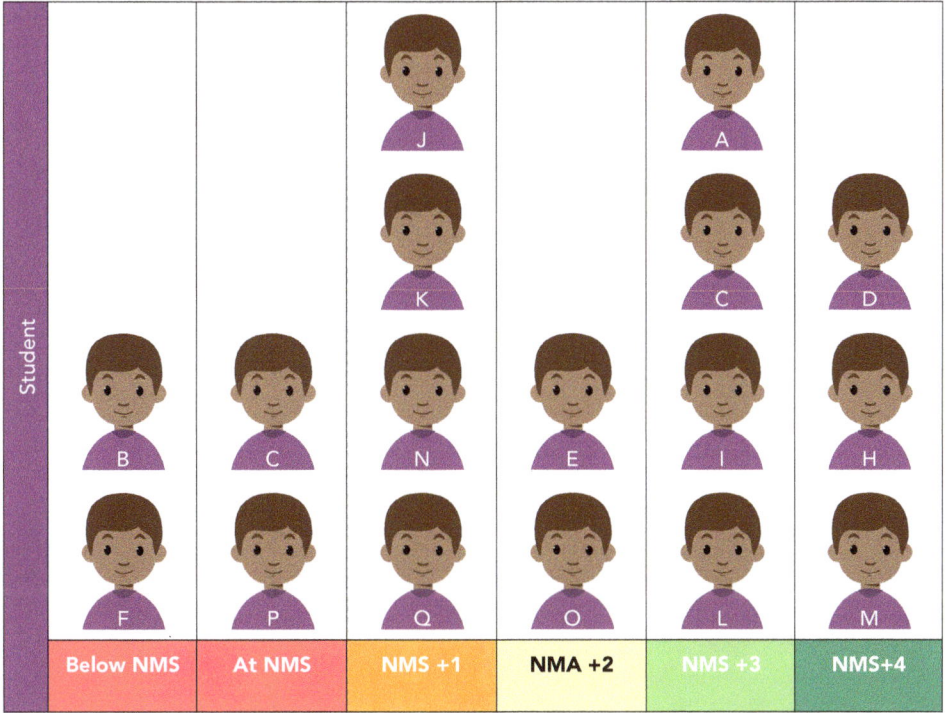

Figure 6.8. Data wall showing NAPLAN achievement data

Tips for implementation

Like the previous example for PAT data, a NAPLAN data wall can help teachers to better understand their students and to plan lessons and units that more appropriately fit their ability and talents. But again, the power lies in feedback to students. This type of data wall can also be shared with students. Why? To celebrate the success of those students who performed really well. To have a conversation with disengaged students about how their results on the NAPLAN tests prove they have ability in a particular learning area. To show students who underperformed that they can do better. Sure, students will not get another chance to take the test for two years, but it is a valuable conversation – particularly for those with whom you are celebrating success.

Example 27b: Data wall showing NAPLAN progress data

NAPLAN data can also be displayed according to achievement or progress. The previous example provided a way that a NAPLAN achievement data wall could so students' position relative to the NMS. But like PAT data, we do not want our students going backwards. In fact, if they stay at the same band in NAPLAN, they will not have achieved at the same standard as in the previous test relative to year-level norms. We also want to be able to celebrate students and teachers who have worked hard to make improvements. The example of a data wall in figure 6.9 shows NAPLAN progress. (Note that from Years 5 to 7 and from 7 to 9, improvement by one band is the same achievement, but from Years 3 to 5 students are expected to jump two bands.)

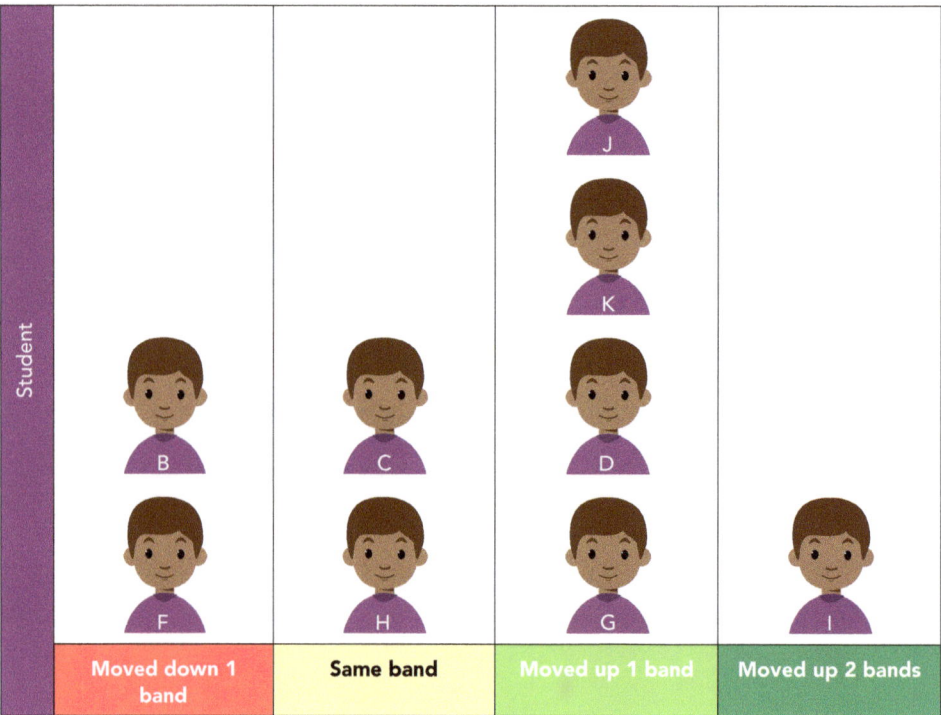

Figure 6.9. Data wall showing NAPLAN progress data

Tips for implementation

NAPLAN progress data is harder to share than ACER data as all students are expected to move up through the bands as they complete the tests, but don't let this deter you! This feedback is still potentially valuable information for students who have made great progress, and it confirms that their efforts are paying off.

Example 28a: Data wall showing all attendance data

Data walls can also be used to display attendance data, which can be particularly useful if attendance is an issue in your context. Figure 6.10 is an example of a data wall I created for a small school that was trying to improve its attendance (and had some quite complex student contexts). Luckily this was a small group of students! A member of the office staff erased the percentages on the laminated cards each week and updated them. The first decision I had to make was what the percentage cut-offs would be for dark green, green, yellow and orange. I used attendance cut-offs of 90 per cent for dark green, 70 per cent for light green, 50 per cent for yellow and 20 per cent for orange. Depending on your context, you might use 95 per cent, 90 per cent, 85 per cent and 80 per cent respectively.

Figure 6.10. Data wall showing all attendance data

USING AND ANALYSING DATA IN AUSTRALIAN SCHOOLS

Tips for implementation

The data wall for attendance shown in this example was solely developed for the purpose of sharing the data with students.

Again, this information is valuable and important for teachers and leaders, but if you want to raise attendance in your school, you need to be talking about attendance with your students. As Tracey Ezard (2015) states, visuals are a superior representation of information; this example taps into this visual superiority and creates a bit of healthy competition. Of course, you need to be sensitive to the fact that some students' attendance is affected by family trauma, sickness and so on. If you would prefer to leave these students off the data wall, you can easily do so.

In the school in which this data wall was used, it worked. It was shared at the Monday morning assembly every week, and every student in the dark-green category was allowed to select a reward from the prize box. When federal and state government funding is so closely linked to attendance and it is a problem at your school, this might be a useful strategy.

Example 28b: Data wall showing top attendance data

The previous attendance data wall was taken to weekly assembly and shared with students. But if, for whatever reason, you are concerned about sharing all the data, you may just want to focus on celebrating the students who are coming to school frequently. If that is your aim, you could choose the cut-off that you would like students to aim for and show just this section of the data wall. Your data wall of the top attendees might look like figure 6.11.

Figure 6.11. Data wall showing top attendance data

This data wall of top attendees might sit somewhere public, or it could be taken to the weekly assembly. Either way, this is about celebrating students who are regularly attending school.

At assemblies, you could make notable mentions of students who enter the data wall for the first time or celebrate students whose attendance is consistently above 95 per cent over a longer time period.

Tips for implementation

If Example 28a (page 169) is a bit too much for your context, or you are worried about multiple students with low attendance and do not want the data wall to discourage them from coming to school, you might choose to show only the top category (or two) at an assembly or on a school noticeboard. This way, students can move in and out of the category, but attention is not drawn to the others who don't make it. You may also like to reward this weekly or monthly at an assembly by recognising those whose attendance is high. Attendance is strongly linked with academic outcomes; don't be afraid of talking to students about it or sharing this data with them. You are, after all, thinking about them first and foremost as young people who need to be in school to learn and achieve outcomes that will set them up for the rest of their lives.

Example 29a: Data wall showing all behaviour reports

In a similar way to the previous examples, the number of behaviour entries or reports made about students can be shown graphically. Although I would not encourage this strategy for large cohorts or a whole school (as it would be extremely time consuming), it could be particularly useful for challenging classes or groups within a school. As shown in figure 6.12, the reports can be grouped into categories for ease of reporting. Like the PAT and NAPLAN data walls, putting faces on the data will maximise the impact of this visual representation.

USING AND ANALYSING DATA IN AUSTRALIAN SCHOOLS

Figure 6.12. Data wall showing all behaviour reports

Tips for implementation

If engagement and disruptive behaviour are commonplace at your school, setting up a data wall to represent the number of behaviour reports for a group of students could be a useful tool for teachers to identify high-flyers. This data wall can be updated weekly or monthly. Again, the power in this data wall lies in the conversations that can be had with students – particularly those at the top and the bottom. Conversations with students who have a large number of behaviour entries are worthwhile to show these students that their behaviour is more disruptive than most. It can lead to great conversations about the challenges these students are facing or the ways they could be better supported. Alternatively, celebrating students with no behaviour entries is also useful. Behaviour and engagement are key factors in improving educational outcomes; start talking about these issues with your students to develop their metacognition around their behaviour choices.

This data wall can also be used in conversations with other teachers, whether it be pastoral leaders, senior leaders, curriculum middle leaders or other teachers of the same students. If you seek strategies and approaches that work or want to build consistency in practice with some students or classes, then a data wall like this can be a great prompt for these conversations.

Example 29b: Data wall showing best behaviour reports

If using this data wall with students, you may either not want to show all the data or only use the data to focus on positive behaviour. One way of doing this is to publish only the students who have had no behaviour reports in a specified period – perhaps a five-week block or a school term.

If you use this system with students to celebrate success, perhaps reset the count each term, or every five weeks, so that the high-flyers have the opportunity to be recognised and make it onto the wall. This recognition could also be paired with small awards at an assembly or positive behaviour rewards, which many schools employ.

Figure 6.13. Data wall showing best behaviour reports

Tips for implementation

If the previous example seems a bit too daunting for your context, you may choose to focus solely on the students who have no behaviour entries. This could be done by showing this section of the data wall weekly or monthly at an assembly, talking about the importance of good behaviour and engagement, and celebrating the students who are consistently doing the right thing. Rather than always focusing on negative behaviours, celebrate the students who are getting it right.

Example 30: Data wall for literacy or numeracy

The data walls in the previous examples focus on one set of data at a time: PAT reading comprehension or mathematics, NAPLAN, attendance or behaviour. Sometimes a more useful representation of student data on a data wall is when more two or more data types are included on the data cards. This increases the challenge of data wall construction, particularly when you're making decisions about whether to display achievement or progress and what it will look like. But just like triangulation, as discussed earlier in this book, including multiple pieces of data on each student's data card ensures there is a fuller picture of each student's potential.

One of the ways that this can be done is by having a data wall for either literacy (or more specifically, reading or writing) or numeracy. On a reading data wall, the data cards might include information on PAT reading comprehension, NAPLAN reading and even English learning area results. A writing data wall might display your system-wide writing task results, alongside NAPLAN writing results and English results. A numeracy data wall might contain information from PAT Mathematics, plus NAPLAN numeracy results and maths learning area results. On one hand, the more types of data you add to the data wall, the more complex it becomes; however, if you can manage these two or three types of data, it minimises the chance of misinterpretation of incorrect data because it is framed in the context of other potentially more accurate data.

Figure 6.14 is an example of a data card for a data wall that focuses on writing. In this example, the system-wide writing analysis tool result for the previous year is shown in the top box, and underneath this the current year writing-analysis tool results for each term are written into four boxes. Underneath these scores there is space for PAT reading comprehension data, both the stanine and percentile, for each student's most recent test. Although the data cards on the data wall were arranged to show the progress and achievement of the students in the writing analysis tool, the additional PAT information and the writing analysis tool results from the previous year aids teachers' interpretation and data storytelling when using the data wall in their planning and department meetings.

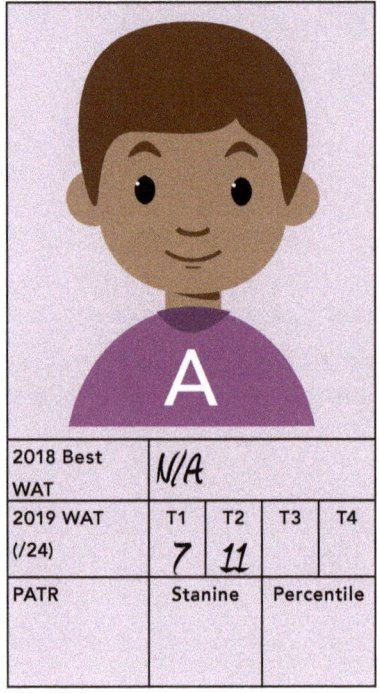

Figure 6.14. Data card for a data wall

Figure 6.15 shows the completed data wall. This data wall is for a relatively small school, meaning that all students from Years 7 to 10 were represented on the same wall. On this data wall, achievement is shown from left to right: from the lowest achievement on the left, through to the highest achievement on the right. Once they were positioned according to their achievement, students were then positioned vertically based on the progress that they made from the previous writing task. Students in the top third of the image achieved a better score than they did the last time they took the test; students in the middle achieved the same result as they did in the previous test; and students in the lower third achieved a score that was lower than their previous result. Because students were all assessed on a similar scale, it was possible to show students from all four year levels on the same wall.

In this image the different colours of the data cards represent the different year levels: pink is Year 7, blue is Year 8, green is Year 9 and yellow is Year 10. In addition, student's names were shaded different colours if they identified as being Aboriginal or Torres Strait Islander or if they required curriculum adjustments due to disability. This colour-coding meant that when teachers were analysing the data for their classes and year levels, they could more easily see how these subsets of the larger population had performed.

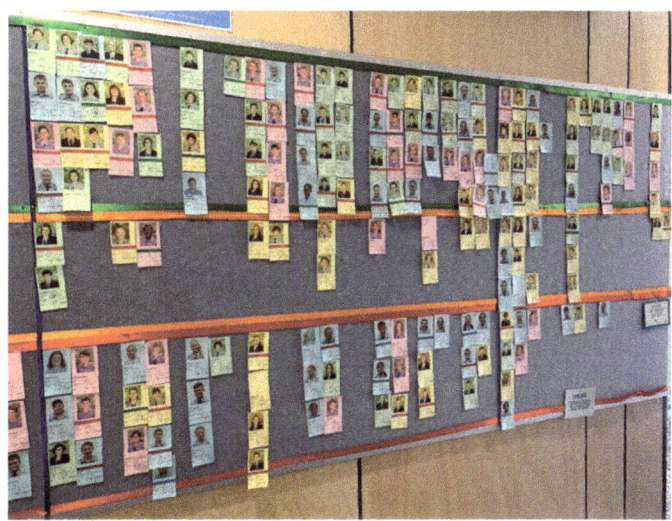

Figure 6.15. Data wall showing achievement and progress

At the end of the year there was an alternate display of the data wall, and this is shown in figure 6.16. In this data wall, students were grouped in their year level and displayed only by their achievement (from left to right). Although the achievement scale is the same for each year level, it was decided to evenly spread all students from left to right. The school had set goals for the number of students to achieve 80 per cent or higher in this assessment. Instead of making the 80 per cent and higher category one set size, a sticker was added so to easily see the different numbers of students from each year level who achieved the goal. The 80 per cent stickers in this image are the four red post-it notes, and this image shows the different numbers for each year group. It is easy to see that there are a lot of yellow cards above the 80 per cent cut off, meaning that the Year 10 cohort did exceptionally well and had a large number of students reached the goal. The second-best year group was Year 8 (blue cards), followed by Year 7 (pink cards). Year 9 (green cards) had the fewest students achieve the target of 80 per cent. Although this example differs slightly from the previous, it is a way of showing achievement while also comparing cohorts with one another.

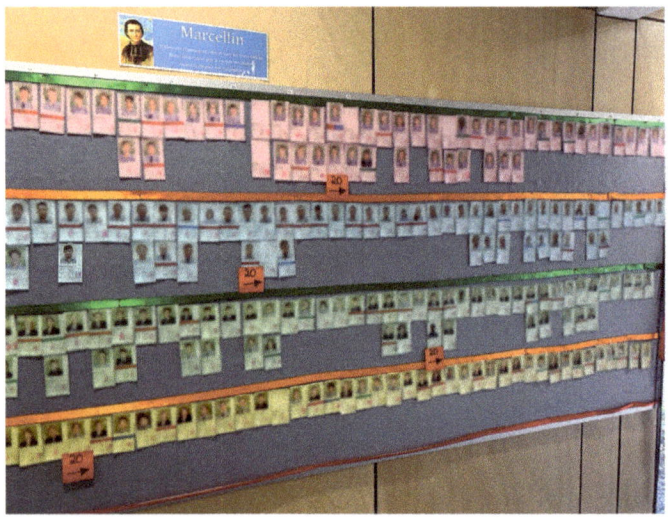

Figure 6.16. Data wall showing achievement at the end of the year

The final data wall example (figure 6.17) shows only progress for a diagnostic reading assessment (DRA). The position of the cards from left to right indicates the year level of the students: prep is on the left, through to Year 6 on the right. Because the school wanted to focus on celebrating progress rather than achievement, this data wall was built to show the growth that students had achieved throughout the year. Students below the bottom ribbon did not move up any levels from the first assessment to the second assessment, students in the middle row progressed one or two levels during this time, and students at the top moved three or more levels. Not only was this representation affirming for many of the teachers (particularly the Year 1 teacher who had a large number of students move three or more levels, and the Year 2 teacher for whom every student made progress), it led to great conversations about reading progress and the strategies that worked for different teachers at different times. It also led to a conversation about reliability and validity of the testing process, which will no doubt benefit the school community in the longer term.

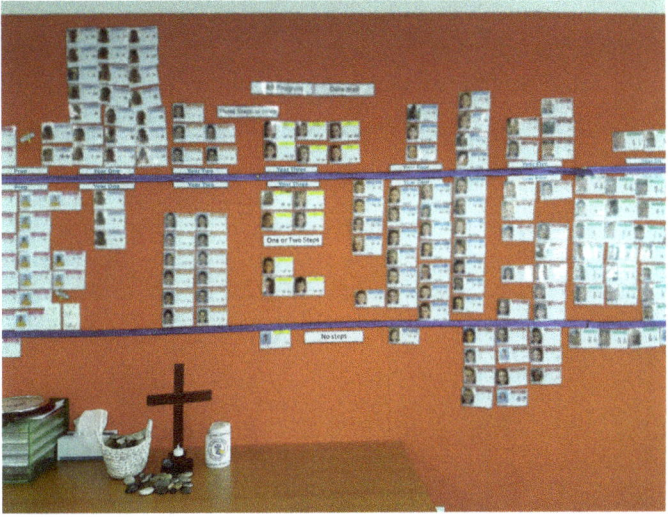

Figure 6.17. Data wall showing progress in a DRA

Tips for implementation

The best use of data walls is for teaching teams, department teams or short cycles of planning teams if they regularly meet at the wall and talk about the data. I have worked with schools where the expectation is that every planning meeting begins at the wall with a conversation about the data and the students that are impacted by the planning. The benefit of doing this, as Lynn Sharratt and Michael Fullan (2012) advocate, is to put faces on the data. This reminds teachers why they're doing what they're doing and which students potentially need additional support. This is most effective when teachers are able to take ownership of the data wall, update their own data cards, and experience the feeling of pride and satisfaction when students move up the wall.

There are many different ways that you can construct your data wall, but I would strongly encourage you to consider the ways in which you can represent both student achievement and progress. Even though not all students will be able to achieve the highest grades, everyone can make progress. A data wall constructed in this way also orients the teacher discussions at the wall, shifting them into conversations focused on progress in learning and growth rather than solely achievement.

Example 31: Thematic analysis of classroom walk-through data

Classroom walk-throughs have great potential, but the data you collect needs to be put to use for them to actually have an impact. One effective way of doing this is through thematic analysis, which is when responses are coded into particular themes so that it is easier to collate and interpret the qualitative information that is collected in a range of different responses.

This example of thematic analysis draws from walk-through data I gathered by asking students in a Year 8 mathematics class 'What skill are you practising in this lesson?' to analyse how well they understood the learning intention. Further discussion of the uses of walk-through data can be found in the tips for implementation.

1. Record and organise the data.

Table 6.25. Student responses to a classroom walk-through question

Student	Response
Student A	Algebra, it's hard!
Student B	Like terms – we are adding them and taking them away.
Student C	Um, I'm not really sure.
Student D	Algebra.
Student E	Identifying like terms.
Student F	Adding and subtracting like terms.
Student G	Algebra.
Student H	Like terms.
Student I	Adding and subtracting like terms.
Student J	We're using letters in algebra to find things that are the same.

2. Decide on the categories that you will use for the thematic analysis. For example, rather than thinking specifically about mathematics, think about your broader goal. Here that's finding out whether students know and understand the learning intention and purpose of the lesson. Categories could be:
    ◆ Vague or unsure about the learning intention
    ◆ broad understanding of the learning intention
    ◆ specific understanding of the learning intention.
3. Categorise each response that you have collected using these labels.

Table 6.26. Coded classroom walk-through responses

Student	Response	Response category
Student A	Algebra, it's hard!	Broad
Student B	Like terms – we are adding them and taking them away.	Specific
Student C	Um, I'm not really sure.	Vague
Student D	Algebra.	Broad
Student E	Identifying like terms.	Specific
Student F	Adding and subtracting like terms.	Specific
Student G	Algebra.	Broad
Student H	Like terms.	Specific
Student I	Adding and subtracting like terms.	Specific
Student J	We're using letters in algebra to find things that are the same.	Broad

4. The thematic data can then be collated (table 6.27) and graphed (figure 6.18). Of these ten students interviewed in this example, one student gave a vague response, four gave a broad response and five gave specific detail.

Table 6.27. Collated response data from classroom walk-through

Response category	Number of student responses
Vague	1
Broad	4
Specific	5

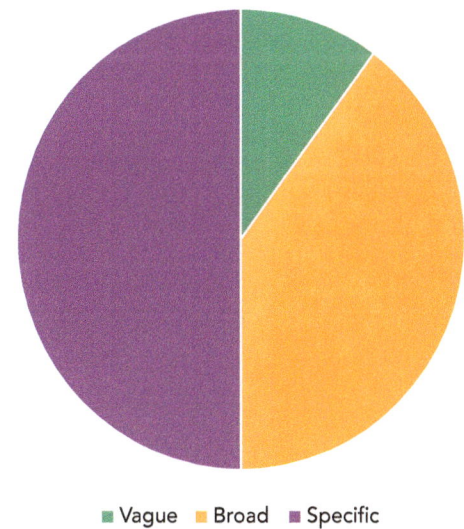

■ Vague ■ Broad ■ Specific

Figure 6.18. Student understanding of learning intentions

Tips for implementation

Classroom walk-throughs are increasingly being used in schools in Australia. Thematic analysis is the best way to deal with the huge amounts of qualitative walk-through data you will accumulate – if you would actually like to do something with it, rather than have it stuck in a computer indefinitely! Think about the broader aims of the walk-through – in this case, students' knowledge of the lesson objectives – and use these to categorise your data.

Once the analysis of the qualitative data is complete, it is incredibly valuable information to share with your teachers, middle leaders, senior leaders and students. If you collect data on lesson objectives, pedagogical practices, the use of technology, seating plans, group work, behaviour, homework, school culture, teacher movement in the classroom or from where students seek academic help (the list really is endless), code the data in a manner that is useable, is transferrable across learning areas and will lead to conversations that will improve outcomes. If students report that they too often jump straight to asking a teacher for help instead of consulting textbooks, looking online or speaking to their peers, challenge the way they see their role as a learner. If students struggle to articulate lesson intentions, ensure that teachers are making them explicit and discuss the importance of students understanding each lesson's purpose. There is so much potential in classroom walk-through data – don't let it go to waste!

Example 32a: Tracking student wellbeing using a purchased product

Student wellbeing is an increasing area of interest in schools. Although educators have discussed student wellbeing for years, the COVID-19 pandemic has really highlighted the need for schools to address the wellbeing of their staff and students.

The foundational Australian Student Wellbeing Framework document outlines five elements of student wellbeing in schools, and in four of the five elements there is reference to monitoring, review, evaluation or evidence-informed practices (Education Services Australia, 2018). Of most interest here is the list of 'Effective practices' under the element of 'Support', which states schools should 'implement a whole school systemic approach to wellbeing' and 'critically analyse and evaluate school data to inform decision-making in order to effectively respond to the changing needs of students and families' (p. 5). In other words, it's not just wellbeing programs, curriculum and events that are important; it is also important for schools to track, in a methodical and planned manner, the wellbeing of students over time. By tracking student wellbeing in this way, we are able to identify trends in individuals in cohorts and be alerted to changes in wellbeing.

There are a range of products on the market that allow you to track the wellbeing of your students; some of these are built for students to engage with regularly (a couple of times a term), while some take the form of annual wellbeing surveys. Different products will suit different schools and contexts in different ways. What is important is that you determine how often you would like information on the wellbeing of your students, what information you would like, and how you can collect, store and visualise this information in a user-friendly format. The best way to do this is to find a product that automates alerts for teachers, prioritises students for check-in or intervention, and (in the best-case scenario) feeds automatically into your learning management system.

If you can take these factors into consideration when planning for a long-term wellbeing tracking solution, you are more likely to collect information that is relevant and useful for you and your teachers, and more likely to be able to use it effectively.

Example 32b: Tracking student wellbeing with a home-grown survey

If you have the resources available and you want to create a bespoke student-wellbeing survey and tracking mechanism, this is certainly possible. Before you begin this journey, there are a couple of things worth considering to ensure the survey is valid, reliable and serves the purpose you intend it to.

The first is that you need a visualisation, communication and action strategy, so you will need someone with a particular interest in this project and skills in building dashboards to support your work. This can be done in platforms such as PowerBI or Tableau, but this does require resources and time. Without a plan to visualise the data so it can be turned into tangible action, there is no point collecting survey data in the first place.

Next, you need to know what type of information you're after. Think about what you'd like to know, how often you'd like to survey students and how you will use the information you gather. Where possible, use questions that generate quantitative or categorised responses – this will make your analysis far easier. If you're into action-research or have staff who have completed masters- or doctoral-level research, tap into their experience to help formulate a plan for the questions.

Consider *how* you ask the questions and ask people in your network who can support you with this. For student surveys, simple is often better. Be clear with what you're asking and, where possible, provide a time period as a point of reference. For example:

- In the last week, how many days have you exercised?
- Over the last week, how many hours, on average, have you slept per night?

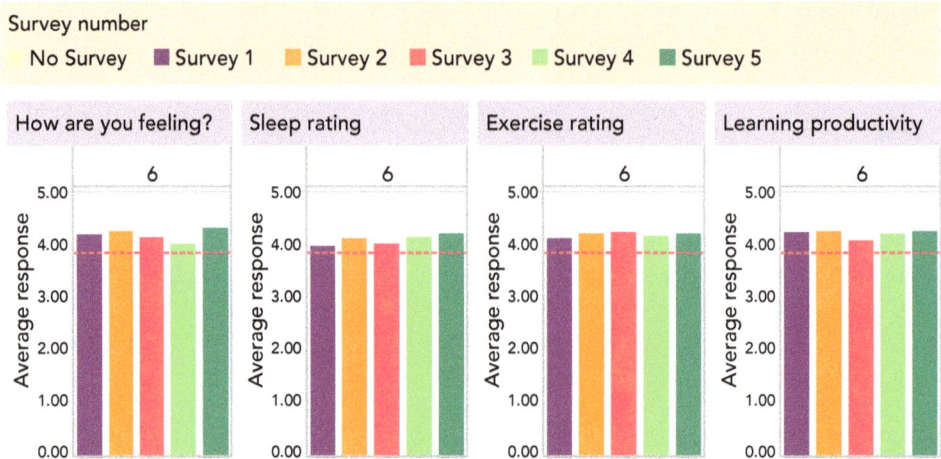

Figure 6.19. Sample reporting of wellbeing questions

Include at least one open-ended question. Although this requires a staff member to read every response, it is really important that students are able to say what they think. Where I've seen this done well, some of the best data has come from this question because it provides additional detail and explanation for the ratings questions. However, don't overdo it. Consider having only one open-ended question at the end of the survey, such as 'If you would like to provide more details or explanation about any of your responses, please do so here.' If you have 600 responses, adding one more short-response question doubles the number of responses you need to read – keep it to one where possible.

Decide how you will implement the survey and when. Microsoft Forms and SurveyMonkey are two options, and both can have set closing times.

Return the data (via visualisation) to key staff as soon as you can. During the COVID-19 pandemic, I was working with a school where we were lucky to have the resources that meant we could return responses to student surveys, which closed 4.00 pm Friday, to the student-wellbeing team first thing Monday morning. Tutor group teachers received the data on Monday afternoon. This quick turnaround meant teachers could act on the data quickly and touch base with students who needed it in a timely fashion.

In your visualisation, assist teachers' analysis and interpretation by colour-coding data to identify 'at risk' responses and, where possible, prioritise students for intervention at the top of the list. This could be done by adding total scores for quantitative results or by the count of cells that are coloured your 'at risk' colour.

Using data in your school

Student wellbeing team – priority view				
Student responses				
Overall, how are you feeling?	How would you explain how you are feeling, in a couple of words? (for example, relaxed, nervous, happy, isolated)	Please rate how productive you have been with your learning, in terms of how much and how well you have been able to learn:	Please rate how well you have been sleeping:	Please rate your level of physical activity and exercise:
4	relaxed, happy	4	2	4
3	isolated	4	5	4
4	good	3	2	3
4	relaxed but also	4	3	5
3	decent, bored	3	4	4
4	Frustrated	3	5	4
3	stressed	3	3	4
5	epic	4	5	1
3	Anxious, isolated	3	4	3
5	Happy, relaxed	4	5	1
3	stressed with as	4	4	4

Figure 6.20. Colour-coded student wellbeing survey responses

If helpful, use a researched instrument to support your data collection. There are plenty around, such as the Adolescent Peer Relations Instrument or the Strengths and Difficulties Questionnaire. In theory, it is possible to use one of these readily available surveys and develop your own visualisations.

Tips for implementation

The priority for wellbeing-tracking data is making the data available to key staff as soon as possible so they are able to action it quickly. The purpose of collecting this data is so it can be used to start conversations with students who need it, so that teachers and support staff can intervene and support students where necessary. It is also a great way of tracking longitudinally; the bar graphs in figure 6.20 shows the tracking of four key measures across five test points in one year level compared with the school average. These cohort averages allow for progress tracking and intervention if results are low or change considerably.

As can be seen in the tips for implementation throughout Chapters 5 and 6, there are many opportunities to use data in providing feedback to students. Most of the examples provided in this book have a practical use with students. Of course, while there is some data that should not be shared, the majority should. Remember, capitalise on the power of feedback, frame the conversation in terms of 'us getting better and working towards our potential', and use the data to celebrate success wherever possible. These good-news stories will stand you in good stead for the future.

CHAPTER 7

ENSURING THAT THE DATA HAS AN IMPACT

Beware of simple ideas and simple solutions. History is full of visionaries who used simple utopian visions to justify terrible actions. Welcome complexity. Combine ideas. Compromise. Solve problems on a case-by-case basis.

(Rosling, 2018, p. 203)

In Chapter 1, I talked about using data to catch out students for the right reasons. All of the examples of data use in classrooms and schools throughout Chapters 5 and 6 should be used to inform your planning, differentiation and programs, and to evaluate the impact you are having. But although collecting, analysing and using data to adjust pedagogy is useful and effective, it does not capitalise on the powerful benefits of feedback and the impact that students knowing and understanding more about their achievement can have. We know that students respond well to transparency in marking, reporting and tracking, and we do this for individual assessment tasks in the classroom. However, this is a leap that is sometimes not made between data and students. To capitalise on the benefits of involving students in this conversation, I believe that – wherever possible – data needs to be used in a five-stage feedback loop (illustrated in figure 7.1).

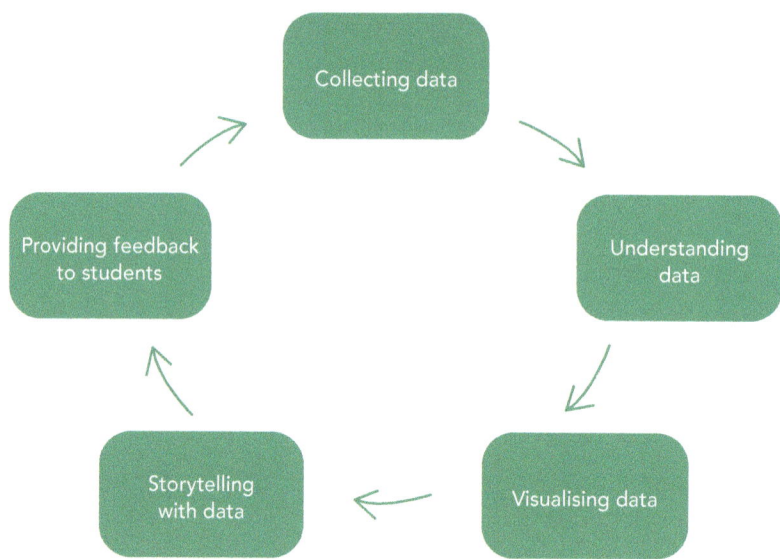

Figure 7.1. Data collection, analysis, use and feedback loop

The first stage is collecting the data, but this means nothing if the data sits on computers and in spreadsheets without any thought or progression to the second stage. The second stage is understanding what the data means, which helps teachers analyse and put a context around the numbers (Chapters 5 and 6 highlight ways this can be done). Once the data is understood, it should then be visualised, and the resulting insights and storytelling should be used to inform individual practice and schoolwide pedagogical approaches, and shape future programs and decision-making. Data might also be displayed on data walls, and student achievement and progress can be celebrated. But to close the feedback loop (and to capitalise on the power of feedback), the data needs to be shared and discussed with students wherever possible. The power of data, particularly when it is used in a formative manner, is wasted if the feedback loop is not closed.

I cycled through this loop a few years ago with a writing assessment in a secondary school in Brisbane. Students are regularly assessed on a writing sample and the results are used to analyse school writing progress and compare schools across the system. Most annual school SMART goals relate to this writing assessment, and schools are measured on the progress they make towards having the majority of their students in the top-grade category (a mark between twenty and twenty-four out of twenty-four). In this example, I went through the data collection, analysis, visualisation and feedback loop twice to improve achievement.

Step 1: Collecting data

Students in Year 8 spent time in classes writing a response to a stimulus question, which was marked by an assessor within the school. The assessor marked the work against eight criteria, awarding a mark of zero to three for each category. Each student received a score for each criterion for a total score out of twenty-four. Following the marking, I was given a spreadsheet listing each student, their eight marks out of three and their total marks out of twenty-four.

Step 2: Understanding data

I chose to view and analyse the data by criterion, showing the average achievement out of three marks. I also collected information on the average total score for students, out of the possible total mark of twenty-four. I analysed the data by comparing the averages to the previous two attempts from Term 1 and Term 2 that were completed earlier in the school year. I considered the changes that I could see in each criterion (For example, which were most different? Had any criterion improved?) and in the total score out of twenty-four.

Step 3: Visualising data

I visualised the data by generating tables and graphs of the data from the three previous tests. I showed the averages for each criterion for all three writing samples in a bar graph alongside one another and compared the average results out of twenty-four. Their results showed:

- Term 1 average – 13.5/24
- Term 2 average – 12.5/24
- Term 3 average – 11.5/24.

If I had stopped at this point and not decided to close the feedback loop, the students would not have been aware of the decline in their scores, they would not have been held to account for this unexplained drop in performance, and there would probably have been fewer conversations about quality writing between teachers and students.

Step 4: Storytelling with data

The table and graph that I developed to display the data indicated quite clearly that the highest results were not the most recent attempt, but from the writing sample from Term 1. In fact, students in this cohort actually achieved lower results in the writing task as the year progressed. I knew this could not be a true reflection of their skill – students did not get worse at writing as the year went on!

This data made me think about what that meant for both the students and their teachers. I thought about the accuracy and reliability of the data and reflected on the effort that I knew teachers had invested in improving writing with students. This storytelling indicated that I needed to go back to students to talk about their results and have them do the assessment again.

Step 5: Providing feedback to students

Due to the poor results, I chose to have the students perform the writing task again, but I also shared these results and the analysis with them to show why I was asking them to re-sit the task. I explained to the students that the results were shared with other people outside of our school and that I did not believe that they had become worse at writing throughout the year. I like to describe my approach as 'tough love' – I actually told them the results were embarrassing and disappointing, because I taught these students and knew they were better than that. (I had strong relationship with the year level as I taught them, so I knew what they were capable of and what I could and couldn't say to them.) I also told them that people were going to make incorrect assumptions about how hard they had worked on their writing throughout the year because the results were not as good as they could have been.

One student put up their hand and said, 'Yeah, but Miss, you are comparing us to other schools, and we are not as good as them.'

'No,' I replied. 'These are your own results that I am comparing you to.'

There was silence. I handed out the students' previous attempts at the task and their marking guides, which showed their previous results, and they were quiet. One girl was particularly quiet – my only student who was working at an A level in mathematics – because she had written nothing during her most recent attempt and been given zero out of twenty-four. Overwhelmingly, students told me that they did not try hard because they did not understand the purpose of the writing task and thought it was a waste of time. In fact, a few students said that if they had known the results and data would be shared with other people, they would have tried harder (and not directly copied the sample shown on the board by the teacher – but that's another story!).

Step 6: Collecting data

Following this conversation, the Head of English and I asked the students to give the writing task another go – to truly show people how good they were at writing. These students were traditionally not high achievers, and they found writing hard and unenjoyable. However, the majority of them enthusiastically wanted to prove that they were better than their previous results, and they furiously wrote and worked on the second task. We connected the purpose of the task to the recent school leadership elections and asked students to write about something that they cared about and affected them directly. This no doubt helped our results. We had allocated fifteen minutes' writing time, but some students were trying so hard that they wrote consistently for thirty minutes. The writing samples were marked by the same in-school assessor and, unsurprisingly, there was a significant improvement in results. The assessor marked students on the same criteria sheet so that when we returned the feedback the second time students could compare the marking on the same sheet as their first attempt and see the improvements that they made.

Step 7: Understanding data

As with the first attempt, I analysed the data by establishing average scores out of three for each of the eight criteria and then considered the average result out of twenty-four.

I compared these results initially with all three of the previous tests to see whether the students had improved.

Step 8: Visualising data

When comparing against the previous three attempts, the results were as follows:

- Term 1 average – 13.5/24
- Term 2 average – 12.5/24
- Term 3 average (attempt 1) – 11.5/24
- Term 3 average (attempt 2) – 18.5/24.

I was absolutely blown away!

Step 9: Storytelling with data

Because of the significant difference between the first and second attempt, I decided to disregard the data from the students' first attempt in Term 3 and instead compare the results of the first two tests of the year with the most recent results. I knew that the second set of data was more accurate and reliable; I had seen the writing process and knew they had done the work independently, and I also knew that it was a better reflection of their ability.

There was not much point keeping the first set of data from that term in the mix – not because I was trying to be deceptive, but because it was not truly reflective of student ability and therefore didn't accurately show the progress students were making nor their areas of weakness. It could also have made it look like we made a significant improvement from Term 3's first assessment to the second assessment, but that would have been deceitful too. We knew we could trust the second set of data, so we used that with students and to inform practice.

Step 10: Providing feedback to students

Given how hard the students had worked, I knew that I needed to give them this feedback to show them that they could achieve good results and to encourage them to work hard on this type of task in the future. I showed students the old graph and table of results, and then showed them the new one. They could see how much the average result had improved, and they could see that their average scores for each of the eight criteria were the highest they had been all year. Needless to say, they were pretty chuffed with their results, and we were proud to share this data with people in the wider system.

If we had looked at the data in the first instance and accepted it how it was, we would have never been able to show the improvements or the effort that had been put in by teachers and students to improve student writing throughout the year. Similarly, if we had not fed this information back to students, and if we had asked them to complete the task again without understanding the data, what it was used for or why it was important for them to be able to write well, we would have probably had to settle for poor results. Given the success of this feedback process, the next time students were asked to complete a writing task, the same preview of the data and a discussion of the purpose and context of the task occurred.

The power in this exercise was not solely in the collection, analysis or display of data (even though the improvements made me proud and excited!), but also in performing data storytelling and providing feedback to students. In both instances, the conversations and the discussion that I had with the students were invaluable. The conversations capitalised on the power of both criterion-referenced and self-referenced feedback because students were provided with feedback that compared them to the average score out of three for each criterion and the total out of twenty-four, as well as the scores that they had attained previously (see Brookhart, 2011, 2017). The visual representation of the data in both graphs and tables capitalised on the superiority of visuals over solely verbal feedback (see Ezard, 2015). The focus of my conversation was about the students' potential and their progress – something that John Hattie argues we should be talking more about (see Hattie, 2017). The feedback that these students received reflects Dweck's (2015) notion of providing pre-test and post-test data, results and feedback to show the potential for improvement. Just as Dweck noted, having an initial test in which students performed poorly and then re-sitting a similar test in which they perform better shows students that they do not have a fixed intelligence – they can and will make progress with effort. In this writing example, one student moved from a seven out of twenty-four to a twenty-four out of twenty-four. Another moved from a zero out of twenty-four to a twenty-one out of twenty-four. As exciting and positive as this data is, the students needed to know that they were capable of producing better work when they put their minds to it. They saw that their intelligence is not fixed, and that with a positive approach, grit and persistence they could succeed.

Given the importance of providing feedback to students, I would encourage you, where possible, to feed back the data that you have analysed in the examples throughout Chapters 5 and 6.

TEACHER DATA CONVERSATION PROTOCOLS AND TEMPLATES

In the first part of this chapter, we considered how the information in our analysis of data can be used with and for students in feedback, both to inform them of, and celebrate, their achievement and progress. But it is likely that many of the data-informed conversations that you will have in your school will be with your colleagues. Working with other staff can, at times, be complex – particularly if staff feel threatened or at risk at any time. In Chapter 1 I talked about Kotter's discussion of a 'survive' or 'thrive' response to the use of data, and his call for people to use data in a way that supports humans to flourish and thrive. Data can trigger fear, and as a leader or facilitator of data-informed conversations in your school you need to be acutely aware of the way that these conversations can be perceived by others. Thus, it is vital that your colleagues trust you and your approaches so that they actively and effectively engage in the conversation and process.

For a school context, the resource *Transformative collaboration: Five commitments for leading a professional learning community* (Flanagan et al., 2016) discusses working in a professional learning community (PLC) and the importance of clarity, trust and evidence-informed action in building effective professional communities that flourish. Of particular relevance to Kotter's views on the use of data and this discussion of teacher data conversations is the importance that the authors of *Transformative collaboration* have placed on trust, which they have identified as Commitment 3 (of five) for leading effective PLCs. They state that high levels of trust in teaching teams lead to improved communication, transparency and teamwork, all of which are vital when staff are de-privatising their work in classrooms. Further, leaders should seek to build, repair and model trust in PLCs more broadly – and these suggestions certainly apply to contexts that involve data-informed discussions. Trust is key.

Although Kotter doesn't explicitly mention trust in his discussion of data, Flanagan et al. (2016) note the survive and thrive concepts in their book on PLCs. They state, 'working within a safe psychological space in which we can share openly our successes and failures, fears and hopes and strengths and weaknesses is paramount to determining whether a PLC culture will thrive or merely survive' (p. 36). It is easy to see how the concepts align. Building trust is hard, but it is vital to ensure that staff feel trusted and supported during data-informed conversations so that the discussions lead to the best possible outcomes.

Even if trust is not an issue in your context, another reason that data-informed conversations can be difficult is that some teachers do not have the data-literacy skills needed to begin the discussion in the first place. Sometimes, teachers do not know how to identify trends and patterns in data, and thus are not particularly skilled at undertaking any analysis. On the other hand, some may not know how to have data-informed conversations, even though they are data literate and are conducting analyses. In this case, they may genuinely not know the types of conversation starters or prompts to use to begin or sustain these conversations. Obviously, this makes things very difficult!

Before these data-informed conversations can begin in your setting, it is important to first identify and acknowledge your own pre-existing assumptions about data and the position from which you are approaching the conversation. For example, I am confident in having data-informed conversations because I believe that if teachers are open and optimistic about the role that data can play in classrooms and schools, data analysis and data-informed conversations will lead to positive changes that will have a significant impact on students and student outcomes. I have also learned how to have these conversations by trying them out, learning with and from others, and being in them regularly. But I can also identify (as I stated in Chapter 1) that I hold particular views on data, and these views are informed by the following seven assumptions:

1. Data provides us with useful information about student potential, which can sometimes be different to what we think.
2. Everyone can learn and improve with effort and application.
3. Using data can motivate and engage students.
4. Data can be inaccurate or may not truly reflect a student's ability.
5. Data should be used to inform planning, programs and differentiation.
6. Data can surprise us – and for the right reasons.
7. Data should be used to catch out students (not teachers), whether they are underperforming, flying under the radar or achieving great results.

I urge you to pause at this point and consider your assumptions about data. Reflect on what you believe data can add in your context. Do you think data adds value? Why do you hold this view? Write your own list of assumptions about data.

When you have reflected on your own assumptions about data, it makes it easier for you to articulate your views to others and, therefore, engage them in data-informed conversations. Both the transparency and the authenticity that you demonstrate once you can articulate your views on data contribute to you building trust among your team as well. To support this process and build trust in your team, it is worth going through a similar process with your teachers and setting aside meeting time with your staff or middle and senior leaders to develop a schoolwide set of data assumptions and beliefs. In this meeting, have all of the participants list their own individual beliefs about data, and then co-construct a list of team data assumptions. As individuals, and then as a team, answer the following questions:

- Why will data be useful for you?
- What do you think data can add in your context?
- What can data teach you that may not have been previously visible?
- What are your core beliefs about learner potential?

If this process truly happens collaboratively and collectively, and if as a staff you can agree on a set of beliefs and assumptions, you will set the tone for future data conversations in your school. This can also be helpful if, in the future, you have concerns or questions about any data-informed conversations, because you can redirect people to these core beliefs and remind them of the bigger picture. When you finish writing the data assumptions, print them out and have everyone sign them to say that these are the principles by which data-informed conversations will be approached. Once your team has formulated your list of data beliefs and assumptions, make sure that you share it with your whole staff. Put the beliefs somewhere that your staff can see and use them regularly and redirect your teachers to them if and when required.

Following the establishment of team or schoolwide data beliefs and assumptions, you might need to rely on some generalised questions to guide data-informed conversations within your staff teams. The problem with considering the most relevant questions is that the types of questions you ask very much depend on the types of data you are analysing and the trends that are present. If you have experience in effective data-informed conversations, you may not need help in identifying which questions to ask. But they might be useful for beginning conversations and building skills, and as you become more familiar with using and discussing data your conversations can (and should) be adapted to your needs.

The following are some examples of questions that might be useful in general data conversations or as guiding questions in staff or team meetings. These don't need to be used in one conversation (unless you have a spare week in your timetable!) or in any particular order. Pick and choose three to five questions that can guide the conversation that you would like to have and use them to start the conversation. Feel free to add your own additional questions and deviate from the plan too!

Questions that can be used in data conversations with individuals or teams:

1. What do we notice about the data? What is it telling us?

2. What do we wonder about the data?

3. What is the data measuring? Is the data reliable? When was the data collected? Who collected the data? What is its purpose?

4. What questions do we have about the data? Who do we need to approach to find out the answers to these questions?

5. What does the data tell us about student achievement?

6. What does the data tell us about student progress?

7. Who are the outliers and why? Why do these anomalies exist?

8. Is there any data that doesn't make sense? Why doesn't it make sense?

9. Are there any immediately identifiable trends in the data? How do we know they are trends?

10. Which individuals or groups have performed well? What is most remarkable about their data? How do we know they performed well? (What evidence is there?)

11. What areas of the data can we celebrate?

12. Which individuals or groups have performed poorly? What areas need our attention? How do we know they performed poorly? (What evidence is there?)

13. Is there anything noteworthy about the middle group of students? Does the data indicate that they require additional support or guidance? How do we know this? (What evidence is there?)

14. Is the data similar to previous results? Is it an improvement or does it show a decline? Are longitudinal comparisons available?

15. What are some possible reasons for the results?

16. What does the data tell us about school programs and approaches? How do we know this is a reflection of the school programs and approaches? (What evidence is there?)

17. What specifically needs to change as a result of the data? How can the data inform teaching? What are the next steps? Why does the data need to change? Who will benefit from the change? What specifically will we do to make this change? What is the timeline for this change? What will we do if there is no improvement in the future?

18. When will we measure this data again? How will we know that this change has been successful?

19. What does the data tell us?

20. What does the data not tell us?

21. How can we use the data to celebrate success and achievement with students?

22. How can we use the data in feedback for and with students?

To support data-informed conversations in your school, you might also choose to use one of the following five templates to guide your conversation about a particular area of focus. These templates are designed to direct your attention to particular areas of the data, with completed analyses for each blank template example.

The first template (page 195) presents a generalised way in which analysis can be performed on three sets of data. The second (page 200) will be useful if you or your team are exploring the data looking for areas of celebration and areas for improvement, and the third (page 204) is helpful for considering the good news stories or 'bright spots' in the data. The fourth template (page 206) looks specifically at areas that require additional attention. All four of these templates can be used for class analysis, subject analysis or cohort analysis by teachers, middle leaders or senior school leaders. The fifth template (page 209) is a little different because it is designed to be used by middle or senior leaders developing a data plan for their team, department or school.

Template 1: Exploring and analysing different types of data

Group:				Focus area:			
Assessment 1:				Assessment 2:			
% of students below average	% of students at the average	% of students above average		% of students below average	% of students at the average	% of students above average	
Assessment 3:				Things I notice about the data:			
% of students below average	% of students at the average	% of students above average					
				Questions I have about the data:			
Things I wonder about the data:							
Specific steps for modifying teaching/programs/approaches:							

Template 1 encourages the user to consider three types of data (triangulation) from the perspective of the percentage of students at, above and below the average. Through this breakdown of the data and by looking at the data, the user will notice and wonder things about the data. This template can be used with a cohort, class or learning area.

I used a similar process recently when working with a primary school in Brisbane to do a 'deep dive' into their data. The school had noticed some inconsistent trends across their NAPLAN, learning area and PAT data and asked me to take a look to identify what might have been the cause. As I began to skim the data, I realised that their numeracy results were largely consistent, but their writing was not. I used this template to consider the number of students above average, average and below average in PAT in Reading, NAPLAN writing and English results. In the learning area results, I considered 'well above' and 'above' standard data as above average, 'at standard' as average, and 'below' and 'well below' standard data as below average. It was immediately clear that their NAPLAN and PAT data told a very consistent story: the cohort was bottom-heavy, with a large number of students below average and very few above. But the school-based English results were more reflective of a bell curve and had a much higher number of students in the 'average' and 'above average' category.

As the consultant, I completed the boxes in the template for the things I'd noticed and wondered about the data as well as any questions I had. In a meeting with the school leadership team, I co-constructed a list of steps and possible options for future steps, based on their knowledge of the school context and our interpretation of the data.

To explain this process further, I will demonstrate using the template with the dataset shown first table 7.1 and then colour-coded in table 7.2.

Table 7.1. Triangulated sample dataset

Student name	PAT in reading comprehension	NAPLAN reading	Learning area result – English	Learning area result – science	Learning area result – mathematics
Ella	Stanine 7	NMS+3	C–	B	B
Melanie	Stanine 6	NMS+2	C	B+	B+
Bobby	Stanine 3	At NMS	D+	C+	D
Markus	Stanine 9	NMS+4	A	A–	A
Jacob	Stanine 7	Below NMS	D+	B+	B
Monique	Stanine 5	NMS+2	C+	B	B–
Cameron	Stanine 8	At NMS	D+	B+	C+
Caitlin	Stanine 8	At NMS	D	A–	C
Ann	Stanine 5	At NMS	C+	B	B–

Table 7.2. Colour-coded sample dataset

Student name	PAT in reading comprehension	NAPLAN reading	Learning area result – English	Learning area result – science	Learning area result – mathematics
Ella	Stanine 7	NMS+3	C–	B	B
Melanie	Stanine 6	NMS+2	C	B+	B+
Bobby	Stanine 3	At NMS	D+	C+	D
Markus	Stanine 9	NMS+4	A	A–	A
Jacob	Stanine 7	Below NMS	D+	B+	B
Monique	Stanine 5	NMS+2	C+	B	B–
Cameron	Stanine 8	At NMS	D+	B+	C+
Caitlin	Stanine 8	At NMS	D	A–	C
Ann	Stanine 5	At NMS	C+	B	B–

Table 7.3. Template 1 completed using the sample dataset

Group: Year 3 students			Focus area: Literacy (reading)		
Assessment 1: PAT in reading comprehension			Assessment 2: NAPLAN reading		
% of students below average	% of students at the average	% of students above average	% of students below average	% of students at the average	% of students above average
1/9 = 11%	3/9 = 33%	5/9 = 56%	5/9 = 56%	2/9 = 22%	2/9 = 22%
Assessment 3: English result			Things I notice about the data:		
% of students below average	% of students at the average	% of students above average	Things I notice about the data: • There is quite a different spread between PAT in reading comprehension (mid–high) and NAPLAN/learning area data (mid–low). • The learning area data spread is similar to the NAPLAN results (low–mid). • Some students have similar results across learning areas (i.e. Markus), but others have quite varied learning area results (i.e. Caitlin). • Some students have learning area data that aligns with their PAT/NAPLAN results (i.e. Bobby) and some that are quite different (i.e. Jacob).		
4/9 = 44%	4/9 = 44%	1/9 = 11%	Questions I have about the data: • What led to the significant improvement in the PAT data? • When was each set of data collected? • Given that NAPLAN reading and the PAT in reading comprehension are reading comprehension assessments and English is more than comprehension alone, is it fair to assume that students are more likely mid–low?		
Things I wonder about the data: • I wonder why students performed so differently in NAPLAN to in the PAT in reading comprehension. • I wonder what genre the assessment result is for English (and whether this aligns with the genre of writing in the NAPLAN test). • I am interested in learning more about the literacy demands of mathematics and science. How relevant is reading comprehension?					

Specific steps for modifying teaching/programs/approaches:

- Break down specific areas of the PAT in reading comprehension and NAPLAN results to see the differences in the strands that were assessed. Are they all very different or are some similar? If they are similar, how can a program be adjusted to cater for this area of weakness?
- Find out the role that reading comprehension plays in mathematics and science and see whether these teachers can embed more explicit reading comprehension strategies in their teaching.
- Consider the English results and the structure/scaffolding required for the next task to help build the skills needed for the students to pass the learning area. Put strategies in place to make these adjustments ASAP.
- Differentiate support for different students (e.g. Bobby has very different needs to Markus).

As we can see, Template 1 encourages teachers to notice and wonder about trends in the data. It translates the triangulated data into percentages of students who are at, below and above standard, and it encourages the user to ask questions and think about the implications for practice.

Template 2: Exploratory analysis

Guiding questions	Response
What is the particular area of interest?	
What trends do you immediately notice in the data?	
Identify three areas of strength in the data.	
What does each of the strengths tell you about your programs/strategies/teaching and learning?	
How can you celebrate the areas of strength?	
Identify three areas of concern in the data.	
What does each of the areas of concern tell you about your programs/strategies/teaching and learning?	
How can you address/make changes to improve the areas of concern?	

This template does something similar to Template 1 (page 195), but the questioning is more detailed. Again, this template can be used by individuals or teams as they reflect on and analyse data from a cohort, class or learning area.

I have used this form as a leader of curriculum to support data-informed conversations with heads of curriculum. At the end of the academic year, I asked the heads of curriculum to complete this form for one of the year groups for which they were responsible. They chose the focus area and completed the table as best they could with their overall learning area results, and relevant NAPLAN and PAT data for the chosen year level. In our review meeting, I sat with the heads of curriculum and helped them flesh out the answers to their questions. Some leaders find this an easy job to do, while others find it difficult. Either way, it is a good starting point to have a data-informed conversation that can lead to tangible steps for improvement in your school. This practice also builds their confidence and ability in having these conversations, meaning they're more likely to start initiating them with members of their team.

When I sat down with the head of humanities she could identify a couple of trends in the data, but found it difficult to list three strengths and three areas of concern. By talking through the dataset and using this template, together we were able to complete the three trends for each field. Following the identification of three strengths and three areas of concern, we then spoke about and completed the boxes on reflecting on the impact of programs, and identifying changes and areas for celebration. Conversely, my head of English was able to complete this template quite easily, but having the review meeting provided an opportunity for us to brainstorm other changes and celebration options that hadn't been considered. I also believe it was a useful process to have him articulate his understanding and the impact of the data. Both leaders went on to make the changes that they detailed in this template and have data-informed reflection conversations in their department meetings.

The following is an example of the way in which Template 2 might be used. I have used the same dataset as in Template 1 (page 195), but rather than colour-coding and looking at percentages of students at, below or above average, I have considered broader bright spots and areas of concern. As highlighted in table 7.4, the three positive trends that are obvious in the dataset are the PAT in reading results, the science learning area results and Markus's results. These are three key bright spots where the data is more positive than in other sections of the table. Even though there may be one or two pieces of data in each category that are not as good, they are largely good news stories.

Table 7.4. Sample dataset highlighting bright spots

Student name	PAT in reading comprehension	NAPLAN reading	Learning area result – English	Learning area result – science	Learning area result – mathematics
Ella	Stanine 7	NMS+3	C–	B	B
Melanie	Stanine 6	NMS+2	C	B+	B+
Bobby	Stanine 3	At NMS	D+	C+	D
Markus	Stanine 9	NMS+4	A	A–	A
Jacob	Stanine 7	Below NMS	D+	B+	B
Monique	Stanine 5	NMS+2	C+	B	B–
Cameron	Stanine 8	At NMS	D+	B+	C+
Caitlin	Stanine 8	At NMS	D	A–	C
Ann	Stanine 5	At NMS	C+	B	B–

Similarly, the data should be considered for areas of concern. As highlighted in table 7.5, the areas of concern identified here are NAPLAN reading, English learning area results and Bobby's individual results. As with the bright spots highlighted in table 7.4, this does not necessarily mean that all students performed poorly; it means that it is an area in which the results were generally lower and something that we should focus our attention on.

Table 7.5. Sample dataset highlighting areas of concern

Student name	PAT in reading comprehension	NAPLAN reading	Learning area result – English	Learning area result – science	Learning area result – mathematics
Ella	Stanine 7	NMS+3	C–	B	B
Melanie	Stanine 6	NMS+2	C	B+	B+
Bobby	Stanine 3	At NMS	D+	C+	D
Markus	Stanine 9	NMS+4	A	A–	A
Jacob	Stanine 7	Below NMS	D+	B+	B
Monique	Stanine 5	NMS+2	C+	B	B–
Cameron	Stanine 8	At NMS	D+	B+	C+
Caitlin	Stanine 8	At NMS	D	A–	C
Ann	Stanine 5	At NMS	C+	B	B–

Table 7.6. Template 2 completed using the sample dataset

Guiding questions	Response
What is the particular area of interest?	Year 3 students' literacy, specifically reading comprehension.
What trends do you immediately notice in the data?	• There is quite a different spread between PAT (mid–high) and NAPLAN/learning area data (mid–low). • The learning area data spread is similar to the NAPLAN results (low–mid) • Some students have similar results across learning areas (i.e. Markus), but others have quite varied learning area results (i.e. Caitlin). • Some students have learning area data that aligns with their PAT/NAPLAN results (i.e. Bobby) and some that are quite different (i.e. Jacob).
Identify three areas of strength in the data.	1. PAT in reading comprehension results — more than half the students are above average. 2. Science results — the overall results in this learning area are generally higher than English and mathematics. 3. Markus's results across standardised testing and learning area results are very good.
What does each of the strengths tell you about your programs/strategies/teaching and learning?	1. Students have good reading comprehension skills — it's not possible to fluke such good results in PAT. 2. The science program is obviously going well. Students are achieving well in this learning area. 3. Markus is a high-performing student who seems to be given the opportunity to be extended.

How can you celebrate the areas of strength?	1. Share the achievement of the group with students / in a newsletter / with staff / at an assembly. See whether much progress has been made from the previous PAT test and celebrate progress too where appropriate. 2. Recognise the achievement of the science department — congratulate the head of the learning area and teachers for their pleasing results. Learn from these teachers about what is working well in science to see whether it is transferable to other learning areas. 3. Share Markus's achievements with his house leader, pastoral care teacher, class teachers, parents and with Markus.
Identify three areas of concern in the data.	1. NAPLAN reading — more than half the students are at or below the national minimum standard. 2. English results — nearly half the students failed the learning area. 3. Bobby's results — his results across standardised testing and learning areas are low.
What does each of the areas of concern tell you about your programs/strategies/teaching and learning?	1. Students' reading comprehension skills were not demonstrated in this assessment — very different results to PAT. 2. Students have not performed as well in English as they did in mathematics and science. 3. Bobby is probably not able to adequately access the curriculum as his literacy levels are low.
How can you address/make changes to improve the areas of concern?	1. More information is required to consider the validity of NAPLAN vs PAT. Which seems to be a more accurate reflection of the students' ability? Do they have strengths/weaknesses in any similar areas across tests? If so, what changes can be made to address these challenges? 2. It raises questions as to what is happening in English — was the genre particularly difficult, was the teaching team consistent, did cross-marking/moderation occur, are these results accurate? What can be done to address this challenge? 3. Reflect on the differentiation strategies in place for Bobby. Could he use additional support staff assistance? Is behaviour a factor? If so, is there somewhere that he should be positioned in the room to maximise progress? Are adequate structures/scaffolding in place for Bobby? Is a disrupted home life, illness or other extenuating circumstance affecting his performance? Put new strategies in place that you believe could help Bobby.

Template 2 is an exploratory template to get your teachers talking about the data and thinking about the broader implications of the trends. If you want to focus primarily on the positives in a class, cohort or school, Template 3 (page 204) is a better option. This template does similar things to Template 2, but it goes into more depth regarding the areas of strength.

Template 3: Bright spots

Guiding questions	Response
What is the particular focus area?	
What positive trends are immediately identifiable in the data?	
What are three bright spots in the data?	
Why are each of these things bright spots?	
What element of your school program/ approaches has led to the bright spots?	
How can you celebrate these bright spots?	
What learning is there from these bright spots for other areas of the school?	

This template can be a useful approach for introducing teachers to using and analysing data in a cohort, class or learning area. It is less confronting than the previous options because it only focuses on the areas of strength and the good news stories in the data. I have found that when I have used this with teachers, it has sent a powerful message about considering the 'why' of the bright spots (rather than ignoring them or merely naming them), how they occurred and whether there is anything to be learned from them. It is a good introductory exercise for sceptics on staff because it does not involve any potential criticisms or negative questions about the impact that they have as a teacher. Remember, build trust first!

As in Templates 1 (page 195) and 2 (page 200), the following is an example of using Template 3 to consider the same sample dataset. For this task, only the positives are required, as this is our focus area. Once this template is completed, you may choose to continue the conversation using some of the guiding questions presented earlier in the chapter.

Table 7.7. Template 3 completed using the sample dataset

Guiding questions	Response
What is the particular focus area?	Year 3 students' literacy, specifically reading comprehension.
What positive trends are immediately identifiable in the data?	• There is quite a different spread between PAT (mid–high) and NAPLAN/learning area data (mid–low). • The learning area data spread is similar to the NAPLAN results (low–mid) • Some students have similar results across learning areas (i.e. Markus), but others have quite varied learning area results (i.e. Caitlin). • Some students have learning area data that aligns with their PAT/NAPLAN results (i.e. Bobby) and some that are quite different (i.e. Jacob).
What are three bright spots in the data?	1. PAT in Reading Comprehension results — more than half the students are above average. 2. Science results — the overall results in this learning area are generally higher than English and mathematics. 3. Markus's results across standardised testing and learning area results are very good.
Why are each of these things bright spots?	1. Reading comprehension is an important skill for all young people to develop. PAT testing is a reliable measure of students' reading comprehension skills. 2. This learning area is outperforming other learning areas. It is good to see success in science; hopefully these results reflect good engagement and effort on the students' behalf. It is also a reflection of the skills of the science department — they are getting better results out of students than other departments. 3. Markus will be pleased to see his results and it is good that he is able to achieve results commensurate with his ability.
What element of your school program/approaches has led to the bright spots?	1. Students have good reading comprehension skills — it's not possible to fluke such good results in PAT. 2. The science program is obviously going well. Students are achieving well in this learning area. 3. Markus is a high-performing student who seems to be given the opportunity to be extended.
How can you celebrate these bright spots?	1. Share the achievement of the group with students/in a newsletter/with staff/at an assembly. See whether much progress has been made from the previous PAT and celebrate progress too, where appropriate. 2. Recognise the achievement of the science department — congratulate the head of the learning area and teachers for their pleasing results. 3. Share Markus's achievements with his house leader, pastoral care teacher, class teachers, parents and with Markus.

(continued)

What learning is there from these bright spots for other areas of the school?	1. *Look at the areas of strength in the PAT in reading comprehension. Consider why a particular strand has a higher success rate — what is happening in the current curriculum for this to occur? Assuming that there is one strand lower than the others, how can we translate this information into practice? How do we explicitly teach the skills the students need?*
	2. *Learn from these teachers about what is working well in science to see whether it is transferable to other learning areas. See whether teachers are explicitly teaching science vocabulary, reading text or doing reading comprehension activities. What could be picked up by other learning areas?*
	3. *Students have the potential to achieve excellent results in this school, and it is important that activities are differentiated across learning areas to ensure that students of all ability levels are being challenged.*

Template 4: Intervention and areas of concern

Guiding questions	Response
What is the particular focus area?	
What are the immediately identifiable trends in the data?	
What are the three most significant areas of concern? *(List from most to least pressing.)*	
Why are each of these areas concerning?	
What does each of these areas of concern tell you about your programs/strategies/learning and teaching?	
How can you address each of the areas of concern (what changes/strategies/approaches could you use to address these concerns)?	
Do these areas of weakness impact or reflect any other areas of your school programs or approaches?	

The fourth template is for considering areas requiring intervention or areas of concern. Again, this can be useful for analysing a class, cohort or school set of data.

As far as these templates go, Template 4 is expert level! This template requires the user to reflect on some pretty tough questions and look for some hard truths in the data. Of the questions raised in the templates shared so far in this chapter, I believe that these are used the least in schools – but they should be used the most. If completed properly, this template asks the tough questions, identifies the reason for poor results, has the user reflect on the changes that can be made and, in turn, forces the user to reflect on their role in the area of weakness. All of these things, if done by the wrong people at the wrong time, run the risk of activating the survive response as discussed in Chapter 1, causing the use and analysis of data to become counter-productive. The answers to these questions may not necessarily be nice to think about because they might not reflect all that well on the teacher, department or school, but until teachers, middle leaders and school leadership teams really address the issues in their classrooms and schools, they will not make progress. Remember, do not lead with this template – if people fear the data, tread lightly!

As in explorations of the previous templates, the following is an example of using Template 4 with the same sample dataset. Unlike Template 3 (page 204), Template 4 focuses on the data that relates to any areas of concern. Once this template is completed, you may continue the conversation about the data by using some of the guiding questions presented earlier in the chapter.

Table 7.8. Template 4 completed using the sample dataset

Guiding questions	Response
What is the particular focus area?	Year 3 students' literacy, specifically reading comprehension.
What are the immediately identifiable trends in the data?	• There is quite a different spread between PAT (mid–high) and NAPLAN/ learning area data (mid–low). • The learning area data spread is similar to the NAPLAN results (low–mid). • Some students have similar results across learning areas (i.e. Markus), but others have quite varied learning area results (i.e. Caitlin). • Some students have learning area data that aligns with their PAT/NAPLAN results (i.e. Bobby) and some that are quite different (i.e. Jacob).
What are the three most significant areas of concern? (List from most to least pressing.)	1. NAPLAN reading – more than half the students are at or below the national minimum standard. 2. English results – nearly half the students failed the learning area. 3. Bobby's results – his results across standardised testing and learning areas are low.

(continued)

Why are each of these areas concerning?	1. Reading is an important skill that all students need so they can effectively engage in society in the future. The school should be working with students to improve their literacy skills as much as possible — particularly when they are below average. 2. Students should be succeeding in English — particularly when they are achieving good results in other learning areas. Is there a problem with the learning area? With the marking? It's important to ascertain details about the issue so it can be addressed. 3. Bobby obviously finds literacy difficult. It's important for his engagement in society in the future that he is able to read and write to a level that enables him to gain employment and live and function as a contributing member of society.
What does each of these areas of concern tell you about your programs/strategies/learning and teaching?	1. Students' reading comprehension skills were not demonstrated in this assessment — very different results to PAT. 2. Students have not performed as well in English as they did in mathematics and science. 3. Bobby is probably not able to adequately access the curriculum as his literacy levels are low.
How can you address each of the areas of concern (what changes/strategies/approaches could you use to address these concerns)?	1. More information is required to consider the validity of NAPLAN vs PAT. Which seems to be a more accurate reflection of the students' ability? Do they have strengths/weaknesses in any similar areas across tests? 2. It raises questions as to what is happening in English — was the genre particularly difficult, was the teaching team consistent, did cross-marking/moderation occur, are these results accurate? 3. Reflect on the differentiation strategies in place for Bobby. Could he use additional support staff assistance? Is behaviour a factor? If so, is there somewhere that he should be positioned in the room to maximise progress? Are adequate structures/scaffolding in place for Bobby? Is a disrupted home life, illness or other extenuating circumstance affecting his performance?
Do these areas of weakness impact or reflect any other areas of your school programs or approaches?	1. Reading comprehension seems to be affecting performance in other learning areas — mathematics teachers report that students struggle with problem-solving and deciphering questions and humanities teachers report students' lack of interest in reading texts. This seems to be a schoolwide problem rather an issue with a standardised test. 2. It is worth considering what is working in other learning areas as English results are much lower. Further analysis is required to ascertain student performance in other learning areas to see whether there are any other trends. 3. Is adequate support/mentoring in place for Bobby? This result could lead to broader conversations across the school about not letting students fall through the cracks.

Template 5: Data plan

Data plan rationale:

Data theme	Types of data considered	Staff involved	Timing	Communication strategy	Analysis required	Actions taken
Academic outcomes		Senior leaders				
		Curriculum middle leaders				
		Teachers				
Student wellbeing						
Student engagement						
Staff wellbeing						
Other school data						
Parents						

School leaders are increasingly seeking to implement a data plan for their staff, but this might also be done by department heads, year-level coordinators or senior leaders. Some of the data plans I've seen have split different datasets into distinct types (for example, attendance, NAPLAN, Year 12 exit results and so on) and have allocated roles for each particular data type. While it's a great start at a plan, and it does help crystallise your ideas on what data will be used and by who, as per the discussion on triangulation throughout this book, I don't believe any dataset should be considered in isolation. Sure, there might be an in-depth NAPLAN analysis that is completed or a thorough investigation of attendance data, but every dataset should always be considered alongside other key data points.

For this reason, the data plan template explored on the following pages groups data into overall aims (academic outcomes, student wellbeing and so on) and then breaks down the ways different subsets of staff within the school might use and act on the data. This may not be a perfect model (because we also know that student wellbeing should also consider academic results), but it is a place to start. There is a completed example following the blank template, but I encourage you to use this template, modify it where appropriate, and add and remove datasets that you do and don't have access to. If you want to make the data plan more complex, go for it; if you want to simplify it, do it! This template is simply a guide from which you can develop your own data plan.

Table 7.9. Template 5 completed using the sample dataset

Data plan rationale: This data plan outlines the intended use of the most important datasets in the school. It categorises the data into broad categories, from which subsets of staff are allocated roles. We believe that data should always inform our practice and that the school is guided by the trends we see emerging from the data. We aim to be responsive to the changing needs of our learners, and this data plan helps us outline the information we will access, who will access it and the intended actions.

Data theme	Types of data considered	Staff involved	Timing	Communication strategy	Analysis required	Actions taken
Academic outcomes	Learning area results Semester reporting NAPLAN results PAT results Year 12 exit results	Senior leaders	End of Semesters 1 and 2	Share findings with middle leaders/teaching staff.	Check overall school spread of results and alignment with standardised tests. Look at both progress and achievement.	Consider class distributions, class structure, teacher resourcing, additional financial and resource requirements, professional learning requirements etc.
	Formative assessment results	Curriculum middle leaders	Mid-term and end of term	Share findings with teachers through department/year-level meetings	Check subject spread of results and alignment with standardised tests. Look at both progress and achievement.	Identify classes to check in with. Identify staff who made need assistance etc.
		Teachers	At least twice per term	Discuss progress and achievement of classes with students individually and with the whole class.	Check class spread of results and alignment with standardised tests. Look at both progress and achievement.	Speak with students during class time, as individuals and as the whole class. Contact home where required for students who are not working well or to their potential.

(continued)

Student wellbeing	Student wellbeing survey Student perception survey Bullying survey 'At risk' list of students	Student wellbeing team (pastoral leaders, senior leader – pastoral, counsellors)	Mid-term and end of term	Share findings with teachers/ tutor-group teachers	Check progress of all 'at risk' students	Update 'at risk' list if required Establish next steps for students who are struggling Plan steps for any identified students who are new to the 'at risk' list
Student engagement	Engagement tracking data Behaviour reports Detention records Attendance	Student wellbeing team and curriculum middle leaders	Mid-term and end of term	Share findings with teachers through full staff meeting	Identify trends in student engagement, year level and/or subject area engagement.	Consider required intervention for individual students, groups, classes or cohorts Design a strategy to address these needs Contact home where necessary for students, classes or cohorts
Staff wellbeing	Staff wellbeing survey Staff absentee rates Staff turn-over rates	Senior leaders	Once per term	Share findings with teachers through full staff meeting	Identify trends across subsets of staff: male/female, year level, department etc.	Consider required intervention for individual teachers or groups of teachers Design a strategy to address these needs Where applicable, communicate your planned changes to the staff.

| Other school data | Enrolment data
Financial information
School HR data
SID funding | Senior leaders | As required — at least once per year | Share findings with teachers through full staff meeting. | Identify trends in across the datasets | Design a strategy to address the needs identified in the data.
Where applicable, communicate your planned changes to the wider community. |
| Parents | Parent perception survey | Senior leaders | Following the annual parent survey | Share findings with community through full staff meeting, newsletter article, social media etc. | Identify trends across year level and/or subject area. | Follow up with parents who requested this in the survey.
Implement any required changes to address the concerns that were identified.
Communicate planned changes to the community. |

This chapter has outlined the ways data can be used to create change in schools through feedback to students and in conversations with colleagues. In closing the feedback loop with students, they become informed of their results and their progress, which can lead to improved accountability, motivation and results. Data can and should be used regularly in meetings with colleagues, and the templates in this chapter can be used to support this process. As with the questions that can be used to guide data-informed conversations with colleagues, these templates can assist with the analysis process and support you in establishing possible solutions and necessary changes. Prior to using these questions and templates, it is important to develop a set of data protocols that are agreed upon for your setting and have a data plan for your school or department. By establishing a common language and expectations, staff in your teams and school know why they are using data and the benefits of knowing how students are tracking.

CONCLUSION

Data are not taken for museum purposes; they are taken as a basis for doing something.

(Deming, 1942, p. 173)

Data analysis and business intelligence strategies and approaches are dominating the corporate world. New data software is being developed at a remarkable speed, and training organisations are rushing to offer data analysis courses online and data science university degrees. As a result, data literacy is becoming incredibly important for Australian schools and educators. Not only are teachers increasingly given data to work with in schools, Australian policy and framing documents are increasing the expectations on teachers to be evidence-informed in their practice. Rather than burying our heads in the sand and ignoring the data, teachers can take charge of it, create our own data stories and lead significant school improvement by knowing more about our students and tailoring our instruction to their needs. Data is not going to disappear from our schools, so skills such as triangulation, using data to differentiate, modifying our programs, knowing which questions to ask and celebrating success will stand us in good stead for the future.

As I said at the beginning of this book, data should be used to catch out students for the right reasons: to celebrate success, identify strengths and establish areas that need attention. It should never be used to catch out teachers, for accountability or to check up on teachers. If data are used in this way, it can activate the survive – rather than thrive – neurological response, and we, our fellow teachers and our students, will never truly flourish. Further, schools should use data in a way that means they are data informed, not data driven. We need to always remember the humans behind the numbers, and our anecdotal and qualitative understanding of students should be used in conjunction with the data at all times.

Data can and should be used with students – in feedback, in conversation, in developing their metacognition around their strengths and weaknesses, and in celebrating their successes. As someone said to me once, if you are trying to lose 5 kilograms, the notion of not weighing yourself at the start, as you progress and at the end would be crazy. So why do some teachers try to avoid this kind of tracking in schools and in conversations with students? We need to capitalise on the accuracy and quantifiable nature of numbers and embrace them for the good that they can offer us and our students, rather than finding reasons to discard them. Teachers inherently want to do the best that they can for their students; using data to inform pedagogy and programs is a way to ensure this occurs.

With this book I aimed to continue the conversation about the practical use of data in schools and develop teachers' understanding of the ways this can be done at a cohort, class or learning-area level. If you've made it this far, well done! You now know what to do and you know how to do it. Your students need you to understand their data and work with them to achieve their best possible outcomes. They are unique and wonderful humans who have much to offer the world – sometimes we need to help them see that. So go ahead and get into the data!

REFERENCES

Alex Linley, P., Joseph, S., Harrington, S., & Wood, A. M. (2006). Positive psychology: Past, present, and (possible) future. *The Journal of Positive Psychology, 1*(1), 3–16. https://doi.org/10.1080/17439760500372796

Allen, R. (2005). *Learning about learning and teaching: Using the evidence of student achievement for improvements at individual, class and school level.* 1997–2008 ACER Research Conference Archive. https://research.acer.edu.au/cgi/viewcontentcgi?article=1014&context=research_conference_2005

Askew, S., & Lodge, C. (2000). Gifts, ping-pong and loops: Linking feedback and learning. In S. Askew (Ed.), *Feedback for learning* (pp. 1–17). Routledge.

Assessment Reform Group. (2002). *Assessment for learning: 10 principles. Research-based principles to guide classroom practice.* https://www.researchgate.net/publication/271849158_Assessment_for_Learning_10_Principles_Research-based_principles_to_guide_classroom_practice_Assessment_for_Learning

Australian Council for Educational Research (ACER). (2016). *National school improvement tool.* https://www.acer.org/files/NSIT.pdf

Australian Council for Educational Research (ACER). (2017, July 26). *Data-driven improvement in schools.* https://rd.acer.org/article/data-driven-improvement-in-schools

Australian Council for Educational Research (ACER). (2019, December 3). *PISA 2018: Australian students' performance.* https://www.acer.org/au/discover/article/pisa-2018-australian-students-performance

Australian Curriculum, Assessment and Reporting Authority (ACARA). (n.d.). *Learning Continuum of Numeracy.* https://www.australiancurriculum.edu.au/f-10-curriculum/general-capabilities/numeracy/learning-continuum/?isFirstPageLoad=false&element=Estimating+and+calculating+with+whole+numbers&element=Recognising+and+using+patterns+and+relationships&element=Using+fractions%2C+decimals%2C+percentages%2C+ratios+and+rates&element=Using+spatial+reasoning&element=Interpreting+statistical+information&element=Using+measurement&level=Level+1a

Australian Curriculum, Assessment and Reporting Authority (ACARA). (2014). *What does the ICSEA value mean?* http://docs.acara.edu.au/resources/About_icsea_2014.pdf

Australian Curriculum, Assessment and Reporting Authority (ACARA). (2019). *NAPLAN Achievement in Reading, Writing, Language Conventions and Numeracy: National Report for 2019.* https://nap.edu.au/docs/default-source/default-document-library/2019-naplan-national-report.pdf?Status=Temp&sfvrsn=2

Australian Institute for Teaching and School Leadership (AITSL). (2011). *Australian professional standards for teachers.* https://www.aitsl.edu.au/docs/default-source/national-policy-framework/australian-professional-standards-for-teachers.pdf

Bain, A., & Swan, G. (2011). Technology enhanced feedback tools as a knowledge management mechanism for supporting professional growth and school reform. *Educational Technology Research and Development, 59*(5), 673–685. https://doi.org/10.1007/s11423-011-9201-x

Bangert-Drowns, R. L., Kulik, C. C., Kulik, J. A., & Morgan, M. (1991). The instructional effect of feedback in test-like events. *Review of Educational Research, 61*(2), 218–238. https://doi.org/10.3102/00346543061002213

Barber, M., & Mourshed, M. (2007, September 1). *How the world's best-performing school systems comeoutontop.*McKinsey&Company.https://www.mckinsey.com/industries/public-and-social-sector/our-insights/how-the-worlds-best-performing-school-systems-come-out-on-top

Bishop, K., & Bishop, K. (2017). Improving student learning outcomes: Using data walls and case management conversations. *Literacy Learning: The Middle Years, 25*(1), i–x. https://search.informit.org/doi/10.3316/INFORMIT.596905678482034

Black, P., & Wiliam, D. (1998). Assessment and classroom learning. *Assessment in Education: Principles, Policy and Practice, 5*(1), 7–74. https://doi.org/10.1080/0969595980050102

Black, P., & Wiliam, D. (2003). 'In praise of educational research': Formative assessment. *British Educational Research Journal, 29*(5), 623–637. https://doi.org/10.1080/0141192032000133721

Bloom, B. S., Hastings, J. T., & Madaus, G. F. (1971). *Handbook on formative and summative evaluation of student learning.* McGraw-Hill.

Brinko, K. T. (1993). The practice of giving feedback to improve teaching: What is effective? *The Journal of Higher Education, 64*(5), 574–593. https://doi.org/10.1080/00221546.1993.11778449

Brookhart, S. M. (2011). Tailoring feedback: Effective feedback should be adjusted depending on the needs of the learner. *The Virginia Journal of Education, 76*(9), 33–36.

Brookhart, S. M. (2017). *How to give effective feedback to your students* (2nd ed.). Association for Supervision & Curriculum Development.

Brown, G. T. L., Lake, R., & Matters, G. (2011). Queensland teachers' conceptions of assessment: The impact of policy priorities on teacher attitudes. *Teaching and Teacher Education, 27*(1), 210–220. https://doi.org/10.1016/j.tate.2010.08.003

Cope, B., & Kalantzis, M. (2015). Interpreting evidence-of-learning: Educational research in the era of big data. *Open Review of Education Research, 2*(1), 218–239. https://doi.org/10.1080/23265507.2015.1074870

Craven, G., Beswick, K., Fleming, J., Fletcher, T., Green, M., Jensen, B., Leinonen, E., & Rickards, F. (2014). *Action now: Classroom ready teachers.* Australian Government.

Crooks, T. J. (1988). The impact of classroom evaluation practices on students. *Review of Educational Research, 58*(4), 438–481. https://doi.org/10.2307/1170281

Deming, W. E. (1942). On a classification of the problems of statistical inference. *Journal of the American Statistical Association, 37*(218), 173–185. https://doi.org/10.2307/2279212

Department of Education and Training. (2018). *Through growth to achievement: Report of the review to achieve educational excellence in Australian schools.* https://www.dese.gov.au/uncategorised/resources/through-growth-achievement-report-review-achieve-educational-excellence-australian-schools

Desautels, L. L., & McKnight, M. (2016). *Unwritten, the story of a living system: A pathway to enlivening and transforming education.* Wyatt-MacKenzie Publishing.

Dixon, H. R., Hawe, E., & Parr, J. (2011). Enacting assessment for learning: The beliefs practice nexus. *Assessment in Education: Principles, Policy & Practice, 18*(4), 365–379. https://doi.org/10.1080/0969594X.2010.526587

Duckworth, A. (2016). *Grit: The power of passion and perseverance.* Scribner.

Dweck, C. S. (2006). *Mindset: The new psychology of success.* Ballantine Books.

Dweck, C. S. (2007). The secret to raising smart kids. *Scientific American, 18*(6), 36–43. https://doi.org/10.1038/scientificamericanmind1207-36

Dweck, C. S. (2010). Even geniuses work hard. *Educational Leadership, 68*(1), 16–20.

Dweck, C. S. (2015. September 22). Carol Dweck revisits the 'growth mindset'. *Education Week.* https://www.edweek.org/ew/articles/2015/09/23/carol-dweck-revisits-the-growth-mindset.html

Education Services Australia. (n.d.). *National learning progressions and online formative assessment initiative.* https://www.esa.edu.au/solutions/our-solutions/national-learning-progressions-and-online-formative-assessment-initiative

Education Services Australia. (2018). *Australian student wellbeing framework.* https://studentwellbeinghub.edu.au/media/9310/aswf_booklet.pdf

Education Services Australia. (2019). *Alice Springs (Mparntwe) Education Declaration.* http://www.educationcouncil.edu.au/site/DefaultSite/filesystem/documents/Reports%20and%20publications/Alice%20Springs%20(Mparntwe)%20Education%20Declaration.pdf

Ezard, T. (2015). *The buzz: Creating a thriving and collaborative learning culture.* Author.

Fisk, S. M. (2017). *A qualitative inquiry of students' and teachers' perceptions on feedback in three Queensland secondary schools* [Doctoral thesis]. Queensland University of Technology. https://doi.org/10.5204/thesis.eprints.112506

Flanagan, T., Grift, G., Lipscombe, K., Wills, J., & Sloper, C. (2016). *Transformative collaboration: Five commitments for leading a PLC.* Hawker Brownlow Education.

Gable, S. L., & Haidt, J. (2005). What (and why) is positive psychology? *Review of General Psychology, 9*(2), 103–110. https://doi.org/10.1037/1089-2680.9.2.103

Gamlem, S. M. (2015). Feedback to support learning: Changes in teachers' practice and beliefs. *Teacher Development, 19*(4), 461–482. https://doi.org/10.1080/13664530.2015.1060254

Hattie, J. (2009). *Visible learning: A synthesis of over 800 meta-analyses relating to achievement.* Routledge.

Hattie, J. (2012). *Visible learning for teachers: Maximizing impact on learning.* Routledge.

Hattie, J. (2017, December 13). *Exclusive: We need to change the conversation around NAPLAN – let's talk about progress.* EducationHQ. https://au.educationhq.com/news/45236/exclusive-we-need-to-change-the-conversation-around-naplan-lets-talk-about-progress/#

Hattie, J., & Timperley, H. (2007). The power of feedback. *Review of Educational Research, 77*(1), 81–112. https://doi.org/10.3102/003465430298487

Hillman, J. (1996). *The soul's code: In search of character and calling.* Random House.

Huck, S. (2012). *Stanine scores.* Reading Statistics and Research. http://www.readingstats.com/Sixth/email2d.htm

Ilgen, D. R., Fisher, C. D., & Taylor, M. S. (1979). Consequences of individual feedback on behavior in organizations. *Journal of Applied Psychology, 64*(4), 349–371. https://doi.org/10.1037/0021-9010.64.4.349

Jackson, R. (2018). *Never work harder than your students and other principles of great teaching* (2nd ed.). Association of Supervision and Curriculum Development.

Jick, T. D. (1979). Mixing qualitative and quantitative methods: Triangulation in action. *Administrative Science Quarterly, 24*(4), 602–611. https://doi.org/10.2307/2392366

Jones, S., & Pickett, M. (2019). *Making the data-driven journey easy* [video]. BrightTALK. https://www.brighttalk.com/webcast/15971/364868

Klenowski, V. (2009). Assessment for learning revisited: An Asia-Pacific perspective. *Assessment in Education: Principles, Policy and Practice, 16*(3), 263–268. https://doi.org/10.1080/09695940903319646

Klenowski, V. (2013). Towards improving public understanding of judgement practice in standards-referenced assessment: An Australian perspective. *Oxford Review of Education, 39*(1), 36–51. https://doi.org/10.1080/03054985.2013.764759

Kluger, A., & DeNisi, A. (1996). The effects of feedback interventions on performance: A historical review, a meta-analysis, and a preliminary feedback intervention theory. *Psychological Bulletin, 119*(2), 254–284. https://doi.org/10.1037/0033-2909.119.2.254

Knapp, M. S., Swinnerton, J. A., Copland, M. A., & Monpas-Huber, J. (2006). *Data-informed leadership in education*. Center for the Study of Teaching and Policy. https://www.education.uw.edu/ctp/sites/default/files/ctpmail/PDFs/DataInformed-Nov1.pdf

Kotter, J. P. (2017). *The problem with data*. Kotter Inc. https://www.kotterinc.com/wp-content/uploads/2017/11/The-Problem-With-Data-Kotter-2017.pdf

Kulhavy, R. W. (1977). Feedback in written instruction. *Review of Educational Research, 47*(2), 211–232. https://doi.org/10.3102/00346543047002211

Kulhavy, R. W., & Stock, W. A. (1989). Feedback in written instruction: The place of response certitude. *Educational Psychology Review, 1*(4), 279–308. https://doi.org/10.1007/BF01320096

Lincoln, Y. S., & Guba, E. G. (1985). *Naturalistic inquiry*. Sage Publications.

Linley, P. A., Joseph, S., Harrington, S., & Wood, A.M. (2006). Positive psychology: Past, present and (possible) future. *The Journal of Positive Psychology, 1*(1), 3–16.

Macquarie Dictionary Publishers. (2021). Progress. In *Macquarie Dictionary*. Retrieved September 15, 2021, from https://www.macquariedictionary.com.au/features/word/search/?search_word_type=Dictionary&word=progress+#result_dict_progress

Marr, B. (2017, July 24). What is data democratization? A super simple explanation and the key pros and cons. Forbes. https://www.forbes.com/sites/bernardmarr/2017/07/24/what-is-data-democratization-a-super-simple-explanation-and-the-key-pros-and-cons

Marzano, R. J. (2006). *Classroom assessment and grading that work*. Association of Supervision and Curriculum Development.

Marzano, R. J. (2017). *The New Art and Science of Teaching: A comprehensive framework for effective instruction*. Association of Supervision and Curriculum Development.

Marzano, R. J. (2011). The Art and Science of Teaching: What teachers gain from deliberate practice. *The Effective Educator, 68*(4), 82–85. http://www.ascd.org/publications/educational-leadership/dec10/vol68/num04/What-Teachers-Gain-from-Deliberate-Practice.aspx

Matters, G. (2006). *Using data to support learning in schools: Students, teachers, systems*. ACER Press. https://research.acer.edu.au/cgi/viewcontent.cgi?article=1004&context=aer

Ministerial Council on Education, Employment, Training and Youth Affairs (MCEETYA). (1989). *The Hobart Declaration on National Goals for Schooling in Australia [the Hobart Declaration]*. http://www.educationcouncil.edu.au/EC-Publications/EC-Publications-archive/EC-The-Hobart-Declaration-on-Schooling-1989.aspx

Ministerial Council on Education, Employment, Training and Youth Affairs (MCEETYA). (1999). *The Adelaide Declaration on National Goals for Schooling in the Twenty–First*

Century [the Adelaide Declaration]. http://www.educationcouncil.edu.au/EC-Publications/EC-Publications-archive/EC-The-Adelaide-Declaration.aspx

Ministerial Council on Education, Employment, Training and Youth Affairs (MCEETYA). (2008). *Melbourne Declaration on Educational Goals for Young Australians [the Melbourne Declaration]*. http://www.educationcouncil.edu.au/site/DefaultSite/filesystem/documents/Reports%20and%20publications/Publications/National%20goals%20for%20schooling/National_Declaration_on_the_Educational_Goals_for_Young_Australians.pdf

Mitroff, I. I., & Sagasti, F. (1973). Epistemology as general systems theory: An approach to the design of complex decision-making experiments. *Philosophy of Social Sciences, 3*(2), 117–134. https://doi.org/10.1177/004839317300300202

Moursched, M., Krawitz, M., & Dorn, E. (2017). *How to improve student educational outcomes: New insights from data analytics*. McKinsey & Company. https://www.mckinsey.com/~/media/McKinsey/Industries/Social%20Sector/Our%20Insights/How%20to%20improve%20student%20educational%20outcomes/How-to-improve-student-educational-outcomes-New-insights-from-data-analytics.pdf

National Assessment Program. (n.d.). *How to interpret*. https://www.nap.edu.au/results-and-reports/how-to-interpret

Natriello, G. (1987). The impact of evaluation processes on students. *Educational Psychologist, 22*(2), 155–175. https://doi.org/10.1207/s15326985ep2202_4

New South Wales Department of Education and Communities. (2015). *Differentiating content, process, product, learning environment*. http://www.ssgt.nsw.edu.au/documents/3_content_pro_etal.pdf

Newton, P. (2007). Clarifying the purposes of educational assessment. *Assessment in Education: Principle, Policy and Practice, 14*(2), 149–170. https://doi.org/10.1080/09695940701478321

O'Neal, C. (2012). *Data-driven decision making: A handbook for school leaders*. International Society for Technology in Education (ISTE).

Organisation for Economic Cooperation and Development (OECD). (2019). *TALIS 2018 results (Volume 1): Teachers and school leaders as lifelong learners*. OECD Publishing. https://doi.org/10.1787/1d0bc92a-en

Qlik. (2019). *3rd-generation BI: Unlocking the possibility in your data*. https://www.qlik.com/us/resource-library/3rd-generation-business-intelligence

Ramaprasad, A. (1983). On the definition of feedback. *Behavioral Science, 28*(1), 4–13. https://doi.org/10.1002/bs.3830280103

Rosling, H. (with Rosling, O., & Rönnlund, A. R.). (2018). *Factfulness: Ten reasons we're wrong about the world – and why things are better than you think*. Hodder & Staughton.

Rowe, A. (2011). The personal dimension in teaching: Why students value feedback. *International Journal of Educational Management, 25*(4), 343–360. https://doi.org/10.1108/09513541111136630

Sadler, D. R. (1989). Formative assessment and the design of instructional systems. *Instructional Science, 18*, 119–144. http://dx.doi.org/10.1007/BF00117714

Scheeler, M. C., Ruhl, K. L., & McAfee, J. K. (2004). Providing performance feedback to teachers: A review. *Teacher Education and Special Education, 27*(4), 396–407. https://doi.org/10.1177/088840640402700407

Scriven, M. (1967). *The methodology of evaluation*. American Educational Research Association (AERA).

Seife, C. (2010). *Proofiness: How you're being fooled by the numbers.* Penguin Publishing Group.

Seligman, M. E. P., & Csikszentmihalyi, M. (2000). Positive psychology: An introduction. *American Psychologist, 55*(1), 5–14. https://doi.org/10.1037/0003-066X.55.1.5

Sharratt, L., & Fullan, M. (2012). *Putting faces on the data: What great leaders do!* Corwin Press.

Sharratt, L., & Fullan, M. (2013). Capture the human side of learning: Data makeover puts students front and center. *Journal of Staff Development, 34*(1), 44–48. https://learningforward.org/wp-content/uploads/2013/02/capture-the-human-side-of-learning.pdf

Sheldon, K. M., & King, L. (2001). Why positive psychology is necessary. *American Psychologist, 56*(3), 216–217. https://doi.org/10.1037/0003-066X.56.3.216

Shen, J., Cooley, V. E., Ma, X., Reeves, P. L., Burt, W. L., Rainey, J. M., & Yuan, W. (2012). Data-informed decision making on high-impact strategies: Developing and validating an instrument for principals. *The Journal of Experimental Education, 80*(1), 1–25. https://doi.org/10.1080/00220973.2010.550338

Shute, V. J. (2008). Focus on formative feedback. *Review of Educational Research, 78*(1), 153–189. https://doi.org/10.3102/0034654307313795

Sinek, S. (2009). *Start with why: How great leaders inspire everyone to take action.* Portfolio.

Sinek, S. (with Mead, D., & Docker, P.). (2017). *Find your why: A practical guide for discovering purpose for you and your team.* Portfolio.

Teacher Education Ministerial Advisory Group. (2014). *Action now: Classroom ready teachers.* Australian Government Department of Education. Skills and Employment. https://www.aitsl.edu.au/docs/default-source/default-document-library/action_now_classroom_ready_teachers_accessible-(1)da178891b1e86477b58fff00006709da.pdf?sfvrsn=9bffec3c_0

The Education Endowment Foundation. (2019). *The EEF guide to becoming an evidence-informed school governor and trustee.* https://educationendowmentfoundation.org.uk/public/files/Publications/EEF_Guide_for_School_Governors_and_Trustees_2019.pdf

Thomson, S., Hillman, K., Schmid, M., Rodrigues, S., & Fullarton, J. (2017, November 5). *Highlights from PIRLS 2016: Australia's perspective: Selected findings from the full report 'Reporting Australia's results PIRLS 2016'.* Australian Council for Educational Research (ACER). https://research.acer.edu.au/cgi/viewcontent.cgi?article=1001&context=pirls

Thomson, S., Wernert, N., Rodrigues, S., & O'Grady, E. (2020). *TIMSS 2019 Australia: Volume 1: Student performance.* Australian Council for Educational Research (ACER). https://doi.org/10.37517/978-1-74286-614-7

Thurmond, V. A. (2001). The point of triangulation. *Journal of Nursing Scholarship, 33*(3), 253–258. https://doi.org/10.1111/j.1547-5069.2001.00253.x

Tomlinson, C. A., & Allan, S. D. (2006). *Leadership for differentiating schools and classrooms.* Hawker Brownlow Education.

Van Sant, G. (Director). (1997). *Good Will Hunting* [Film]. Miramax Films.

Wiliam, D. (2011). What is assessment for learning? *Studies in Educational Evaluation, 37*(1), 3–14. https://doi.org/10.1016/j.stueduc.2011.03.001

Wylie, E. C., & Lyon, C. J. (2015). The fidelity of formative assessment implementation: Issues of breadth and quality. *Assessment in Education: Principles, Policy & Practice, 22*(1), 140–160. https://doi.org/10.1080/0969594X.2014.990416

Zacharias, N. T. (2007). Teacher and student attitudes toward teacher feedback. *RELC Journal, 38*(1), 38–52. https://doi.org/10.1177/0033688206076157

Zhao, Y. (2014). *Who's afraid of the big bad dragon?* Jossey-Bass.

INDEX

A

ability and potential of a class
    differentiating teaching for different ability levels, 68–69, 73–78
    setting up a spreadsheet to establish, 70–73
Aboriginal and Torres Strait Islander students, 5
academic growth in learning areas *see* measuring and comparing academic growth in learning areas
ACARA (Australian Curriculum, Assessment and Reporting Authority), 122
ACER (Australian Council for Educational Research), 11, 20, 25
    understanding ACER data, 50–52
ACER Middle Years Ability Test (MYAT), 47, 50
ACER Online Assessment and Reporting System (OARS), 82
ACER Progressive Achievement Testing (PAT), 25, 47, 50
achievement and progress measures, 21–24
    achievement reported by media, 1
    tracking achievement *versus* question difficulty, 129, 161–163
    using ACER scale scores to measure progress, 158–161
    see also PAT; PIRLS; tracking performance in formative, summative and homework tasks
Action now: Classroom ready teachers (Teacher Education Ministerial Advisory Group), 6
AITSL (Australian Institute for Teaching and School Leadership), 3
AITSL standards, 3, 18–19
Alice Springs (Mparntwe) Education Declaration, 1, 4, 5, 18
Allan, SD, 63, 75
Allen, R, 67
Allwell testing, 47
American Psychological Association, 41–42
analysis of data *see* use and analysis of data
APST (Australian Professional Standards for Teachers), 1
Askew, S, 26
assessment
    conceptions of assessment, 32–34
    formative and summative assessment, 30–32, 35, 45, 47, 69–70
    investigating strengths and gaps in assessment tasks, 82–84
    of, for and as learning, 34–35
    tracking progress of students in assessment using GPA system, 92–95
Assessment Reform Group, 34
assumptions about data, 14–16, 192–193
at-risk students
    using cohort data to identify, 133–135
attendance data walls, 169–171
attendance records, 48
Australian Council for Educational Research *see* ACER (Australian Council for Educational Research)
Australian Curriculum, 1, 3
Australian Curriculum, Assessment and Reporting Authority (ACARA), 122
Australian Institute for Teaching and School Leadership (AITSL), 3
Australian media reporting, 1
Australian Professional Standards for Teachers (APST), 1
Australian Student Wellbeing Framework, 180

B

Bain, A, 28
bands, NAPLAN testing *see* NAPLAN
Bangert-Drowns, RL, 29
Barber, M, 6
behaviour reports using data walls, 171–173
beliefs and presuppositions about data (the author), 14–15
Black, P, 26–27, 30, 31, 34
Bloom, BS, 31
box and whisker plots, 112–116
bright spots for areas of celebration and improvement, 194, 204–206
Brinko, KT, 28
Brookhart, SM, 30, 87
Brown, GTL, 32
Bush, President George W, 7
The buzz (Ezard), 41

C

calculating individual student GPAs across learning areas, 142–143
Carnegie Mellon University, 44
celebrating success, 194, 204–206
class streaming groups *see* identifying groups in a cohort for intervention, extension or class streaming
classroom walk-through data, 177–180
Cole, Kat, 37
collection and interpretation of data, 10, 47–65
    analysing data using colour-coding, 56–59
    examples of data available in Australian schools, 47–48
    five-stage feedback loop, 185–190
    interpretation and context of data, 10–11
    triangulating data, 59–65
    understanding ACER data, 50–52
    understanding GPA, 52–53
    understanding NAPLAN data, 48–50
    understanding Z-scores, 53–56
Collins, Sir Kevan, 3
colour-coding in analysing data, 56–59
    see also triangulating in analysing data; using data in the classroom, examples of; using data in your school, examples of
comparing growth across classes – value added, 144–146
comparing performance of different classes, 139–142
comparison of states and individual schools, 1
competencies and module completion, tracking performance in, 91–92
conceptions of assessment, 32–34
conclusion, 215–216
context and interpretation of data, 10–11, 48
conversations with students
    tracking class performance, 78, 80–82
    see also impact of data; triangulating in analysing data
conversations with teachers
    data conversation protocols and templates, 190–214
    data-informed culture, 190–194
Cope, B, 33–34
COVID-19 pandemic *see* student wellbeing
creating data walls, examples of, 130
    attendance (all) data, 169–170
    attendance (top) data, 170–171
    behaviour (all) reports, 171–173
    behaviour (best) reports, 173
    literacy or numeracy, 173–177
    NAPLAN achievement data, 167
    NAPLAN progress data, 168
    PAT achievement data, 164–165
    PAT progress data, 165–166
criticism of data use in schools, 7–10
Crooks, TJ, 30
Csikszentmihalyi, M, 42–43

D

Dann, B, 5–6
dashboards
    in school learning management systems, 56, 64, 67, 119–120
    visualisation dashboard, 119–120
data, purpose and importance of
    and AITSL standards, 3, 18–19
    assumptions about data, 14–16, 192–193
    criticism of data use in schools, 7–10
    data democratisation, 12–14
    data literacy, 1, 4, 11, 191–192, 215
    data plan for middle and senior leaders, 209–213
    data storytelling, 11–12, 56, 185–190
    data visualisation, 11
    examples of data available in Australian schools, 47–48
    negative perception of, 4
    orienting school improvement, 3
    use as pastoral care, 16–18
    why use data in schools, 6–7
    see also collection and interpretation of data; data-informed culture; feedback to students; impact of data; using data in the classroom; using data in your school
data driven culture, 7, 215
'Data-driven improvement in schools' (ACER), 11
data-informed culture, 37–46, 215
    data-informed conversations with teachers, 190–194
    grit, 38, 43–46
    mindset, 38–41
    positive psychology, 38, 41–43
data literacy, 1, 4, 11, 191–192, 215
data walls *see* creating data walls, examples of
Datnow, Professor A, 21
decision-level assessment, 32
Deming, WE, 1, 215
democratisation of data, 12–14
Deng Xiaoping, 8
DeNisi, A, 26, 29, 30
Desautels, LL, 17
developmental scale for using data in the classroom, 13–14
Diagnostic Reading Assessment (DRA), 47
differentiating teaching for different ability levels, using data, 68–69
    identifying differentiation strategies for small groups within a class, 75–78
    identifying individual intervention strategies, 73–78
DRA (Diagnostic Reading Assessment), 47
Duckworth, A, 4, 38, 43–46, 106
Dweck, CS, 22–23, 39–40, 107, 190

E

Education Declaration, Alice Springs (Mparntwe), 1, 4, 5, 18
educational change driven by data, 3
educational feedback *see* feedback to students
educators negative perception of data, 4
effective feedback, 27–29
    definition of, 29
    see also feedback to students
effort
    in experiencing achievement, 44–45
    role in developing growth mindset, 40
emerging assessment model, 33–34
evidence, use of, 3, 20
evidence-informed teachers, 215
examples
    of triangulating data for individual students, 61–65
    of using data in the classroom, 70–126
    of using data in your school, 130–184
extension groups *see* identifying groups in a cohort for intervention, extension or class streaming
Ezard, T, 41

F

feedback to students
    assessment and learning, 34–35
    conceptions of assessment, 32–34
    contributor to student mindset, 40
    definitions of, 26–27
    effective feedback, 27–29
    five-stage feedback loop, 185–190
    formative and summative assessment, 30–32, 45
    impact of, 25, 29–30, 185–190
    opportunities for providing feedback, 184
    student perceptions of, 2
    types of, 87
fixed mindset, 39–40
Flanagan, T, 191
Flynn, J, 45
Ford, Henry, 40
formative assessment, 30–32, 35, 45, 47, 69–70
Fullan, M, 9–10, 17, 18, 43, 164, 177

G

Gamlem, SM, 25
Golden Circle model (Sinek), 6–7
Good Will Hunting (film), 3, 4
Google templates, 117–119
GPA (grade point average), 48
    calculating individual student GPAs across learning areas, 142–143
    understanding GPA, 52–-53
    used in comparing performances of different classes, 139–142
    used in tracking progress of students, 92–95
    grades used to rank order student achievement, 95–100
    grades used to rank order student progress, 104–107
graphing numerical data, 163–164
grit, in using data in schools, 38, 43–46
Grit: The power of passion and perseverance (Duckworth), 4, 38, 43
growth mindset, 39–41
Guba, EG, 59

H

Handbook on formative and summative evaluation of student learning (Bloom et al.), 31
Hattie, J, 23, 27, 30, 41, 85, 190
high achieving students
    using cohort data to identify, 130–133
homework tasks, tracking performance in, 88–90
'how' and 'what' of using data in the classroom, 68
How the world's best-performing school systems come out on top (Barber & Mourshed), 6
human aspect behind the data, 17

I

identifying differentiation strategies for small groups within a class, 75–78
identifying groups in a cohort for intervention, extension or class streaming, 127, 128
    using cohort data to identify at-risk students, 133–135
    using cohort data to identify top performers, 130–133
    using data to assist with streaming classes and timetabling, 135–139
identifying individual intervention strategies, 73–75
impact level assessment, 32
impact of data
    five-stage feedback loop, 185–190
    teacher data conversation protocols and templates, 190–214
impact of feedback to students, 25, 29–30, 185–190
importance of data *see* data, purpose and importance of
Indigenous students, 5
intelligence quotient (IQ) scores, 45
international comparisons of students, 3–4
    see also standardised testing
'The international context' (Dann), 5–6
interpretation and context of data *see* collection and interpretation of data
intervention
    and areas of concern, 194, 206–208
    strategies for individuals, 73–75
    see also identifying groups in a cohort for intervention, extension or class streaming
IQ scores, 45

J

Jackson, R, 29
judgement-level assessment, 32

K

Kalantzis, M, 33–34
Kaufman, S, 44
Klenowski, V, 34
Kluger, A, 26, 29, 30
Knapp, MS, 10
Kotter, JP, 8–9, 190, 191
Kulhavy, RW, 26, 29

L

learning areas
    access to data in, 48
    see also measuring and comparing academic growth in learning areas
learning management systems in schools, 56, 64, 67, 119–120
Lincoln, YS, 59
line graphs used to track progress of individual students over time, 116–122
literacy and numeracy test
    in initial teacher education programs, 6
literacy data, 1, 4, 11
    data wall for, 173–177
Lodge, C, 26
Lyon, CJ, 28–29

M

marks used to rank order student achievement, 100–104
marks used to rank order student progress, 107–109
Marshall, R, 21, 22
Marzano, RJ, 13
Matters, G, 47
McKinsey and Company report 2017, 38–39, 40
McKnight, M, 17
measuring and comparing academic growth in learning areas, 127, 128–129
    calculating individual student GPAs across learning areas, 142–143
    comparing growth across classes – value added, 144–146
    comparing the performance of different classes, 139–142
media in Australia, 1, 4
Melbourne Declaration on Educational Goals for Young Australians 2008, 18, 35
mentoring programs in schools, 6
Middle Years Ability Test (MYAT), 47, 50
mindset in using data in schools, 38–41
module completion, tracking performance in, 91–92
Mourshed, M, 6

My School website, 4, 129
    used to compare NAPLAN achievement compared to national averages, 153–154
    used to compare NAPLAN growth compared to national averages, 154–155
    used to compare NAPLAN growth compared to schools with similar students, 155–157
    used to compare NAPLAN growth compared to students with the same starting score, 157–158
MYAT (Middle Years Ability Test), 47, 50

N

NAPLAN (National Assessment Program – Literacy and Numeracy)
    analysis of criteria and question types used in, 82
    reviewing NAPLAN data (*see* reviewing NAPLAN data)
    understanding NAPLAN data, 48–50
National Assessment Program – Literacy and Numeracy *see* NAPLAN
National Learning Progressions and Online Formative Assessment Initiative, 24
national minimum standard (NMS) NAPLAN, 48–50
National School Improvement Tool (NSIT), 3–4, 18, 20–21
Natriello, G, 30
NCCD (Nationally Consistent Collection of Data), 69, 75
negative perception of data by educators, 4
The New Art and Science of Teaching (Marzano), 13, 14
Newton, P, 32
NMS (national minimum standard) NAPLAN, 48–50
No Child Left Behind Act 2001 (USA), 7
non-Indigenous students, 5
NSIT (National School Improvement Tool), 3–4, 18, 20–21
numeracy and literacy test
    in initial teacher education programs, 6
numeracy data walls, 173–177
numerical data, graphing of, 163–164

O

OARS (ACER Online Assessment and Reporting System), 82
OECD (Organisation for Economic Co-operation and Development), 5
other school data measures, including wellbeing, 127, 130
    graphing numerical data, 163–164
    thematic analysis of classroom walk-through data, 177–180
    tracking student wellbeing using a purchased product, 180–181
    tracking student wellbeing with a home-grown survey, 181–184

outcome measures reported by media, 1
overview of *Using and analysing data in Australian schools, second edition*, 2

P

pastoral care responsibility of data, 16–18
PAT (Progressive Achievement Testing), 25, 47, 50
    reviewing ACER PAT data (*see* reviewing ACER PAT data)
patterns and trends in student learning
    using common data in schools, 47–48
    using triangulation, 59–61
pedagogy and programs informed by data, 216
percentiles, ACER tests *see under* ACER (Australian Council for Educational Research)
performance
    affected by feedback, 25, 29–30
    comparing performance of different classes, 139–142
    tracking class performance, 78–82
    see also tracking performance in formative, summative and homework tasks
PIRLS (Progress in International Reading Literacy Study), 5
PISA (Programme for International Student Assessment), 3, 5
placemats, differentiation, 75–78
PLC (professional learning community), 191
positive psychology
    in using data in schools, 38, 41–43
potential of a class *see* ability and potential of a class
Power BI program, 11
power of 'why' in data, 6–7
power of 'yet' in growth mindset, 40
preparing for beginning of a term or semester, using data, 68
    setting up a spreadsheet to establish ability and potential of a class, 70–73
'The problem with data' (Kotter), 8–9
professional learning community (PLC), 191
Programme for International Student Assessment (PISA), 3, 5
progress *see* achievement and progress measures
Progress in International Reading Literacy Study (PIRLS), 5
Progressive Achievement Testing (PAT), 25, 47, 50
Proofiness: How you're being fooled by the numbers (Seife), 10
protocols and templates for teacher data conversations *see* templates for teacher data conversations
purpose of assessment, 32–33, 35
purpose of taking data, 1
putting faces on the data, 9–10

Q

question difficulty *see under* achievement and progress measures

R

Ramaprasad, A, 26
rank order of student achievement using grades, 95–100
rank order of student achievement using marks, 100–104
rank order of student progress using grades, 104–107
rank order of student progress using marks, 107–109
research reports, 6
reviewing ACER PAT data, 127, 129
    creating an ACER difficulty *versus* percentage correct scatterplot, 161–163
    data wall showing achievement data, 164–165
    data wall showing progress data, 165–166
    using ACER scale scores to measure progress, 158–161
reviewing NAPLAN data, 127, 129
    considering scale scores over time – tracking a cohort, 146–150
    considering scale scores over time – tracking a program, 150–153
    data wall showing achievement data, 167
    data wall showing progress data, 168
    My School NAPLAN achievement compared to national averages, 153–154
    My School NAPLAN growth compared to national averages, 154–155
    My School NAPLAN growth compared to schools with similar students, 155–157
    My School NAPLAN growth compared to students with the same starting score, 157–158
Rosling, H, 185

S

Sadler, DR, 29
Scheeler, MC, 28
school improvement, use of data for, 3
school learning management systems, 56, 64, 67, 119–120
school mentoring programs, 6
Scripps National Spelling Bee, 44
Scriven, M, 31
Seife, C, 10
Seligman, MEP, 41–43
setting up a spreadsheet to establish ability and potential of a class, 70–73
sharing data with students, 12–14, 24, 73, 75, 78, 80–82
    see also feedback to students
Sharratt, L, 9–10, 17, 18, 43, 164, 177
sight words testing, 48

Sinek, S, 6–7
social multiplier, 45
spreadsheet to establish ability and potential of a class, 70–73
standardised testing
  access to, 12–13
  and classrooms and school communities, 5
  NAPLAN, 1, 4, 5
  PIRLS, 5
  PISA, 3, 5
  research reports on, 6
  TIMSS, 5
  use of standardised testing data, 31, 32
standards for teacher professional practice, 3, 18–19
stanines, ACER tests *see under* ACER (Australian Council for Educational Research)
Stock, WA, 29
storytelling using data, 11–12, 56
  five-stage feedback loop, 185–190
strategies for small groups within a class, 75–78
strategies for using line graphs to track progress of individual students over time, 116--121
streaming classes and timetabling *see* identifying groups in a cohort for intervention, extension or class streaming
student data *see* data, purpose and importance of
student wellbeing, 180–184
students with diverse needs, 6
summative assessment, 30–32, 35, 45, 48, 69–70
surveys of principals, teachers, parents and students, 5
survive and thrive concept, 9, 191, 215
Swan, G, 28

T

Tableau program, 11
teachers
  data conversation protocols and templates for, 190–214
  data literacy skills, 1, 4, 11, 191–192, 215
  evidence-informed, 215
  as learners, 41
  literacy and numeracy test in initial teacher education programs, 6
  mindset of, 40–41
  standards for, 3, 18–19
templates for teacher data conversations
  bright spots for celebration, 194, 204–206
  data plan for middle and senior leaders, 209–213
  exploratory analysis of data, 194, 200–203
  exploring and analysing different types of data, 194, 195–200
  intervention and areas of concern, 194, 206–208
  protocols and templates, 190–194
testing *see* standardised testing
thematic analysis of classroom walk-through data, 177–180
Thomson, W, 4
thrive and survive concept, 9, 191, 215
Through growth to achievement (Australian Government Department of Education and Training), 6
timetabling and streaming classes *see* identifying groups in a cohort for intervention, extension or class streaming
Timperley, H, 27, 30
TIMSS (Trends in International Mathematics and Science Study), 5
Tomlinson, CA, 63, 75
top performers
  using cohort data to identify, 130–133
tracking performance in formative, summative and homework tasks, 69–70
  class performance, 78–82
  competencies and module completion, 91–92
  developing a table of values, 109–112
  displaying spread of achievement in a box and whisker plot, 112–116
  graphing progress of individual students over time, 122–126
  homework completion, 88–90
  investigating strengths and gaps in assessment tasks, 82–84
  progress of individual students over time using line graphs, 116–122
  progress of students using GPA system, 92–95
  rank order of student achievement using grades, 95–100
  rank order of student achievement using marks, 100–104
  rank order of student progress using grades, 104–107
  rank order of student progress using marks, 107–109
  value adding for students, 85–87
tracking student wellbeing
  with a home-grown survey, 181–184
  using a purchased product, 180–181
traditional assessment model, 33–34
traditional psychology, 42
Transformative collaboration: Five commitments for leading a professional learning community (Flanagan et al.), 191
Trends in International Mathematics and Science Study (TIMSS), 5
triangulating in analysing data, 59–65
  see also colour-coding in analysing data; using data in your classroom, examples of; using data in your school, examples of
trust in a professional learning community, 191
'turnaround teachers', 17

U

University of Cambridge, 44
University of the Sunshine Coast, 4
Unwritten: The story of a living system (Desautels and McKnight), 17
use and analysis of data, 1, 4, 5, 13
    colour-coding in, 56–59
    exploratory analysis of data, 194, 200–203
    exploring and analysing different types of data, 194, 195–200
    see also using data in your classroom; using data in your school
using data in your classroom, 67–126
    differentiating teaching for different ability levels, 68–69, 73–78
    examples of, 70–126
    preparing for beginning of a term or semester, 68, 70–73
    tracking performance in formative, summative and homework tasks, 69–70, 78–126
    see also feedback to students
using data in your school, 127–184
    creating data walls, 127, 130, 164–177
    examples of, 130–184
    identifying groups in a cohort for intervention, extension or class streaming, 127, 128, 130–139
    implementing other school data measures, including wellbeing, 127, 130, 163–164, 177–184
    measuring and comparing academic growth in learning areas, 127, 128–129, 139–146
    reviewing ACER PAT data, 127, 129, 158–166
    reviewing NAPLAN data, 127, 129, 146–158, 167–168
    see also feedback to students

V

value added for students, 85–87, 144–146
values, table of, 109–112
    visualisation dashboards in school learning management systems, 56, 64, 67, 119–120
visualisation of data, 11
    box and whisker plots, 112–116
    five-stage feedback loop, 185–190

W

W questions for feedback, 28
walk-through data *see* thematic analysis of classroom walk-through data
wellbeing data measures *see* other school data measures, including wellbeing
wellbeing of students, 180–184
Who's afraid of the big bad dragon? (Zhao), 7
why use data in schools, 6–7
William, D, 26–27, 30, 31, 34
Wylie, EC, 28–29

Y

Yale University, 44
Year 12 exit results, 48

Z

Z-scores, 48, 53–56
Zacharias, NT, 29
Zhao, Y, 7–8

www.ingramcontent.com/pod-product-compliance
Lightning Source LLC
Chambersburg PA
CBHW051310110526
44590CB00031B/4359